FACE TO FACE

Marc Quinn
meets
Franz Xaver Messerschmidt

Verlag der Buchhandlung Walther und Franz König

ACKNOWLEDGEMENTS

Our thanks go to:

Authors: Georg Lechner, Cat Marnell,
Tim Smith-Laing, Lou Stoppard
Contributors: Shadi Al-Atallah, Adiam Yemane
Graphic Designers: Eva Kellenberger,
Maria Candanoza (Kellenberger–White, London)
Sponsor: Martin Böhm (Dorotheum, Vienna)
Marc Quinn Studio, London: Margaree Cotton,
Tanya Moulson, Helen Neven, Catrin Owen,
Damian Simpson, Amy Stafford, Elizabeth Wayne
Belvedere, Vienna: Tanja Angermann-Cekinmez,
Johanna Hofer, Eva Lahnsteiner, Beba Pikall-Kotyza
Editorial Team: Yoel Noorali, Katharina Sacken,
Tas Skorupa

Stella Rollig and Marc Quinn

COLOPHON

This catalogue is published on the occasion of the exhibition *Face to Face. Marc Quinn meets Franz Xaver Messerschmidt*, Upper Belvedere, Vienna, from February 24 to July 3, 2022.

Artistic Director, CEO: Stella Rollig
CFO: Wolfgang Bergmann

Curator: Stella Rollig
Assistant Curator: Johanna Hofer

Exhibition Management and Loans: Stephan Pumberger
Exhibition Production: Tanja Angermann-Cekinmez
Chief Curator: Harald Krejci
Education: Michaela Höß
Communications and Marketing: Katharina Steinbrecher
Visitor Services: Margarete Stechl
Research Centre: Christian Huemer
Conservation Department: Stefanie Jahn

Belvedere
Prinz Eugen-Strasse 27
1030 Vienna
Austria
www.belvedere.at

PUBLICATION

Editors: Stella Rollig, Marc Quinn

Authors: Georg Lechner, Cat Marnell, Marc Quinn,
Stella Rollig, Tim Smith-Laing, Lou Stoppard
Graphic Design: Kellenberger–White, London
Publication Management: Eva Lahnsteiner,
Helen Neven, Catrin Owen, Beba Pikall-Kotyza
Contributors: Shadi Al-Atallah, Adiam Yemane
Copy-editing (German): Katharina Sacken
Copy-editing (English): Yoel Noorali, Tas Skorupa
Translations (German-to-English): Jeremy Gaines
Translations (English-to-German): Barbara Hess
(Tim Smith-Laing), Thomas Raab (Lou Stoppard,
Interview)
Picture Editing: prints professional
Printed and bound by: DZA Druckerei zu
Altenburg GmbH

Paper: Bio Top 3, Igepa IBO One, Maxi Satin
Typeface: Practice by Optimo

Published by:
Verlag der Buchhandlung Walther und Franz König
Ehrenstrasse 4
50672 Cologne
Germany

Bibliographic information published by the Deutsche Nationalbibliothek. The Deutsche Nationalbibliothek lists this publication in the Deutsche Nationalbibliografie; detailed bibliographic data are available on the Internet at https://www.dnb.de.

Printed in Germany

DISTRIBUTION

Europe
Buchhandlung Walther König
Ehrenstrasse 4
50672 Cologne
Germany
Tel.: +49 (0) 221 205 9653
verlag@buchhandlung-walther-koenig.de

DANK

Unser Dank geht an

Autor*innen: Georg Lechner, Cat Marnell,
Tim Smith-Laing, Lou Stoppard
Mitwirkende: Shadi Al-Atallah, Adiam Yemane
Grafische Gestaltung: Eva Kellenberger,
Maria Candanoza (Kellenberger–White, London)
Sponsor: Martin Böhm (Dorotheum, Wien)
Marc Quinn Studio, London: Margaree Cotton,
Tanya Moulson, Helen Neven, Catrin Owen,
Damian Simpson, Amy Stafford, Elizabeth Wayne
Belvedere, Wien: Tanja Angermann-Cekinmez,
Johanna Hofer, Eva Lahnsteiner, Beba Pikall-Kotyza
Lektor*innen: Yoel Noorali, Katharina Sacken,
Tas Skorupa

Stella Rollig und Marc Quinn

IMPRESSUM

Dieser Katalog erscheint anlässlich der Ausstellung *Face to Face. Marc Quinn meets Franz Xaver Messerschmidt*, Oberes Belvedere, Wien, vom 24. Februar bis 3. Juli 2022.

Wissenschaftliche Geschäftsführerin /
Generaldirektorin: Stella Rollig
Wirtschaftlicher Geschäftsführer: Wolfgang Bergmann

Kuratorin: Stella Rollig
Assistenzkuratorin: Johanna Hofer

Ausstellungsmanagement und Sammlungsverwaltung:
Stephan Pumberger
Ausstellungsproduktion: Tanja Angermann-Cekinmez
Chefkurator: Harald Krejci
Kunstvermittlung: Michaela Höß
Kommunikation & Marketing: Katharina Steinbrecher
Besucher*innenservice: Margarete Stechl
Research Center: Christian Huemer
Restaurierung: Stefanie Jahn

Belvedere
Prinz Eugen-Straße 27
1030 Wien
Österreich
www.belvedere.at

PUBLIKATION

Herausgeber*innen: Stella Rollig, Marc Quinn

Autor*innen: Georg Lechner, Cat Marnell, Marc Quinn,
Stella Rollig, Tim Smith-Laing, Lou Stoppard
Grafische Gestaltung: Kellenberger–White, London
Publikationsmanagement: Eva Lahnsteiner,
Helen Neven, Catrin Owen, Beba Pikall-Kotyza
Mitwirkende: Shadi Al-Atallah, Adiam Yemane
Lektorat (Deutsch): Katharina Sacken
Lektorat (Englisch): Yoel Noorali, Tas Skorupa,
Adiam Yemane
Übersetzung (Deutsch – Englisch): Jeremy Gaines
Übersetzung (Englisch – Deutsch): Barbara Hess (Tim
Smith-Laing), Thomas Raab (Lou Stoppard, Interview)
Bildbearbeitung: prints professional
Druck und Bindung: DZA Druckerei zu
Altenburg GmbH

Papier: Bio Top 3, Igepa IBO One, Maxi Satin
Schrift: Practice von Optimo

Erschienen bei:
Verlag der Buchhandlung Walther und Franz König
Ehrenstraße 4
50672 Köln, DE

Bibliografische Information der Deutschen Nationalbibliothek
Die Deutsche Nationalbibliothek verzeichnet diese Publikation in der Deutschen Nationalbibliografie; detaillierte bibliografische Daten sind im Internet über https://www.dnb.de abrufbar.

Gedruckt in Deutschland

VERTRIEB

Europa
Buchhandlung Walther König
Ehrenstraße 4
50672 Köln, DE
Tel.: +49 (0) 221 205 9653
verlag@buchhandlung-walther-koenig.de

IMAGE CREDITS

Photo: Elizabeth Wayne: pp. 9–12, 43, 73–136 & 143–146, 179;
Various photographers, courtesy of Marc Quinn studio; pp. 15, 57–72 & 149;
Photo: Adiam Yemane: pp. 16 & 150;
Photo: Austrian National Library, Vienna: pp. 19, 48 & 153, 186;
Photo: Høstland, Børre: pp. 36 (fig. 1) & 172 (Abb. 1);
Photo: Metropolitan Museum of Art, New York / Fletcher Fund, 1919: pp. 36 (fig. 2) & 172 (Abb. 2);
Photo: Metropolitan Museum of Art, New York / Harris Brisbane Dick Fund, 1932: pp. 37 & 173;
Photo: Courtesy Shadi Al-Atallah and Guts Gallery: pp. 38 & 174;
Photo: Courtesy Shadi Al-Atallah and Cob Gallery: pp. 39 & 175;
Photo: Lyon MBA, Photo Alain Basset: pp. 40 (fig. 6) & 176 (Abb. 6);
Photo: 2004 Musée du Louvre / Angèle Dequier: pp. 40 (fig. 7) & 176 (Abb. 7);
Photo: MSK Gent, www.artinflanders.be, Photo: Hugo Maertens: pp. 40 (fig. 8) & 176 (Abb. 8);
Photo: Bethlem Museum of the Mind, London: pp. 41 (fig. 9) & 177 (Abb. 9);
Photo: Museo Reina Sofía, Madrid: pp. 41 (fig. 10) & 177 (Abb. 10);
Photo: Museum of Fine Arts, Houston / Bridgeman Images: pp. 42 & 178;
Photo: Belvedere, Vienna: pp. 49 & 187;
Front cover: Marc Quinn, *Fear of Fear*, 1994, photo by Elizabeth Wayne, artwork by Kellenberger–White, London;
Back cover: Franz Xaver Messerschmidt, *Second Beak Head*, 1777/1781, photo by Elizabeth Wayne, artwork by Kellenberger–White, London

BILDNACHWEIS

Foto: Elizabeth Wayne: S. 9–12, 43, 73–136 & 143–146, 179;
Verschiedene Fotograf*innen, Courtesy Marc Quinn Studio; S. 15, 57–72 & 149;
Foto: Adiam Yemane: S. 16 & 150;
Foto: Österreichische Nationalbibliothek, Wien: S. 19, 48 & 153, 186;
Foto: Høstland, Børre: S. 36 (fig. 1) & 172 (Abb. 1);
Foto: Metropolitan Museum of Art, New York / Fletcher Fund, 1919: S. 36 (fig. 2) & 172 (Abb. 2);
Foto: Metropolitan Museum of Art, New York / Harris Brisbane Dick Fund, 1932: S. 37 & 173;
Foto: Courtesy Shadi Al-Atallah and Guts Gallery: S. 38 & 174;
Foto: Courtesy Shadi Al-Atallah and Cob Gallery: S. 39 & 175;
Foto: Lyon MBA, Foto Alain Basset: S. 40 (fig. 6) & 176 (Abb. 6);
Foto: 2004 Musée du Louvre / Angèle Dequier: S. 40 (fig. 7) & 176 (Abb. 7);
Foto: MSK Gent, www.artinflanders.be, Foto: Hugo Maertens: S. 40 (fig. 8) & 176 (Abb. 8);
Foto: Bethlem Museum of the Mind, London: S. 41 (fig. 9) & 177 (Abb. 9);
Foto: Museo Reina Sofía, Madrid: S. 41 (fig. 10) & 177 (Abb. 10);
Foto: Museum of Fine Arts, Houston / Bridgeman Images: S. 42 & 178;
Foto: Belvedere, Wien: S. 49 & 187;
Cover (Vorderseite): Marc Quinn, *Fear of Fear*, 1994, Foto: Elizabeth Wayne, Gestaltung: Kellenberger–White, London;
Cover (Rückseite): Franz Xaver Messerschmidt, *Second Beak Head*, 1777/1781, Foto: Elizabeth Wayne, Gestaltung: Kellenberger–White, London

ISBN 978-3-7533-0201-0

belvedere

With the kind support of /
Mit freundlicher Unterstützung von

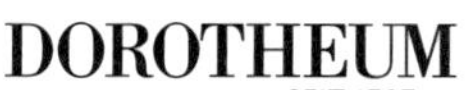

CONTENTS

INHALTSVERZEICHNIS

The Hands of the Sculptor
Stella Rollig

This is the story of two men at the beginning of their fourth decade, no longer in the first flush of youth but on the brink of their 'best years'—except that it doesn't turn out that way for either of them.

Marc Quinn was thirty in 1994 when he started working on the series of busts that now, under the title *Emotional Detox*, form one of the artist's most impressive groups of works. He was going through alcohol withdrawal, and when he talks about it, it sounds like a life-or-death decision. *Emotional Detox* comprises self-portraits of this experience.

Franz Xaver Messerschmidt was thirty-four years old in 1770 when he began work on what are now known as the *Character Heads*. It was the year in which his continual rise thus far to the status of a well-employed sculptor, commissioned artist of the imperial house, and member of the Vienna Academy went slightly off the tracks. In the following decade, he was denied a professorship that the Academy had been dangling in front of him for years, his commissions declined, and he turned his back on the Austrian capital, ultimately settling in what is now Bratislava. He is said to have suffered from a mental illness, but sources substantiating the diagnosis are scarce, and he was probably a difficult person, perhaps paranoid or schizophrenic, as various researchers have later attempted to prove. He was to live another thirteen years, years in which he continued to work on the 'heads', as he simply called them, eventually leaving behind a few dozen to an initially uncomprehending posterity.

A good two centuries later, the group of *Character Heads* has long since been scattered and become a highly prized artefact of art history, represented in important museum collections including that of the Belvedere, which holds the largest contingent. In 1994, three years have passed since Marc Quinn created *Self* (1991), the most radical and shocking self-portrait imaginable. This iconic work is the one with the most potential to make him immortal: it is the artist's head cast from his own blood, dipped in frozen silicone. How, I ask myself, do you carry on after having produced such a work, committed such a deed, at age twenty-seven?

It is said that nobody can ever know what an artist has done, only they themselves. 'But I don't know myself', they often reply. Rarely in the face of historical artworks is there such a compelling desire to talk to the artist about his work as there is with the *Character Heads*. Mr. Messerschmidt, why did you do that? 'Oh, I just tried this and that. I liked making faces in front of the mirror. Why should only children be allowed to pull faces and amuse themselves that way? I wanted to form heads that fine art had never seen before, instead of the heads of majesties and scholars. I don't even know why myself.'

Quinn discovers one of these heads in the Victoria and Albert Museum: *The Strong Smell*, by a certain Franz Xaver Messerschmidt. But does the portrait show someone smelling? (We know that the titles of the heads were assigned not by the artist but by someone else after his death.) If you care to see it, the crinkled nose and the pursed upper lip do seem to correspond to the disgust of an unpleasant odour. But if you find yourself faced with this during a life crisis, doesn't the expression then more closely resemble one of existential pain? Perhaps Quinn sees a man squeezing his eyes as tightly shut as possible in order to lock the agonising images in his head behind ramparts of black and starbursts, stretching his neck and hyperextending his muscles in order to feel his body instead of his soul—to banish the terrible thoughts for a moment in the corset of physical exertion?

And perhaps, then and there, he suddenly knows how to go on after the absolute artistic divestment of *Self* and after the physical and emotional agonies of withdrawal. He will go on to create a series of works that portray him in his living hell. He will draw inspiration from the traditional iconography of the seven deadly sins. And he will show the demon that is at his throat: it is himself.

The sculptor's hands choke and poke his likeness, punch his face, press on his skull. The bust, which extends down to the waist, is lumpy, raw, riddled with holes. The hands are detached from the arms and have taken on a sadistic life of their own. And yet, were it not for the tortured facial expression, these hands could also be playing a game of the kind that children like. Little children who poke adults in the face—look how funny that looks when I pull your cheeks apart!

The sculptor takes matter into his own hand and lays them on himself. The great thing about *Emotional Detox*, besides the gripping presentation and masterful technique, is the pictorial ambiguity. The sculptor shows the basic principle of his work, moulding with his own hands; life runs through the body leaving scratches and scuffs. We are our own worst tormentors but, like Baron Munchausen, we can pull ourselves out of the morass by our own hair.

List of Works

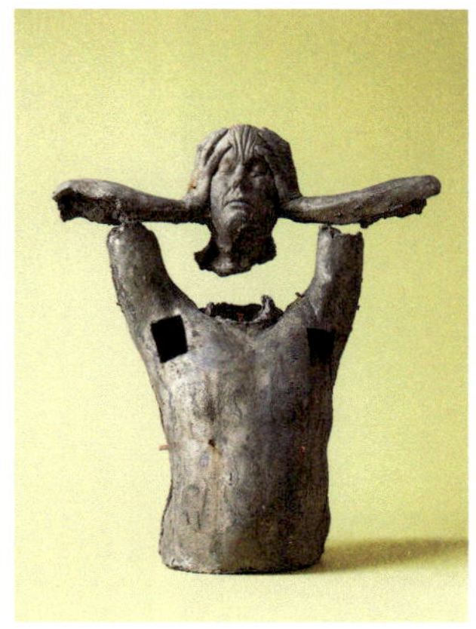

Marc Quinn
Emotional Detox IV, 1995
Edition of 3 with 2 APs
Cast lead and wax
90 h × 80 w × 30 d cm

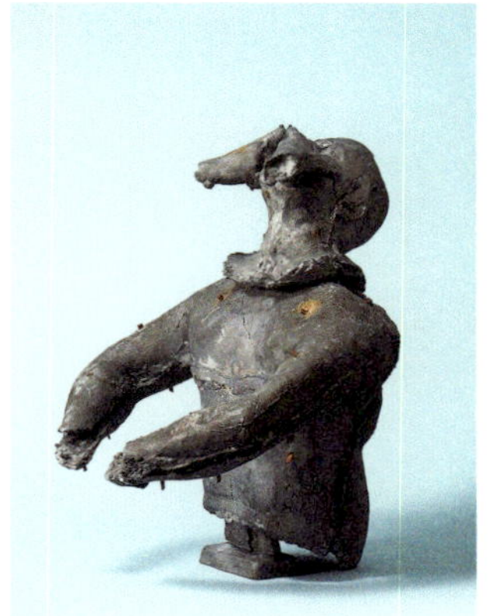

Marc Quinn
Emotional Detox III, 1995
Edition of 3 with 2 APs
Cast lead and wax
83 h × 75 w × 55 d cm

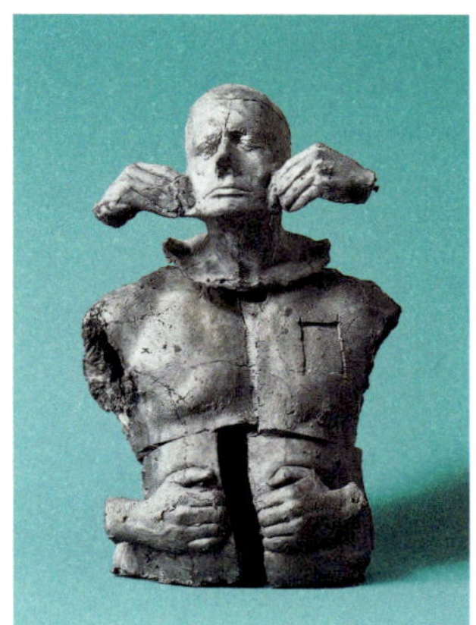

Marc Quinn
Emotional Detox V, 1995
Edition of 3 with 2 APs
Cast lead and wax
86 h × 52 w × 36 d cm

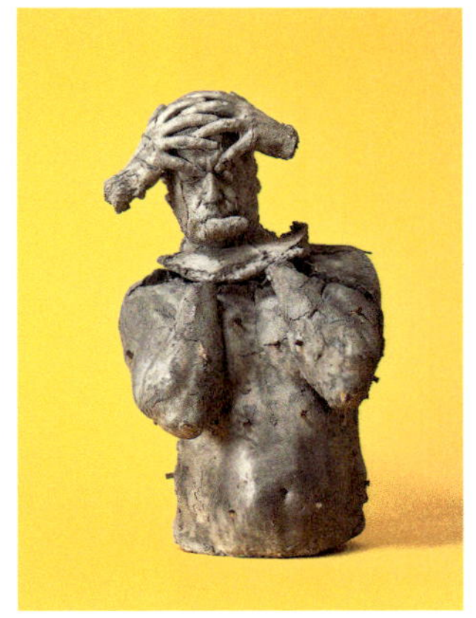

Marc Quinn
Emotional Detox II, 1995
Edition of 3 with 2 APs
Cast lead and wax
86 h × 47 w × 37 d cm

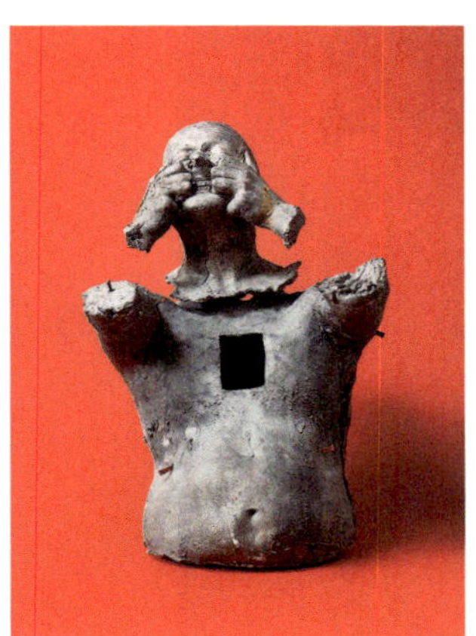

Marc Quinn
Emotional Detox VII, 1995
Edition of 3 with 2 APs
Cast lead and wax
90 h × 80 w × 30 d cm

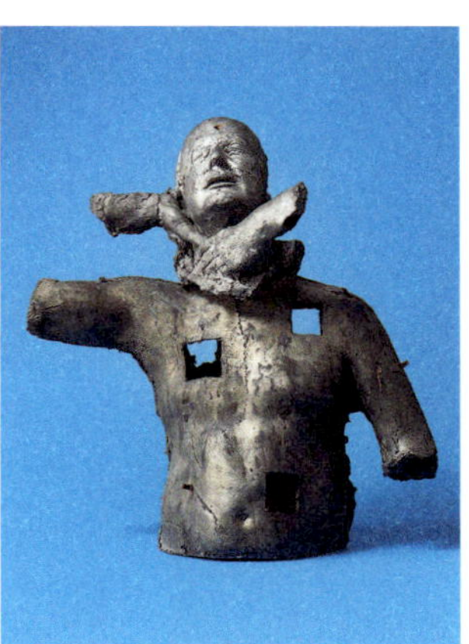

Marc Quinn
Emotional Detox I, 1994
Edition of 3 with 2 APs
Cast lead and wax
80 h × 65 w × 35 d cm

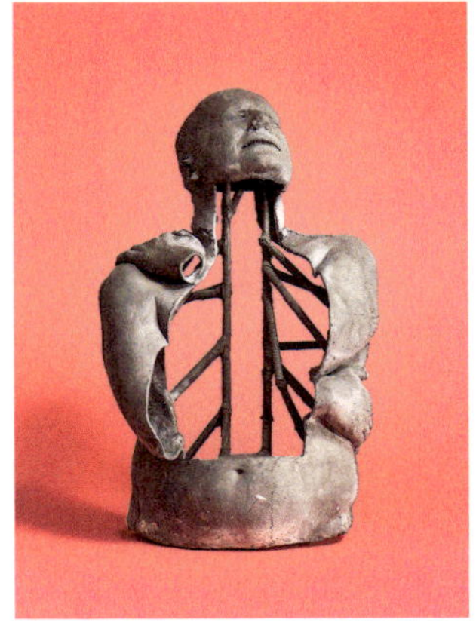

Marc Quinn
Fear of Fear, 1994
Edition of 5 with 2 APs
Cast lead
76 h × 43 w × 37 d cm

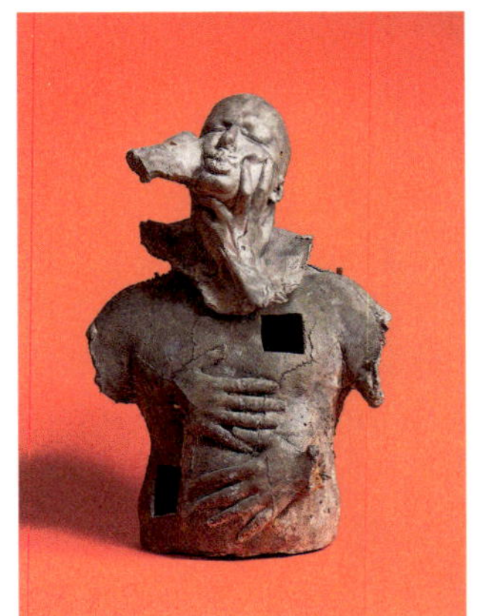

Marc Quinn
Emotional Detox VI, 1995
Edition of 3 with 2 APs
Cast lead and wax
86 h × 55 w × 40 d cm

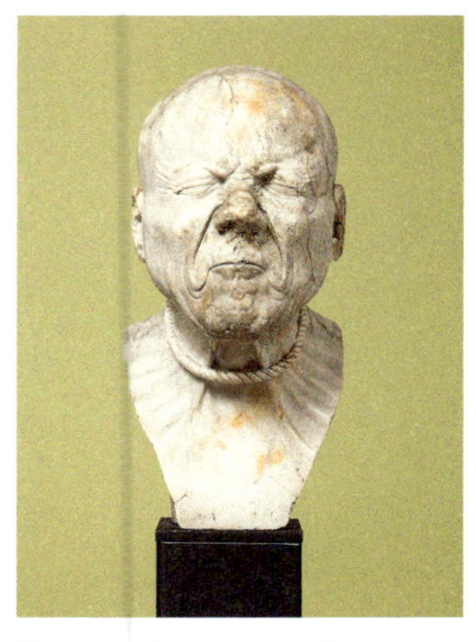

Franz Xaver Messerschmidt
A Hanged Man, 1771/1783
Alabaster, grey white stone with brownish spots
38 h × 20 w × 27 d cm

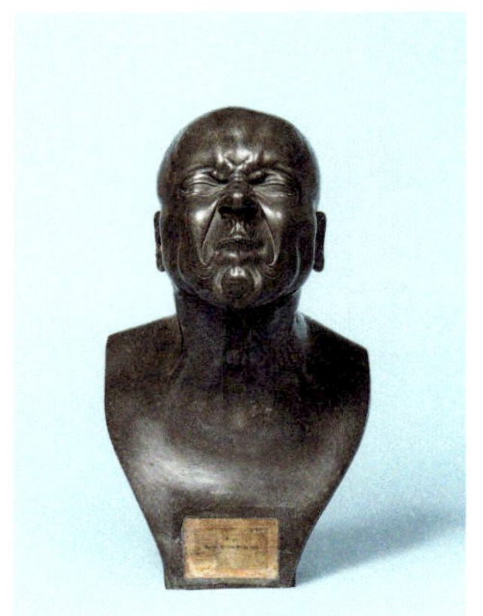

Franz Xaver Messerschmidt
The Sneeze-Inducing Odour, 1777/1783
Lead cast
47 h × 27 w × 33 d cm

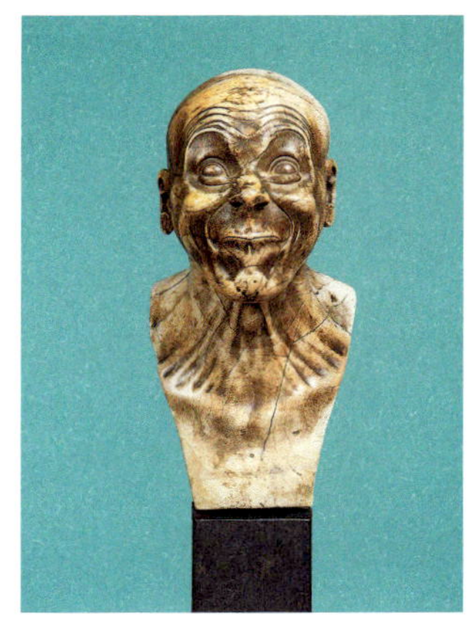

Franz Xaver Messerschmidt
The Simpleton, 1777/1783
Brown-flecked alabaster
43,5 h × 21 w × 33 d cm

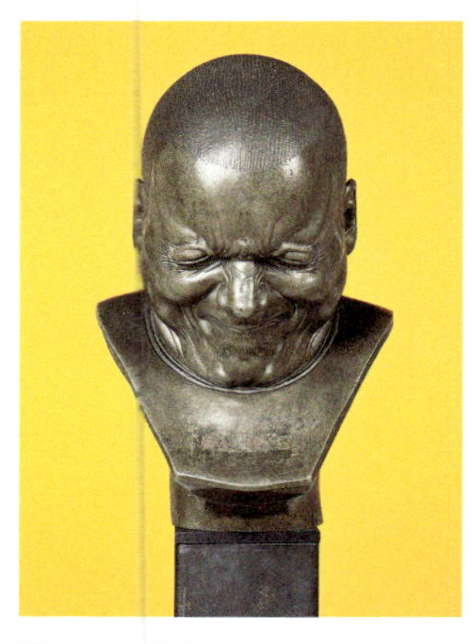

Franz Xaver Messerschmidt
An Arch-Rascal, 1777/1783
Tin alloy
39 h × 26 w × 25 d cm

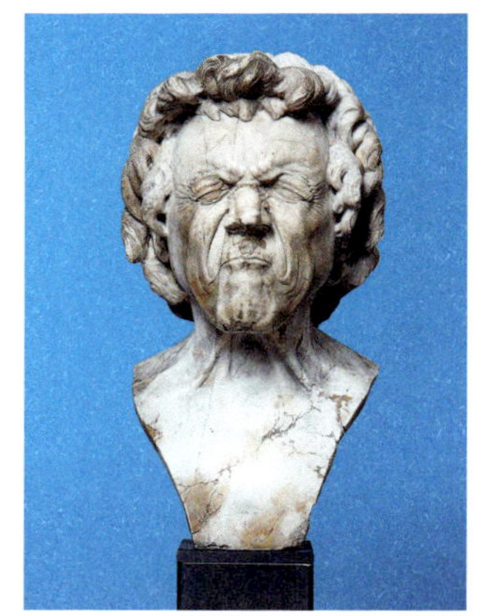

Franz Xaver Messerschmidt
A Haggard Old Man with Aching Eyes, 1771/1783
Alabaster, mottled brownish-grey stone
44 h × 23.5 w × 26 d cm

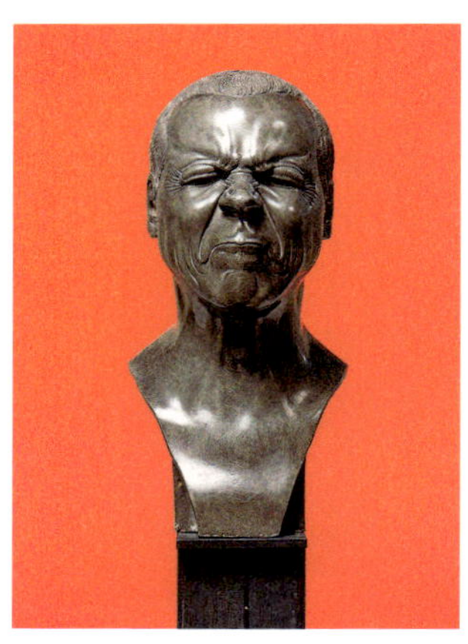

Franz Xaver Messerschmidt
A Dismal and Sinister Man, 1770/1783
Lead alloy
43 h × 22 w × 24 d cm

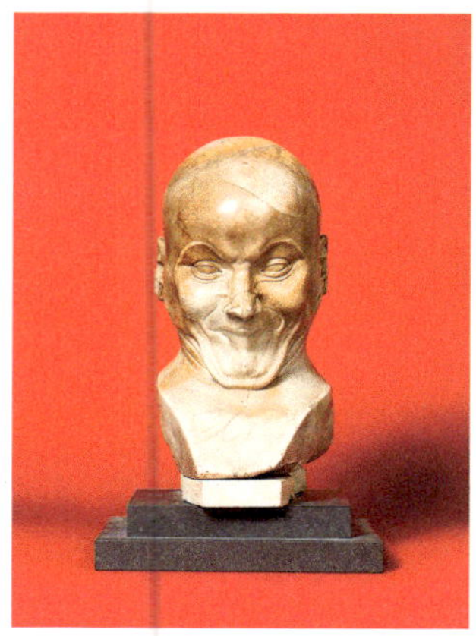

Franz Xaver Messerschmidt
A Mischievous Wag, 1777/1783
Alabaster, brown-flecked stone
37 h × 18 w × 23 d cm

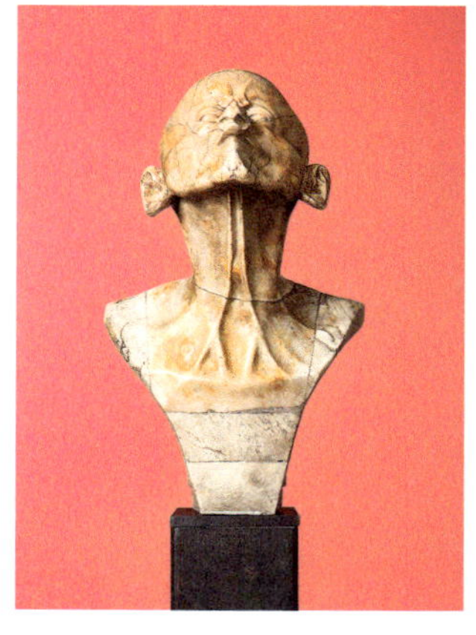

Franz Xaver Messerschmidt
Second Beak Head, 1777/1781
Alabaster, mottled brownish stone
42.5 h × 26 w × 24.5 d cm

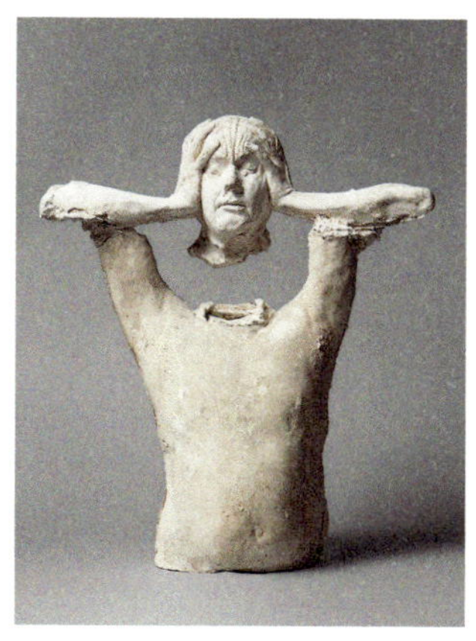

Marc Quinn
The Oneironaut IV (Emotional Detox), 1995
Plaster
92 h × 81 w × 37 d cm

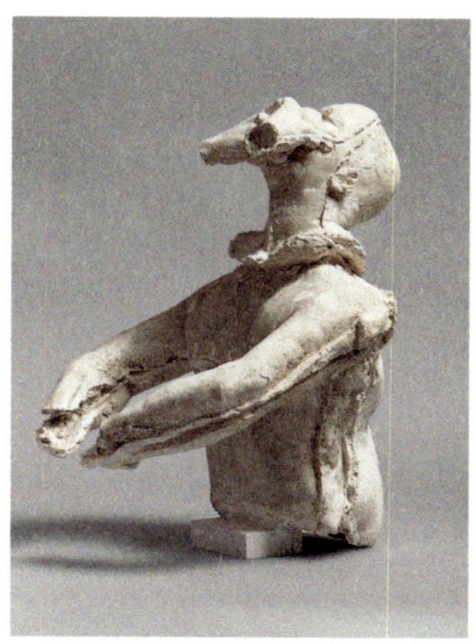

Marc Quinn
The Oneironaut III (Emotional Detox), 1995
Plaster
80 h × 56 w × 64 d cm

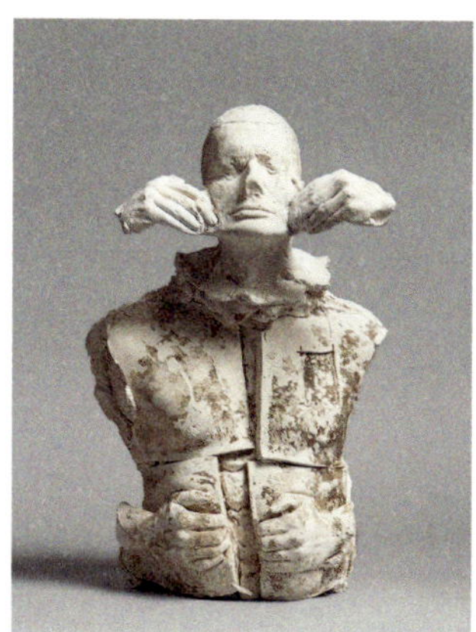

Marc Quinn
The Oneironaut V (Emotional Detox), 1995
Plaster
81 h × 52 w × 39 d cm

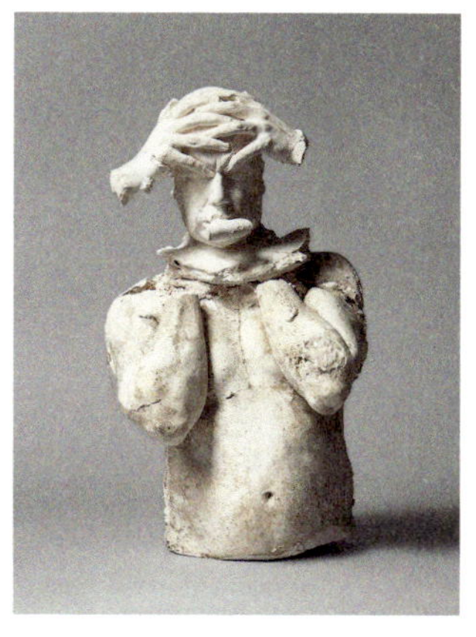

Marc Quinn
The Oneironaut II (Emotional Detox), 1995
Plaster
81 h × 46 w × 35 d cm

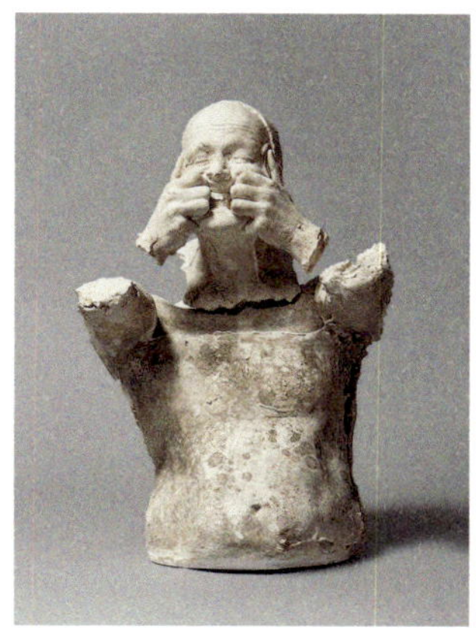

Marc Quinn
The Oneironaut VII (Emotional Detox), 1995
Plaster
75 h × 52 w × 46 d cm

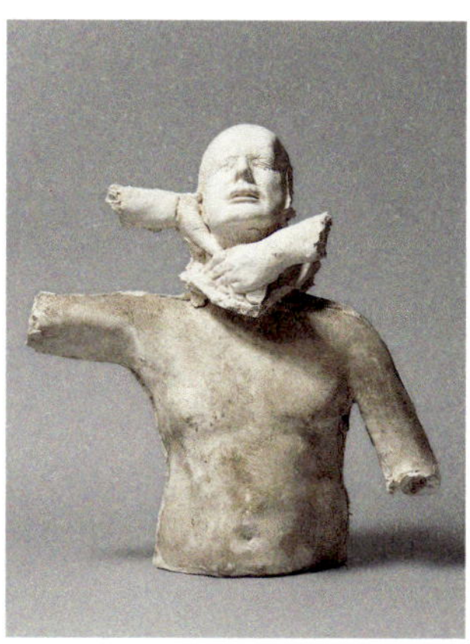

Marc Quinn
The Oneironaut I (Emotional Detox), 1995
Plaster
80 h × 70 w × 34 d cm

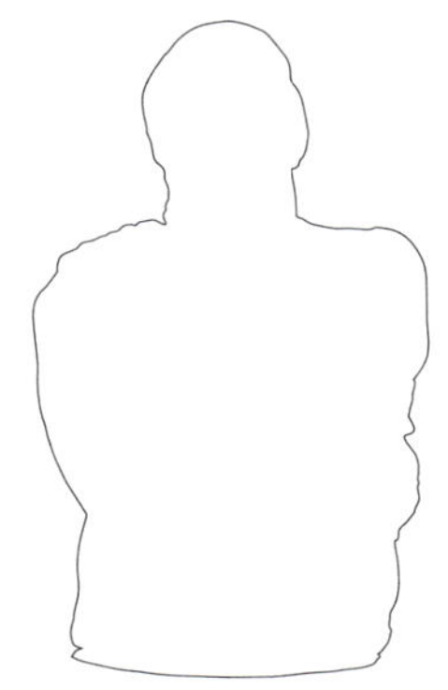

Marc Quinn
Fear of Fear, 1994

The original cast has been lost since its creation.

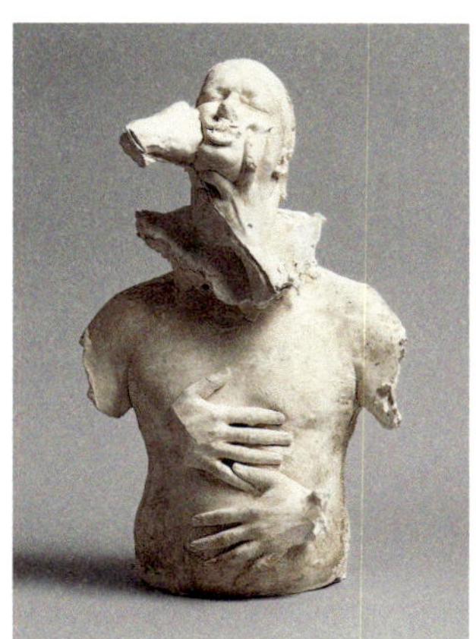

Marc Quinn
The Oneironaut VI (Emotional Detox), 1995
Plaster
86 h × 51 w × 30 d cm

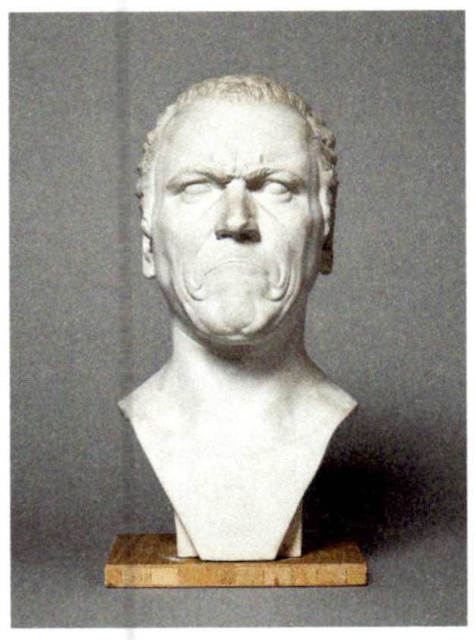

After Franz Xaver Messerschmidt
A Surly Old Soldier, 1964
Plaster cast
Height: 42 cm

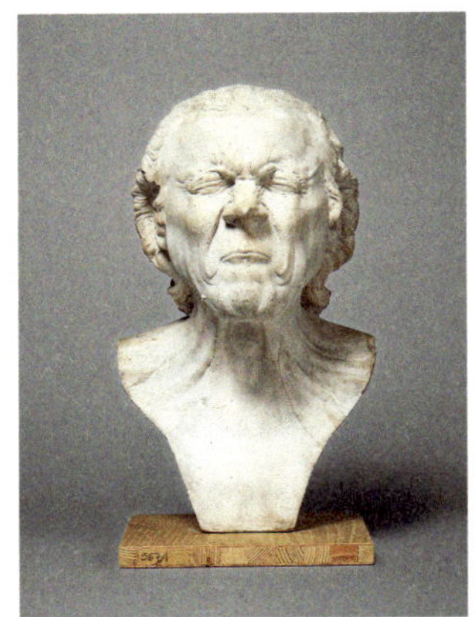

After Franz Xaver Messerschmidt
The Vexed Man, before 1923
Plaster cast
Height: 42 cm

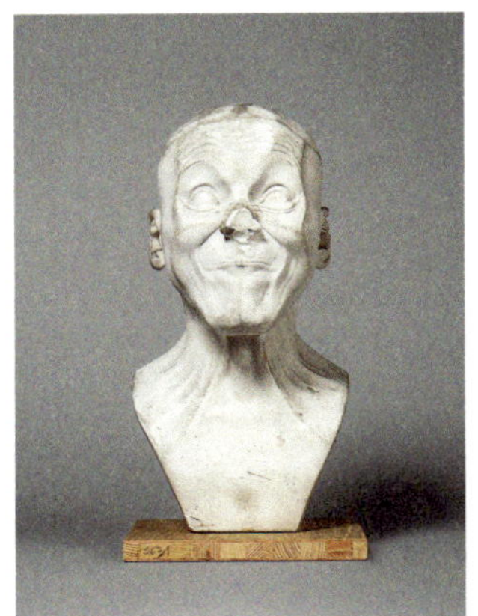

After Franz Xaver Messerschmidt
A Lecherous and Careworn Fop, before 1923
Plaster cast
Height: 42 cm

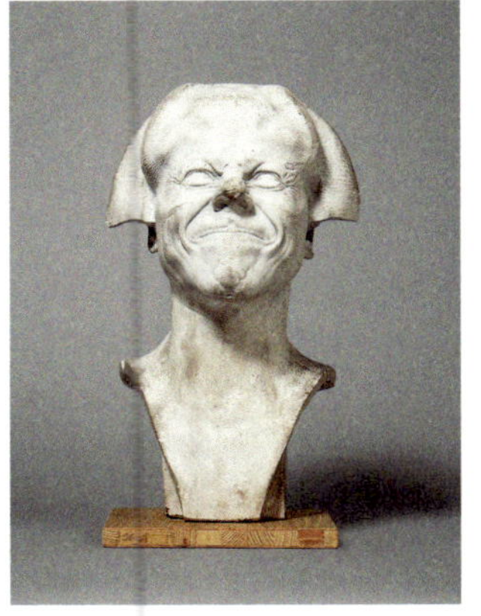

After Franz Xaver Messerschmidt
A Grievously Wounded Man, before 1923
Plaster cast
Height: 45 cm

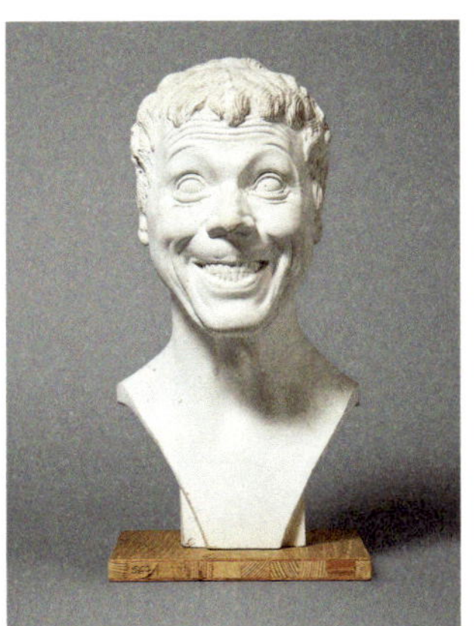

After Franz Xaver Messerschmidt
The Enraged and Vengeful Gypsy, before 1923
Plaster cast
Height: 45 cm

The historical titles of the *Character Heads* are not derived from Franz Xaver Messerschmidt; these titles were introduced posthumously by Franz Friedrich Strunz in his essay *Merkwürdige Lebensgeschichte des Franz Xaver Messerschmidt, k. k. öffentlichen Lehrer der Bildhauerkunst* (Remarkable Life Story of Franz Xaver Messerschmidt, Imperial and Royal Public Teacher of Sculpture), which was published in Vienna in 1793 in conjunction with an exhibition. These improvised titles continue to be used and are considered to be part of the provenance of the works. Due to their subjective and pejorative nature, current research discourse is in favour of replacing the titles with numbers.

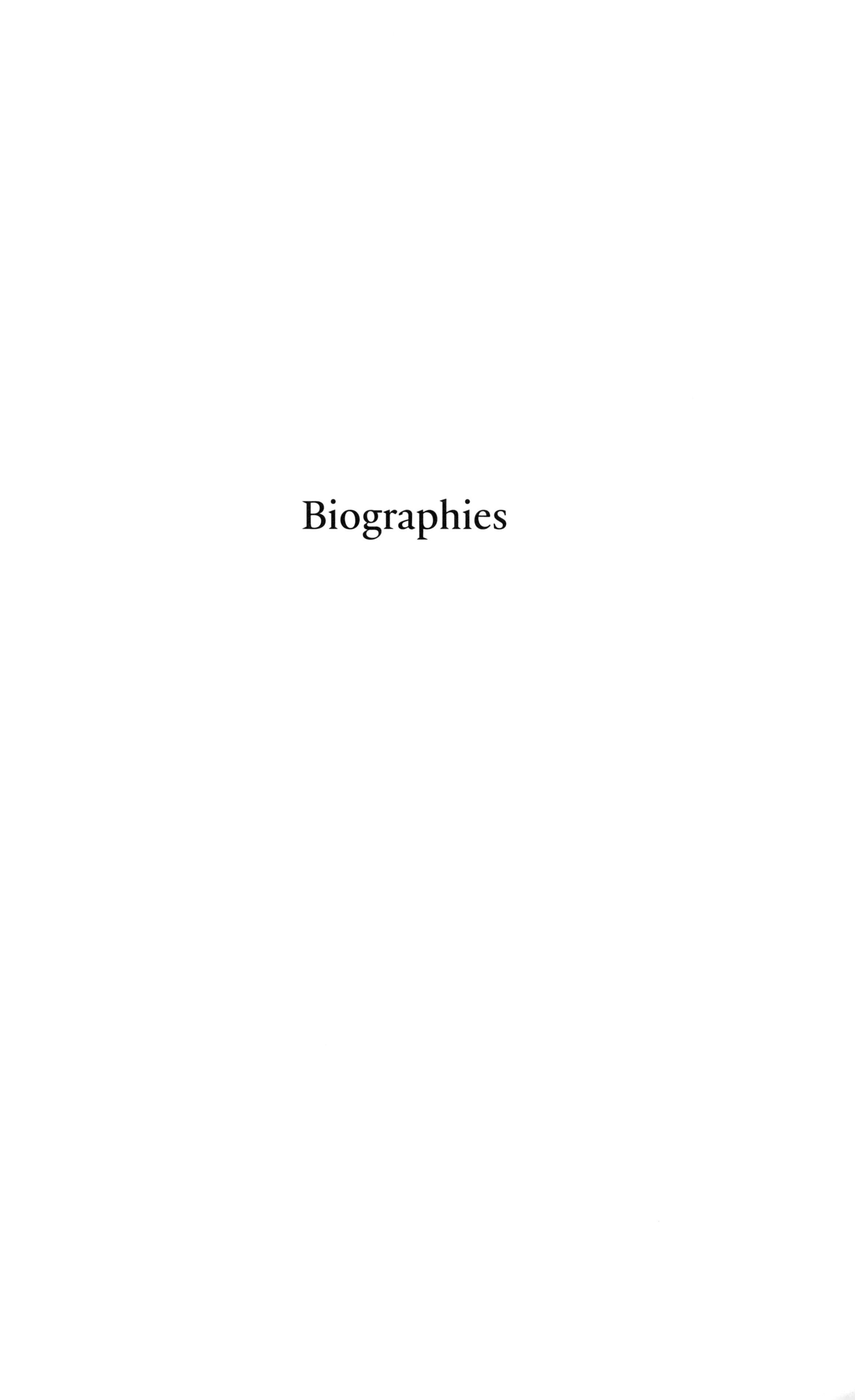

Biographies

Marc Quinn

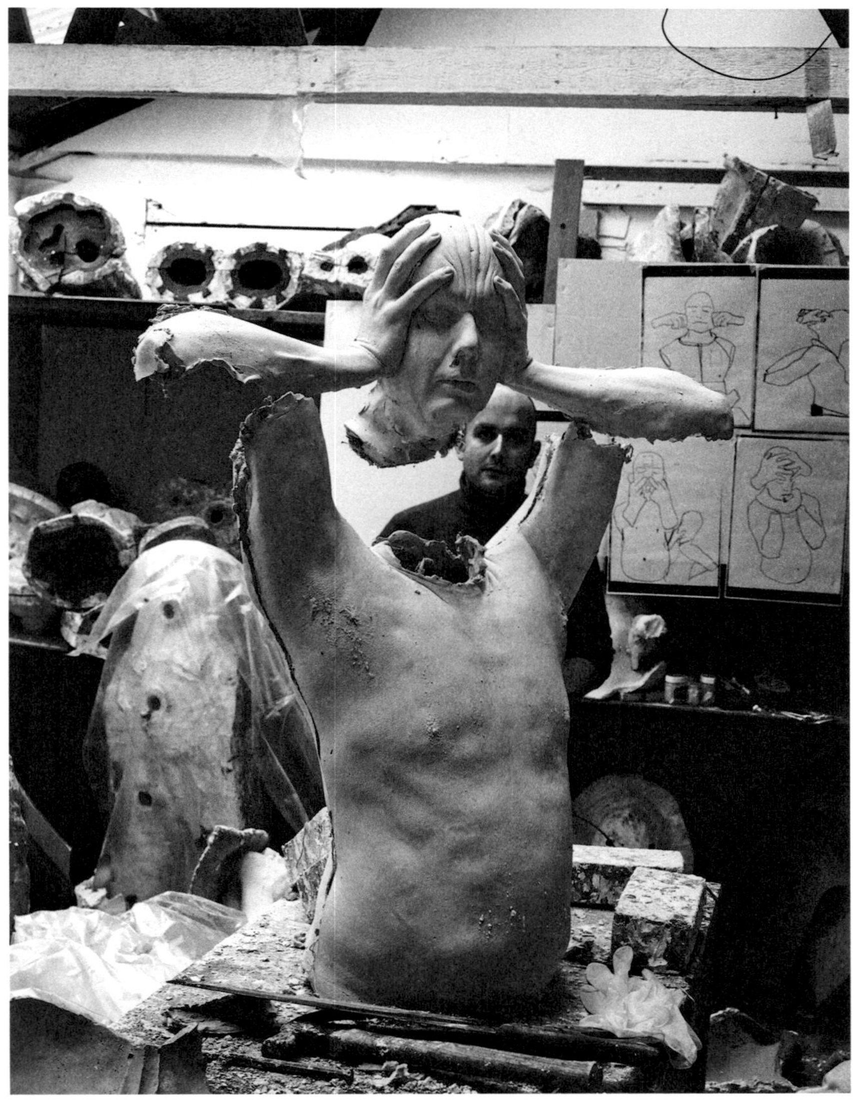

Fig. 1

Marc Quinn, born 1964, is one of the leading artists of his generation. His sculptures, paintings, and drawings explore what it means to be human in the twenty-first century. His work connects frequently and meaningfully with art history, from modern masters right back to antiquity. Quinn came to prominence in 1991 with his sculpture *Self* (1991), a cast of the artist's head made from eight pints of his own frozen blood. While much of his early work focused on explorations of self, Quinn soon became fascinated with reflecting the experiences of other people, questioning value, perception, and the fault lines of society. Critically acclaimed works include *Alison Lapper Pregnant* (2005), exhibited on the Fourth Plinth of London's Trafalgar Square; *Siren* (2008), a solid gold sculpture of Kate Moss shown at the British Museum coinciding with the 2008 financial breakdown, posing questions of value and belief systems in society; *Breath* (2012), a colossal replica of *Alison Lapper Pregnant* commissioned for

Fig. 1
Marc Quinn pictured in the studio with *The Oneironaut IV (Emotional Detox)*, 1995.

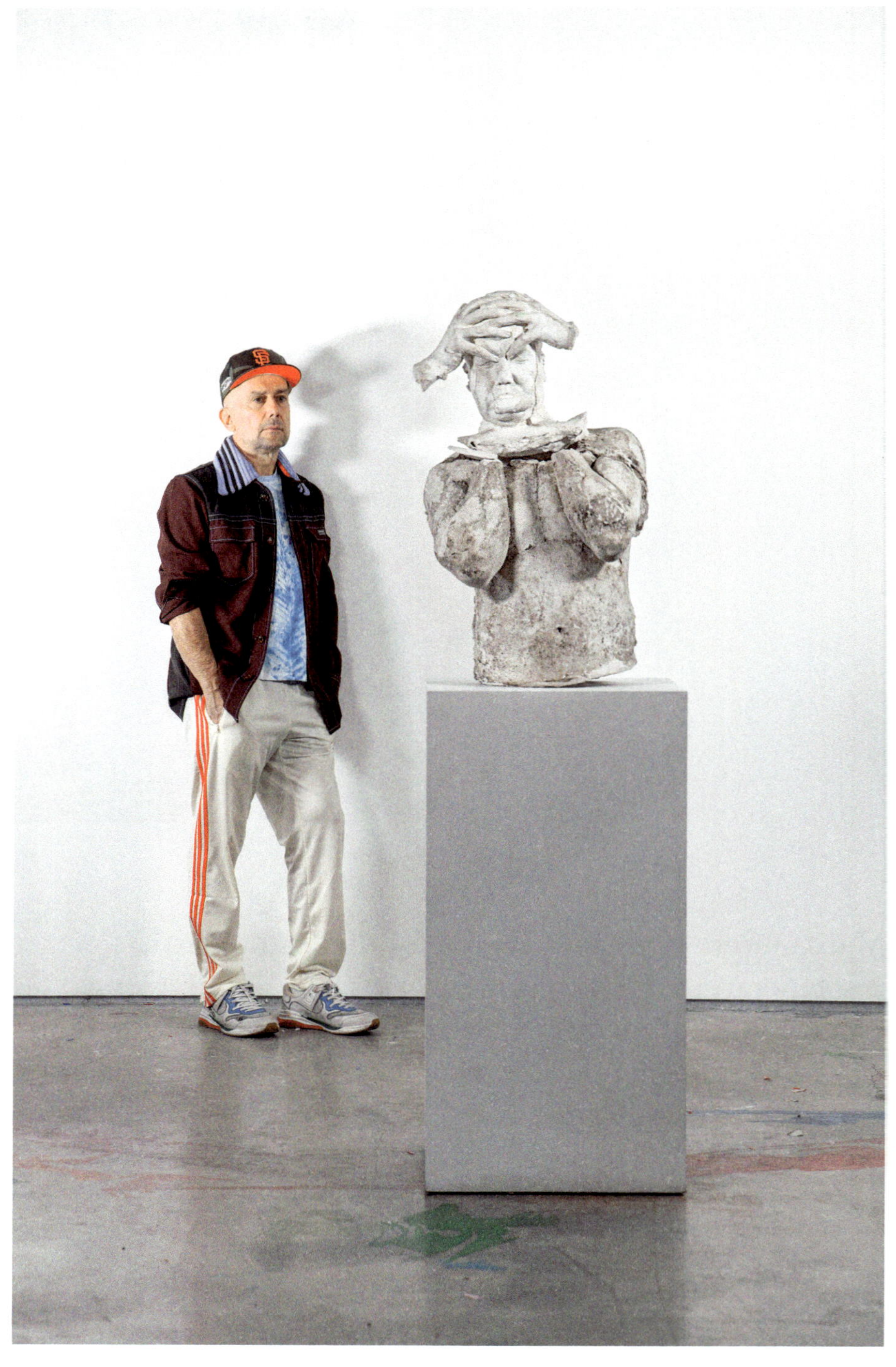

Fig. 2

Fig. 2
Marc Quinn with *The Oneironaut II (Emotional Detox)*, photographed by Adiam Yemane in late 2021.

the opening ceremony of the 2012 London Paralympics; and *Self-conscious Gene* (2019) a 3.5-metre bronze sculpture of 'Zombie Boy' Rick Genest, now on permanent display at the Science Museum, London. Over the last decade, Quinn's work has become increasingly engaged with the media, current affairs, and world events. *History Paintings* (2009–present) is his ten-year series of hyperreal oil paintings of pivotal moments in recent history, drawn directly from press photography. During the COVID-19 pandemic, as news cycles accelerated, Quinn created HISTORYNOW (2020–present), a series of paintings derived from iPhone screenshots of news stories and Instagram posts.

Since 2015 Quinn has developed several not-for-profit projects, which seek to raise awareness of the ongoing global refugee crisis and raise funds for the International Rescue Committee and further refugee organisations. This includes *100 Heads* (2019–present), a significant series of sculptures, comprising one hundred concrete portrait busts of refugees living today.

Quinn's work is included in collections around the world, including Tate in London, the Metropolitan Museum of Art in New York, the Solomon R. Guggenheim Museum in New York, SFMOMA in San Francisco, Fondazione Prada in Milan, the Stedelijk Museum in Amsterdam, and the Centre Pompidou in Paris.

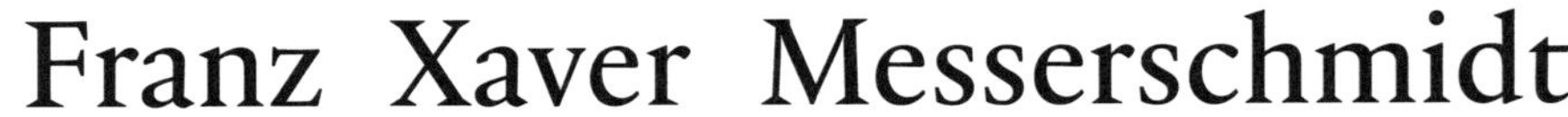

Franz Xaver Messerschmidt

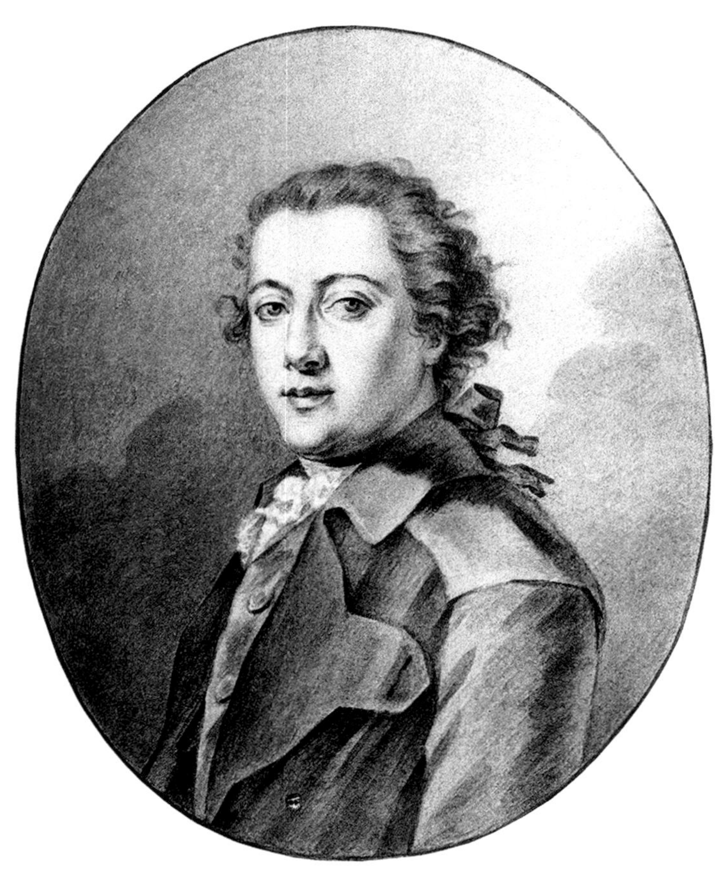

Franz Xaver Messerschmidt was born in 1736 in Wiesensteig, Swabia. After the death of his father, he completed an apprenticeship as a sculptor with his uncle, Johann Baptist Straub, in Munich in 1746. In 1752 the young Messerschmidt joined the workshop of another uncle, Philipp Jakob Straub, in Graz as a journeyman. In 1755 Franz Xaver Messerschmidt began his studies at the Academy of Fine Arts in Vienna. There, he was supported by his mentor, the painter Martin van Meytens the Younger, who was also director of the academy starting in 1759. This relationship gave him his first job as a stucco cutter in the imperial armoury, gaining him both material and technical expertise. In 1760 Messerschmidt began receiving commissions as a sculptor from high-ranking members of the nobility and the imperial family itself. His statues of Maria Theresa and Francis I are now on display in the Sala Terrena in the Upper Belvedere. The first *Character Heads* can be traced back to 1770. Disappointed that he was overlooked as a potential member of the academy during the 1774 professorial election, Messerschmidt left Vienna in 1775. After working in Munich and Wiesensteig, he settled in Pressburg (now Bratislava), where he worked on the *Character Heads* until his death in 1783.

Fig. 3
Unknown artist
Supposed portrait of Franz Xaver Messerschmidt in his youth, undated
Austrian National Library, Vienna

Marc Quinn
in Conversation with
Cat Marnell

CM I'm not the most focused of interviewees.

MQ Maybe that's fitting for a conversation about art and addiction.

CM And Messerschmidt?

MQ The heads do look quite intense.

CM Was he?

MQ Well, one of the weirder things about the collection for me is the technical mastery behind each head. That's why they're so great. They're so raw and emotive but technically perfect—that doesn't usually go together. I mean, he must have at least had lucid periods while he was making them. Because I don't think he could have made them otherwise—from out of the grips of a full-blown psychosis.

CM Yeah. I feel like in those times—whenever I was fucked up—I used to just feel the urge to smear my lipstick. [*Laughs.*] Those substances would make me feel completely loopy; suddenly I'd be in a twenty-four-hour hardware store, I hadn't slept for days. It was some of the craziest stuff you could imagine, and it's just such a great relief now to be taking care of myself. One of my favourite books about addiction is *Narcissus in Wonderland* by Richard B. Ulman and Harry Paul [New York, 2006], which basically equates the addict to a fantasy-junkie who—like Narcissus in the mirror—gets transfixed by themselves, because addiction (the book posits) mimics narcissism.

MQ Messerschmidt spent a lot of time in front of the mirror too, observing his facial expressions. That's how he sculpted them in such a lifelike way. That was one of the things that struck me most about your book actually: how factual and true to life it was, and how relentlessly upbeat the tone was, but with all these crazy things happening at the same time. I was really sucked in. How did the book come about?

CM Well, I've worked in publishing my entire adult life, starting as a teenager, but I had always wanted to be a magazine editor. I was at *Vanity Fair* and *Teen Vogue* and *Glamour*, and finally wound up at *Lucky*, which was a shopping magazine. But because of my prescription-drug addiction I lost my magazine career and ended up writing for the internet, which at that time—2010—was frowned upon by magazine people. I was so embarrassed. But when I was publishing online I went viral and then I got this book deal. I was so sick at the time, though: I was a drug addict. And of course, deep in my addiction I couldn't write. It was like running a marathon with an iron leg. But eventually I started the book in recovery, in a treatment centre in Thailand, at a desk in the dark with all these monkeys … hooting.

MQ [*Laughing.*] That's a surreal image. You know, I remember thinking that if I stopped with the alcohol, I'd stop being creative. I worry that a lot of people carry on because of that. They're scared that what they see as that crazy, creative part of themselves will die if they give up, but it's the opposite, like with you in Thailand: you gain the ability to do something with it instead, in a controlled way, without destroying yourself.

CM I think that if I was a painter or a sculptor—anything *besides* a writer—I'd probably have that same self-defeating belief. But the writing's just so technical for me that there's no way addiction could ever be anything but an impediment. Because it's so muddled; it's hell. Creativity-wise, that dark trance you can get it in with your addiction *can* be gold, but health—that's *diamonds*. It turns you into an athlete! I mean, all the fantastic ideas, those are still with me—and clearly for you as well—but now we can communicate them. I wouldn't trade my clarity for anything.

MQ Yeah, it's a nightmare living without it. You never get the best out of yourself.

CM I try to apply exercise principles to my work now. Have you heard of high-intensity interval training? It's about making the maximum impact in the shortest amount of time. You keep it tight and don't take a break, and then it's just *done*. That's how I like to write: tight, organised, as early in the morning as possible.

MQ So your addictions are work and exercise now?

CM You know, it could be even better than that? Now I'm getting into *cleaning*.

MQ [*Laughing*.] It's kind of amazing though, to have a way of dealing with things through these creative means? Both of us are really lucky that we're able to do that.

CM It's the great privilege of my life. You have to apply all your addict energy somewhere because it's not going away. You know, trainers love working with former addicts? There's that famous Hollywood trainer who's like, 'Bring on the former alcoholics, they'll always show up.' But yeah, it's a dream to get to here. I mean, how magnificent is it for you to have your show at a palace? Which I know is par for the course for Europe, but it's still fabulous.

MQ It's a little surreal: I couldn't even look at the *Emotional Detox* pieces for a long, long time. They reminded me too much of that period in my life. I made them, then moved on.

CM Again, it's amazing how creative work can purge things. For me personally, with everything I write, once it's out of me I'm over it.

MQ It's a really fundamental part of art's appeal for artists: one theory was that—with the heads—Messerschmidt was trying to scare off evil spirits that frightened him in the night.

CM You know that's funny, given my own memory of Austria at night. Have you ever been to the Prater amusement park in

Vienna? I swear it's like wandering through the human brain. There are giant clown mouths, a haunted house, dragons, snakes, and I was walking around like, 'What the fuck is this place?' I'm a big carnival person, actually. I used to feel like my brain was so flat and uninteresting during the day, like the way amusement parks rides are: they look like nothing, and then as soon as it gets dark, the lights come on. So my whole life I've been drawn to those places, but now I'm realising the good stuff comes in the morning. I really hate to tell that to anyone young who's reading our conversation.

MQ_ You're shattering all their illusions. I get up early and exercise now, which is something I never thought I'd do. I feel really weird if I don't do it.

CM As Gwen Stefani once said, 'I would never even think about not doing it.' All the best ideas I have now are from running.

MQ_ Yeah, any kind of movement can unblock ideas for me too; I find it makes things happen in my head. I figure out how to express what I'm thinking.

CM Have you heard of the poet John Berryman? He won the Pulitzer Prize for *The Dream Songs* and at some point jumped off a bridge—he was a terrible alcoholic. Anyway, his book was the first thing I thought of when I looked at your work. They're quite uncomfortable to look at, your pieces. And his poetry is so muddled and murky. When I used to come home drunk I would pull it off my shelf and it would make perfect sense, and then if I ever read it sober I'd be like, 'What is this?' It's so surreal—but ugly. It's just a very, very sick person; it's the subconscious. Did you go to treatment for your addiction in the end?

MQ_ Yeah. I woke up one morning after coming back from a holiday to France with my girlfriend, which had not gone well, and I was in this kind of squat I was living in, surrounded by bottles, and I picked up this magazine and was flicking through it when I saw this list titled something like 'London's

Top Doctors.' And the doctor I had visited when I was giving blood for my blood sculpture *Self* was in there, so I started to read, and it said he specialised in addiction. And then something just happened, and I picked up the phone and asked him, 'Can I come and see you?' And when I did, he said 'Oh I was wondering when you might turn up to talk to me about this.' He got me into a rehab clinic, and I went that day. I decided pretty quickly that it was what I wanted to do: I don't know how, after being so incapable of stopping before.

CM How old were you?

MQ Thirty. And then I couldn't work for about a year and a half after that, and then I started making these sculptures, which, now, I can look at again.

CM I understand why you couldn't. You know, I love tear sheets, and even just the photos and people I want tacked up around me, that's changed. As I get older, I just want the healthy people up—not Marilyn Monroe. It's nothing conscious, but you keep yourself distant from the sick stuff.

MQ But also there *is* something helpful, I think, about how in treatment you meet other sick people, because it's quite isolating—life as an addict—and you tell yourself this is so unique to you and that nobody has ever felt this way before, but then you say, 'Oh my god, this is normal, it's not a big deal.' And it relaxes you to realise there are other people that feel the same way that you do. When I used to go to meetings what worked was how quickly they stopped the fantasy. You're walking in and telling yourself that maybe drinking wasn't so bad, it was great that one night, et cetera et cetera, and then there's someone talking about what it was *really* like, yesterday, and the fantasy just withers. Because the human mind loves to fantasise. But it's very hard for people to even *risk* a confrontation with a reality check like that. Take the titles of the Messerschmidt heads: when he died, a guy from a carnival bought them and then just gave each one a really ridiculous name. 'A Know-It-All Quibbling

Quipster,' 'The Ultimate Simpleton.' And those are *still* the names they're stuck with today. It's funny, because without the names they're powerful and disturbing—because they show unnameable emotions. You have to feel them, which is challenging, and it's as if it was only with these silly names that people were able to start accepting them. Naming tames them. I think there's something of this juxtaposition at play in your own book [*How to Murder Your Life*, New York, 2017] actually, between the content and the tone. It's *appalling*, and yet *really funny*.

CM Right, I really wanted my narrator to sound kind of... 'perky.'

MQ Perky in hell, yeah. That uncanniness gave it such an edge, I thought. It's like a really extreme version of that impulse to hide everything that's actually happening to you behind a weird layer of... perkiness.

CM Thank you, I'm glad, because that was definitely a choice. I wanted the book to have the same feeling as pop music, as opposed to something like 'Heroin' by The Velvet Underground—the more typical thing for this kind of topic. And when you're a woman and you write about yourself, I've found people can sometimes discredit a little bit the technical work and the choices you make. They just say it's 'confessional', and yes, I'm using autobiographical material, but I constructed every single beat on every page, you know? I wrote it so that every chapter had the same word count, 4,400 words.

MQ I think your book will last. I think in art it's realness that endures. Maybe that's why we're still talking about Messerschmidt. It doesn't matter what people think about something at the time, because if it comes from a real place it has centuries of life ahead of it. People in a thousand years will still have the same problems that we have—the human brain isn't going to change. So all of this work about human strength and weakness—for better or worse—will still be relevant.

Making Faces
Tim Smith-Laing

When the soul is agitated, the human face becomes a living painting, where the passions are rendered with as much delicacy as energy, where every movement of the soul is expressed in a line, every action by a character whose prompt and lively impression outpaces the will, reveals us, and shows on our outside, by pathetic signs, the images of our most secret agitations.

– Buffon, *Natural History*[1]

There is no art / To find the mind's construction in the face

– Duncan, in Shakespeare's *Macbeth*[2]

Emotional Detox shows us Marc Quinn's body suffering, over and again, at its own hands. They fly free to oppose it, pushing, beating, strangling, even multiplying to perform different tasks at once. In number VI, one hand holds the head still while the other punches it; in number V, one pair stretches the cheeks as if to open out the face, a second neatly splits the belly below. Terrible violence is done. And yet the face at the centre of it all remains curiously calm. Literally detached, balanced on the body, Quinn's bust takes its punishment with strange composure. Across the series the eyes are shut, but not screwed tight with fear or agony. The closest thing to visible pain occurs in sculpture I: a frown, an inaudible gasp at the tightening strangle. Otherwise, the expressions, such as they are visible beneath the manipulations wrought on them, might be called patient. Perhaps some kind of understanding has been reached that the work of the hands is not violence for violence's sake. Here, in number VI, one pair caresses the torso as if to soothe. In number IV it even seems as if a kind of repose has been reached through their ministrations. Wholly separate from the body at last, the head rests between the hands, aloft and cradled. Or so.

Or so, because of how much turns on that expression and what we make of it. *Emotional Detox* offers up a series of interpretative trails to follow, gathering meaning as we go, but there are so many that they become a maze. Here is the proffered key of the title: *detox*; catharsis by another name; and yet the sequence ends

1 'Lorsque l'ame [*sic*] est agitée, la face humaine devient un tableau vivant où les passions sont rendues avec autant de délicatesse que d'énergie, où chaque mouvement de l'âme est exprimé par un trait, chaque action par un charactère dont l'impression vive & prompte devance la volonté, nous décèle & rend au dehors, par des signes pathétiques, les images de nos plus secrettes [*sic*] agitations.' Georges-Louis Leclerc, Comte de Buffon, *Histoire naturelle, générale et particulière, Tome second* (Paris, 1749), p. 519.

2 Shakespeare, *Macbeth*, I.4.11–12.

3
See *Merkwürdige Lebensgeschichte des Franz Xaver Messerschmidt, k. k. öffentlichen Lehrer der Bildhauerkunst* (Vienna, 1794). The author has recently been identified as one Franz Friedrich Strunz. See Anna Schirlbauer, 'Die Charakterköpfe F. X. Messerschmidt und ihr erster Aussteller Franz Strunz', *Ars* 46, no. 2 (2013), pp. 292–308.

4
Respectively: private collection, Belgium; collection of Gerolamo and Roberta Etro; Belvedere, Vienna, inv. no. 2284; Metropolitan Museum of Art, New York, acc. no. 2010.24.

not with the equilibrium of number IV, but with the forcefully retracted lips and bared teeth of number VII. Is this what purity looks like, or does the process never end? Here is the biography: Quinn's one-time alcoholism; but this alone is too slim to describe what is going on. Here is the art history and inspiration: Franz Xaver Messerschmidt's *Character Heads*; but Quinn's response is at least as tangential as it is direct. Here is the significant material: lead, with its toxicity, its alchemical symbolism, its malleability, baseness, and potential... Here are the concerns that run across Quinn's career: identity and the self, the mind-body problem, transformation... All these we know are at play; each one adds to how we might read and react. None helps us pause. If there is a point where the significations could halt, it must be the face.

What to make of the face is a vexed question, though, and not just for *Emotional Detox*. It is one that ties Quinn to Messerschmidt more deeply than even direct inspiration. In *Emotional Detox* our attempts to understand what is happening to the subject—the person, as it were, *within* the body—run up against what might be called a paucity of expression. We are some distance from the hovering smile of *Self* (1991), and further still from the ecstatic contortion of *Blind Leading the Blind* (1995). Across *Emotional Detox* there is a kind of minimisation of expression: no clear *look on the face* emerges for us to endow with meaning. Turn to Messerschmidt's work and the same problem arises, but from the opposite: a superabundance of expression. The so-called *Character Heads* offer nothing but *looks on the face*. But what looks! Across the heads, the human face contorts in a welter of abstruse configurations: wrinkles radiate in deep incisions from clenched eyes; brows ruck into thick folds; cheeks and chins dimple, strain, and undulate into taut symmetries. We have, within the bounds of the sculptures themselves, nothing to go on except the face, shorn of all but the merest sliver of body; but the face's meaning, serially and individually, escapes us.

The escape matters because as with *Emotional Detox* we feel ourselves to be in the presence of a subject, or subjects. The *Character Heads* are, at first glance, realist sculptures, hyper-realist even; such that, setting aside the special visions of the *Beaked* heads, we find ourselves naturally trying to intuit the state of the mind or minds that seem to exist within them. The attempt, however, is doomed. Hence the straining titles the heads remain lumbered with today, conferred upon them by their first cataloguer and exhibitor.[3] The flimsiness of narrative tags like *Just Rescued from Drowning* or *The Incapable Bassoonist*, or moral descriptions like *A Mischievous Wag* or *A Hypocrite and a Slanderer* suggests more than anything else the heads' refusal to submit to interpretation.[4] Even as seemingly simple a case as *The Yawner* runs into problems. In the silence of sculpture, might that yawn not just as easily be a scream?[5]

The interest that Messerschmidt's heads stimulated in his own life has only grown over the two and a half centuries since he created them. The famous contemporary description by Friedrich Nicolai, depicting Messerschmidt as a quite literally haunted recluse, hard at work on the heads as an apotropaic device against 'the god of proportion', continues to stoke fascination.[6] More or less presumptuous retrodiagnoses have seen him variously labelled a schizophrenic, an anal retentive, or a sufferer of dystonia.[7] The still-growing body of modern scholarship has set him more carefully in his own life and times: in the intrigues and politics of the Viennese court and art academies, in the swirling eddies of protoscience and pseudoscience that characterised Enlightenment Europe and Vienna.[8] Alongside art-historical parallels, eighteenth-century physiognomy, spiritualism, and Hermeticism line up to offer possible interpretative paths. Numerology rears its head. The sculptor's relationship to Franz Anton Mesmer, charismatic quack father of 'animal magnetism', exerts a particular draw.[9] But the speculation and the archaeology alike fall short of explaining. As Michael Yonan observes, grasp as we will, Messerschmidt's heads remain 'semantically slippery'.[10] They escape us, even as we stand in front of them.

Here, opposite *Emotional Detox*, however, it is possible to look at this escape as a specific instance of a general problem: what we might call the 'knowledge problem' of the face. On the one hand faces present a special point of certainty in human relations: the crux of our identity in the seeing world, they are the anchor of our social selves. Alternative options are available—we might know a loved one by their voice, their gait, their smell—but all these

5
Szépművészeti Múzeum, Budapest, inv. no. 53.655.

6
Friedrich Nicolai, *Beschreibung einer Reise durch Deutschland und die Schweiz im Jahre 1781* (Berlin and Stettin, 1788), pp. 6, 401–20. For an English translation, see Maria Pötzl-Malikova and Guilhem Scherf, eds., *Franz Xaver Messerschmidt* (New York/ Paris, 2010), 207–11.

7
The trend was inaugurated by psychoanalyst and art historian Ernst Kris, and has continued ever since. See Ernst Kris, 'Die Charakterköpfe des Franz Xaver Messerschmidt: Versuch einer historischen und psychologischen Deutung', *Jahrbuch der kunsthistorischen Sammlungen in Wien*, Neue Folge 6 (1932), pp. 169–228, republished as 'A Psychotic Sculptor of the Eighteenth Century', in *Psychanalytic Explorations in Art* (New York, 1952), pp. 128–50. On dystonia, see Michal Maršálek, 'Dystonia in Art: The Impact of Psychiatric and Neurological Disease on the Work of the Sculptor F. X. Messerschmidt', in *Dystonia and Dystonic Syndromes*, ed. Petr Kaňovský, Kailash P. Bhatia, and Raymond L. Rosales (Berlin, 2015), pp. 227–44.

8
See, for example, Maria Pötzl-Malikova, *Franz Xaver Messerschmidt* (Vienna, 1982) and Miriam Szőcs, 'Intrigue or Insanity? The Case of Franz Xaver Messerschmidt', *Sculpture Journal* 20, no. 1 (2011), pp. 55–70.

9
See Michael Yonan, *Messerschmidt's Character Heads: Maddening Sculpture and the Writing of Art History* (London, 2017), ch. 3, pp. 196–262.

10
Yonan 2017 (see note 9), p. 26.

are more tenuous and more intimate. The face is certain and open to the world. This is why, twelve decades into the age of the fingerprint, and four into DNA profiling and retinal scans, the passport photograph still dominates identity documents. Quinn himself has used all these other means of self-portraiture, but only *Self* has had the capacity, in all its ongoing iterations, to keep up with the changing continuity of his identity in the world. We look and know, and trust that means of knowing so much that we have even, in the last few years, imperfectly and with vast technical cunning, trained our phones and our computers to do the same.

Beyond this lies the openness of faces as conduits. They are the point where our inner and outer selves meet most nearly; where what happens inside our heads crosses over, in the semaphore of our facial muscles, to the outside. The dead metaphor of *expression* sums up the assumption. It entered English first in the double sense of 'pressing out' and 'putting into language'; when, in the mid-eighteenth century, it expanded to include our faces, it did so in recognition of their passing meaning from inside to outside.[11] At opposite poles, when expressions cease to convey meaning, they are no longer *expressions* at all: they point to some sort of defect in the emotional landscape within. To be expressionless, in modern clinical language, is to *lack affect*: to be unmoved by the world around us. To move beyond expression is to *make faces*, or to *gurn*: the facial equivalent of babble, signifying nothing. Between the two poles, our faces make meaning.

That meaning is useful enough when instrumentalised by the bearer—the smile, the glare—but all the more special as a form of knowledge when beyond the bearer's control. Expressions beyond our control display, as the eighteenth-century *savant* Buffon put it, 'our most secret agitations'—the internal emotions we would ideally wish to conceal from external view. Knowledge otherwise inaccessible. They offer the possibility of what Buffon's and Messerschmidt's contemporary Johann Caspar Lavater called *pathognomy*: [12] interpreting the passions of the soul.[13] It promises a way of seeing through to truths that others might not wish to reveal.

11
See OED, *expression*, I.1.a: 'The action of pressing or squeezing out' (earliest citation 1594); II.4.a: 'Manner or means of representation in language' (earliest citation 1628); and II.5.a: 'Of the countenance, voice, or (occasionally) attitude, etc.: Capacity or fact of expressing feeling or character; expressive quality' (earliest citation 1774).

12
See also Maria Pötzl-Malikova, *Franz Xaver Messerschmidt 1736–1783. Monograph and Catalogue Raisonné* Vienna 2015, p. 119f.: "The nature of the 'Heads' is such that it cannot have been an easy matter for [Franz Friedrich] Strunz to invent titles for them. While his reliance on Johann Caspar Lavater is obvious he was unable to make concrete use of the Swiss physiognomist's teachings. The mainstay of his interpretation of Messerschmidt's busts was not the individual characteristics of the skull so dear to Lavater but the changeable expressions of the face. Georg Christoph Lichtenberg's pathognomics would have been more to the point but Strunz is unlikely to have benefited from it."

13
Johan Casper Lavater, *Physiognomische Fragmente zur Beförderung der Menschenkenntnis und Menschenliebe*, 4 vols. (Leipzig/Winterthur, 1775–78).

Here, though, is where the problem occurs. Precisely because faces might offer special knowledge, they are untrustworthy. Our understanding might be off, or more importantly it might be being manipulated. Expressions are not *altogether* beyond our control. And those who can maintain conscious control of their faces earn an unfair advantage. *Macbeth*'s King Duncan, just betrayed by one man and soon to be murdered by another, is far from the only Shakespearean character to lament the lack of a reliable 'art to find the mind's construction in the face'. Hamlet, good student that he is, takes special care to 'set it down' in his notebook that 'one may smile, and smile, and be a villain'.[14] All forms of communication offer the possibility for deception; the face is unique because it dangles at the same time the promise of being able to see through deception.

14
Shakespeare, *Hamlet*, I.v.105.

In art there is no urgent need to see through untruth in quite the same way. Even if we could talk of being deceived we are not about to be betrayed. And yet the problem of the face presses still: in the mute worlds of painting and sculpture we have so little else to go on. Wherever it appears the expressive face engages our attention like almost nothing else, and all the more so when what appears *as expression* refuses to render up its secrets. Taken opposite each other, *Emotional Detox* and the *Character Heads* appear, among all their other qualities, as counterposed experiments upon that engaged attention. Over the series of *Emotional Detox* it is as if Quinn's face hovers just precisely above the boundary of the expressionless: it expresses, but in a whisper so low we cannot hear the words. Across the *Character Heads*, the human face hovers just precisely below the boundary of *making faces*: like a crowd of raised voices, they express so loudly and so urgently that we cannot make their messages out. Both keep us leaning forward, in the hope we might.

The Expression of Madness

Lou Stoppard

'He lived and dressed like an ordinary citizen', wrote the eighteenth-century German writer and bookseller Christoph Friedrich Nicolai of the Austrian sculptor Franz Xaver Messerschmidt in an essay on their June 1781 meeting.[1] It is a sentence shaded with ideals and expectations; who, or what, is the normal citizen? How does one live—or perform—a regular life; does it depend on what you eat, wear, buy, and consume? Can one be ordinary and make art? Be ordinary and suffer mental illness? Be ordinary and slip, at times, away from the present into a frenetic inner world of chaos and confusion? Be ordinary and electrified with worry? Be ordinary and drink, constantly, morning, day, night, drink until one escapes, transcends, reality for some softer, slower but brighter place? Can one be ordinary and an addict (an experience, of Marc Quinn's, that has given rise to this project)?

Curiously, the above-mentioned sentence seems to contradict the majority of Nicolai's other assertions about Messerschmidt. While Messerschmidt favoured a modest style of dress, rejecting the pomposities of some of his artist peers, he was, in Nicolai's own words, 'peculiar'. He suffered outbursts and frenzies, and he threatened to kill another member of the Academy of Fine Arts in Vienna (he was rejected for the role of professor at the Academy, not due to the weakness of his practice, but because others were alarmed by his temperament and fits). Other times, he apparently flew into rages and destroyed bodies of work, disgusted if they were not sufficiently expressive, or angered by those who wanted to buy them. And, even when he left his work behind, when he tried to sleep at night, to escape from the difficulty of the day-to-day, he saw ghosts descending, jeering, swirling; they came to threaten and torture and mock him.

Consensus—shaped by accounts such as Nicolai's—is that when Messerschmidt began work on his *Character Heads*, as they later became known, he was losing his grip on reality. Such theories were bolstered in 1932, when the

1
Friedrich Nicolai, *Beschreibung einer Reise durch Deutschland und die Schweiz im Jahre 1781*, vol. 4 (Berlin/Stettin 1785). Translation from 'Description of a Journey through Germany and Switzerland in the Year 1781', translated by Herbert Ranharter, *The Paris Review* (30 September 2010); https://www.theparisreview.org/blog/2010/09/30/the-heads-of-franz-xaver-messerschmidt/ (accessed on 15 February 2022).

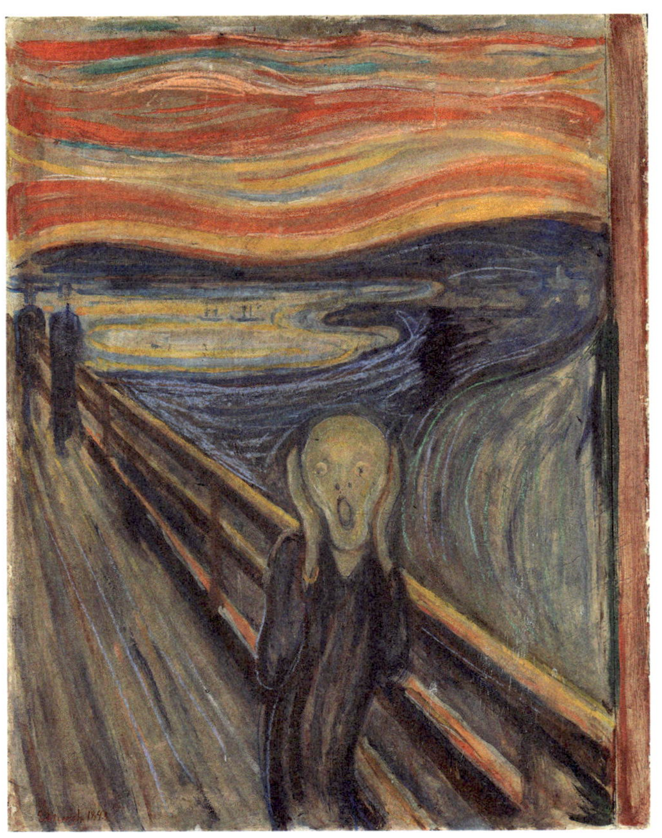

Fig. 1

Viennese art historian Ernst Kris published a study of the *Heads*, which argued that the artist had begun to show symptoms of schizophrenia from around 1770 onward, and that the *Heads* must be seen in connection with this disorder. Others too have been quick to proffer diagnoses; a narcissistic personality disorder, repressed sexuality, lead poisoning. Even those biographers and critics less inclined to speculative medicine and pseudoscience have tended to agree that the *Heads* were the result of some bout of psychosis or delusions.

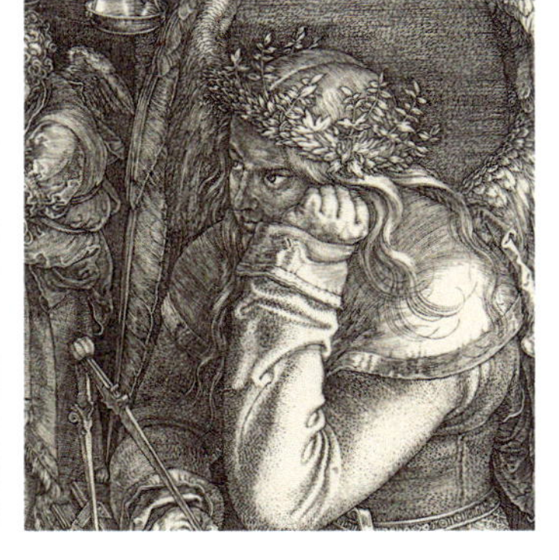

Fig. 2

Messerschmidt saw the *Heads* as a help, a solution, a defence against the ghosts that tormented him; he felt that if he could just capture the right expressions, in the right way, then the spirits would leave him be. (It is, of course, relevant to note, when judging Messerschmidt, that belief in ghosts was widespread during his era). He set about this project—bizarre and grand in its ambition and scope, encompassing over sixty *Heads*, intended to show all the expressions of the human face, all the glory of the forty-three muscles—without commission or guarantee of remuneration; it was a greater, more personal sense of requirement that spurred him. We can interpret that, to him, the face was a portal; to understanding, to control,

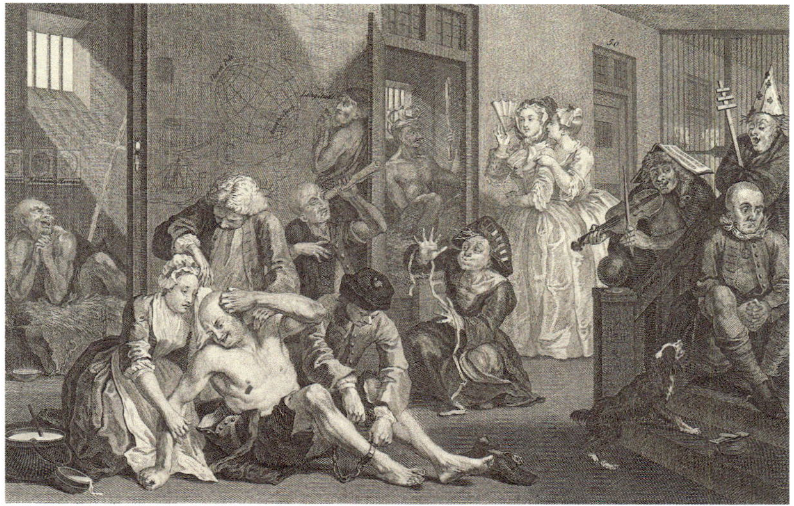

Fig. 3

to knowledge, to the soul. With this in mind, it would be fair to say, if one accepts a psychosis diagnosis, that Messerschmidt had that special quality of the insane, put forward in Michel Foucault's *Madness and Civilization* (1961): an ability to reveal the distinction between what men are and what they pretend to be.[2]

2
Michel Foucault, *Histoire de la folie* (Paris, 1961); published in English as *Madness and Civilization: A History of Insanity in the Age of Reason*, translated by Richard Howard (New York, 1965).

Of course, to return to Nicolai's point, clothes and possessions can do a lot of the work in showing who we are, or who we want to present ourselves as, and in signalling that one is losing one's way; that one is strung out or sinking below the lines of appropriateness and formality—the stains, the smells, the oversized volumes, and rips of the homeless, the abandoned, the unlucky, the unwell. These can be universal symbols of pain and inequality. But the face, not the wardrobe, conveys the particularities, the depths, the personal record, of one's affliction. They say the body keeps the score, but it is the face that reveals it, in all its blazing individuality, to others. Predictably, then, artistic projects about madness often focus on the face, the expressions; the scream (Edvard Munch, 1893, fig. 1); the despondent, depressed stare (*Melencolia I*, Albrecht Dürer, 1514, fig. 2); the grimaces and baroque gestures (*A Rake's Progress*, William Hogarth, 1734, fig. 3). One can see a synergy between Messerschmidt's heads and Richard Avedon's 1963 portraits of patients at East Louisiana State Mental Hospital; the differing characters, the faces, all records of the traumas and the fantasies, the various muscles groups pulled in a plethora of ways, depending on situation, experience, state. One sees a strong connection with the vibrant works of Shadi Al-Atallah

Fig. 1
Edvard Munch
The Scream, 1893
National Museum of Art, Architecture and Design, Oslo

Fig. 2
Albrecht Dürer
Melencolia I, 1514
Metropolitan Museum of Art, New York

Fig. 3
William Hogarth
A Rake's Progress, plate 8, 1735
Metropolitan Museum of Art, New York

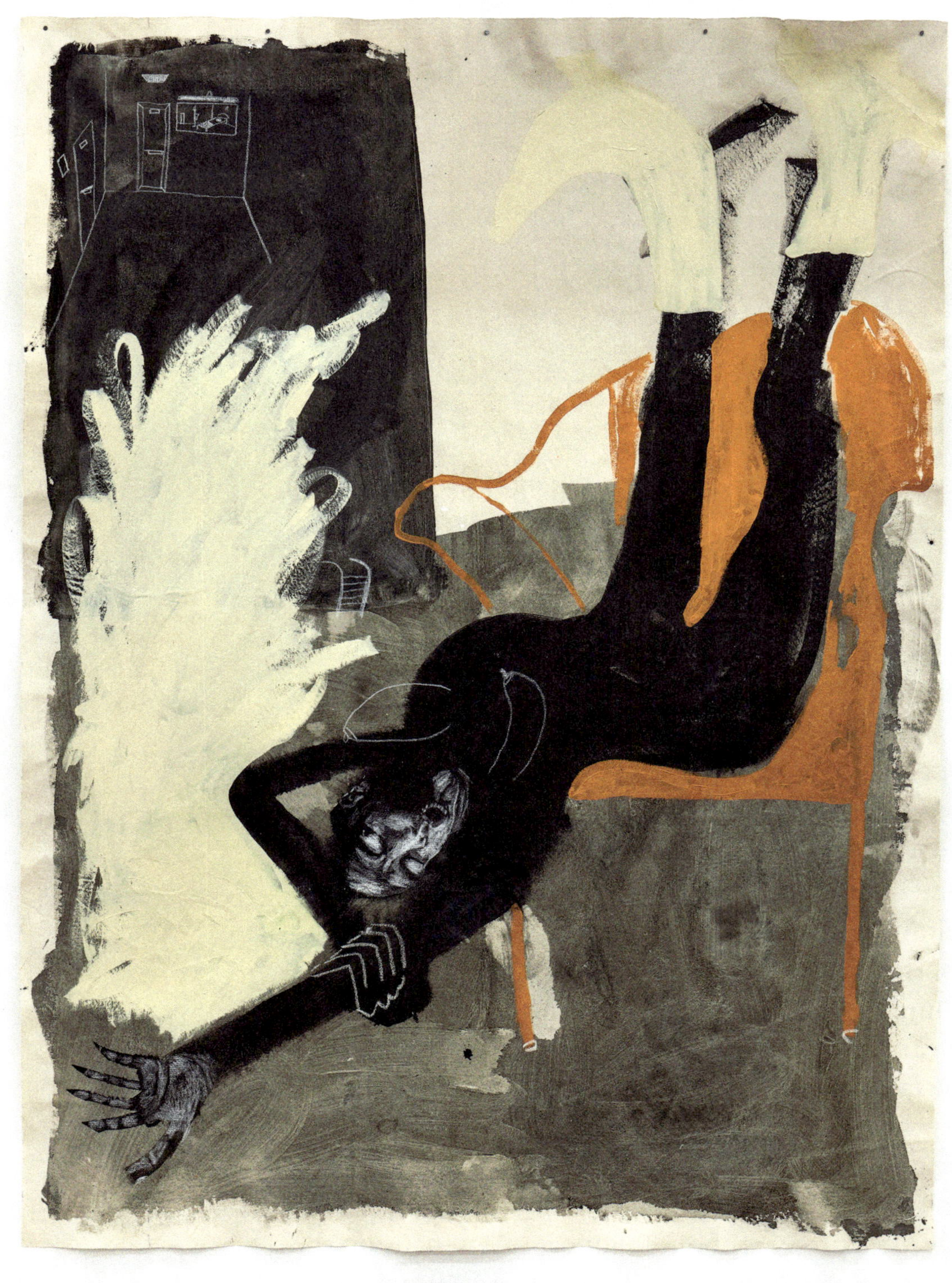

Fig. 4

Fig. 4
Shadi Al-Atallah
GROUP THERAPY AT 8, 2021
Courtesy Shadi Al-Atallah and
Guts Gallery

Fig. 5
Shadi Al-Atallah
Kris croker stole my tears, 2018
Courtesy Shadi Al-Atallah and
Cob Gallery

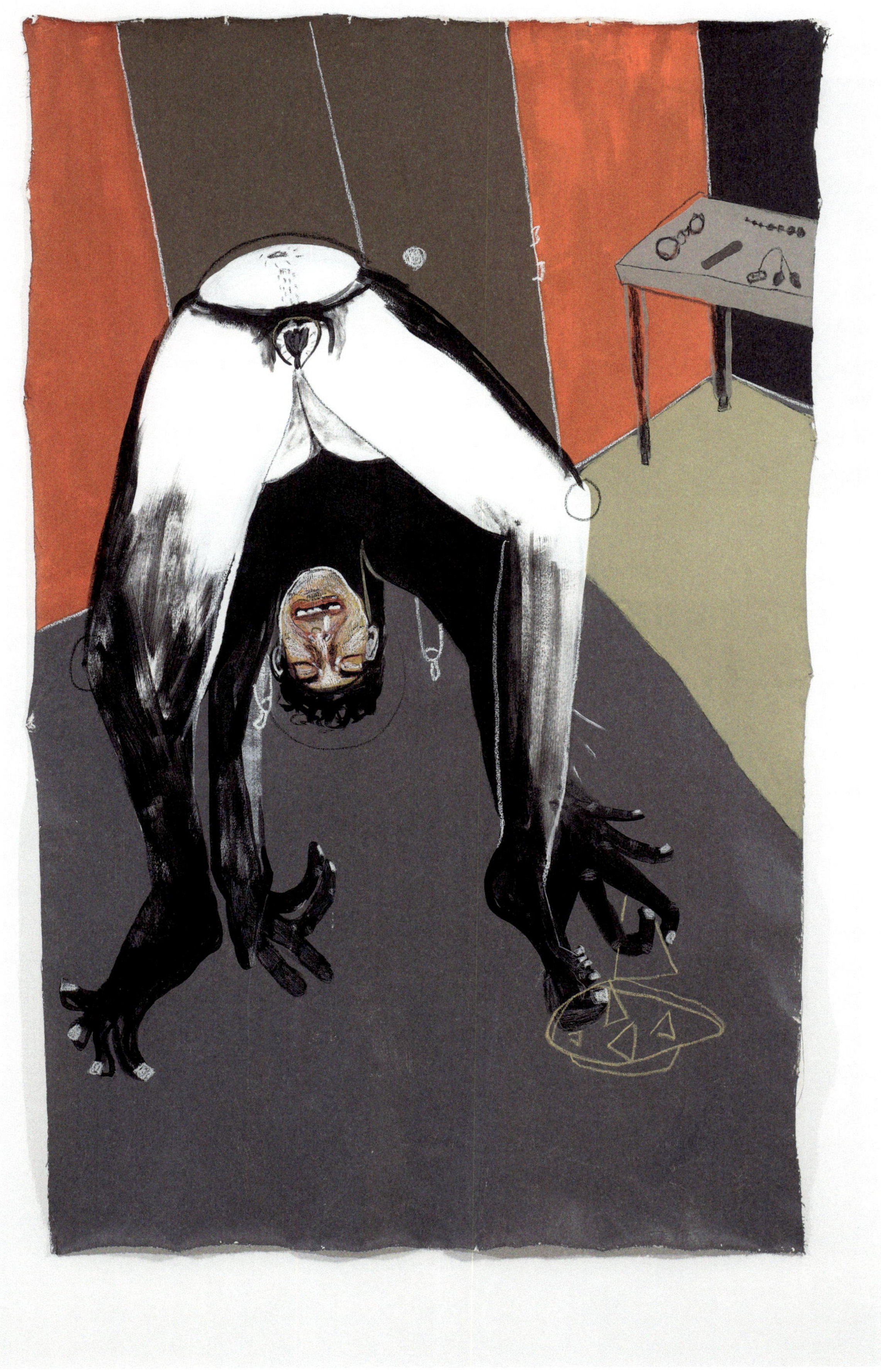

Fig. 5

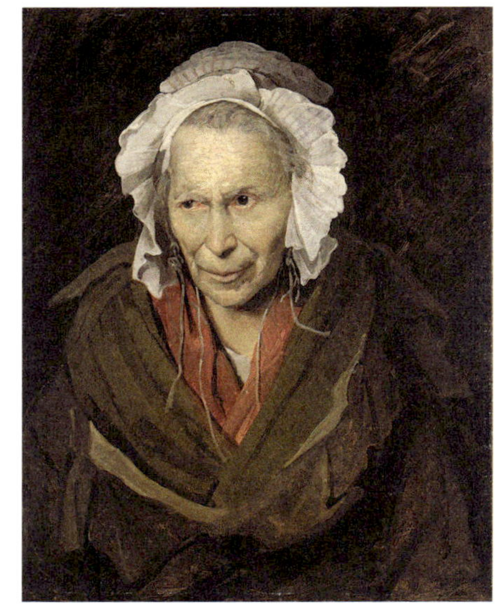

Fig. 6

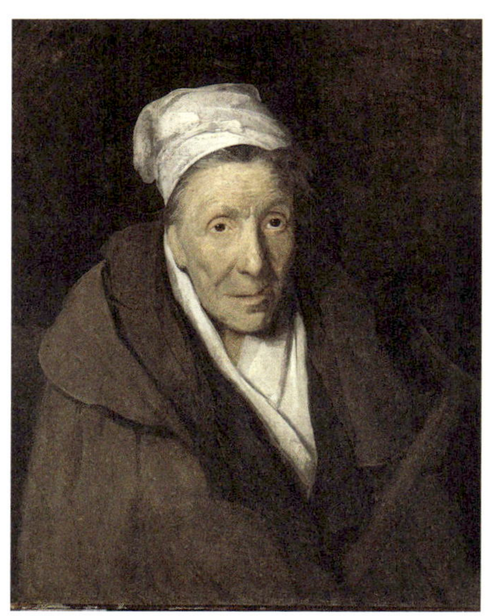

Fig. 7

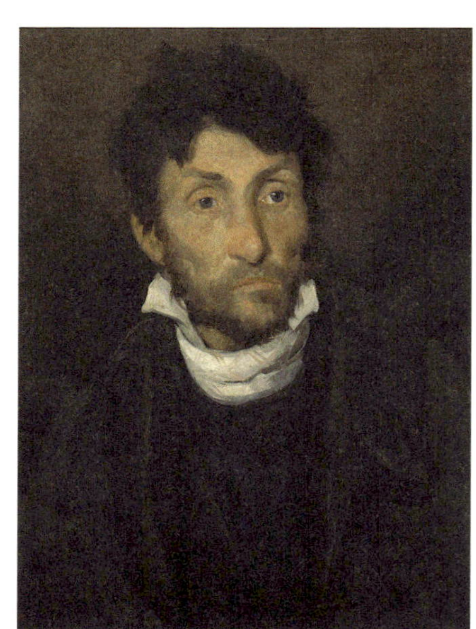

Fig. 8

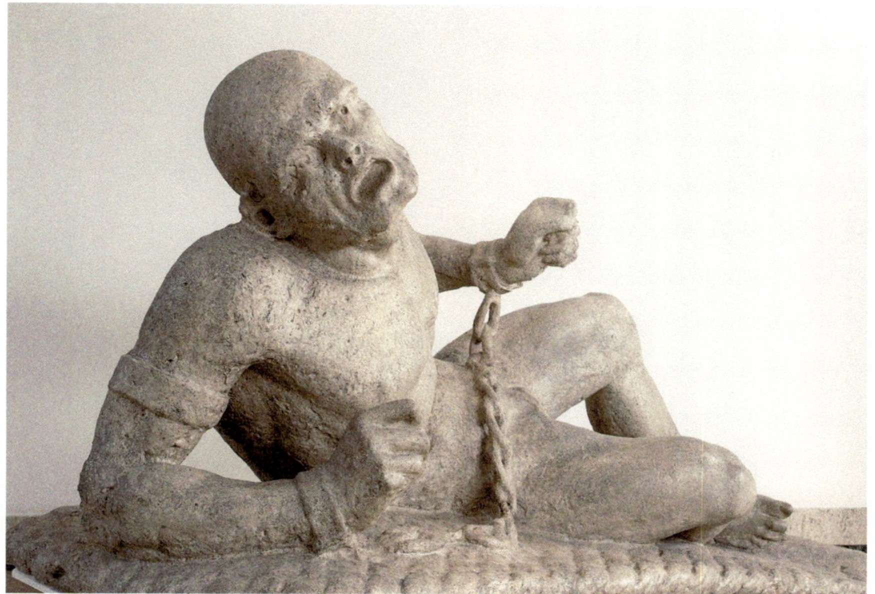

Fig. 9

(figs. 4, 5), who looks inwards, exploring themes of mental health and catharsis through striking self-portraits; faces and bodies undulating, distorting and gesturing in response to seemingly overwhelming, unendurable sensation. Visually, you could relate Messerschmidt to Théodore Géricault's painting series *Portraits of the Insane* (1819–24) (fig. 6–8), or even with Caius Gabriel Cibber's sculptures *Raving Madness* (fig. 9) and *Melancholy Madness* (both 1676), displayed at the gates of Bethlem Hospital in London, defining the image, the possibilities, of those inside. Of course, there are exceptions, works that convey chemical imbalance or strength of feeling or bursts of emotions in the abstract—Antonio Saura's *Grito n.º 7* (1959, fig. 10), with its kinetic brushstrokes, is surely one of the finest examples—but if one is looking for projects about madness, one usually finds a rich well of scowls and howls, snarls and grimaces. This can be seen as a comment on the intangibility, the mystery, of the brain and the mind. Artists show the conditions—the physical symbols, the demonstration, the side effects of mental distress. They show what they can see, what they can understand.

Indeed, Messerschmidt's *Heads*, and many works inspired by them, serve as a statement of art and of face as mutual gateways to the inner secrets of the human mind; as attempts to probe, to know, to desperately find an answer. To Messerschmidt, expressions were, it seems, a universal language, a way of explaining the unexplainable. In this sense, both scientifically and artistically, he was a pioneer.

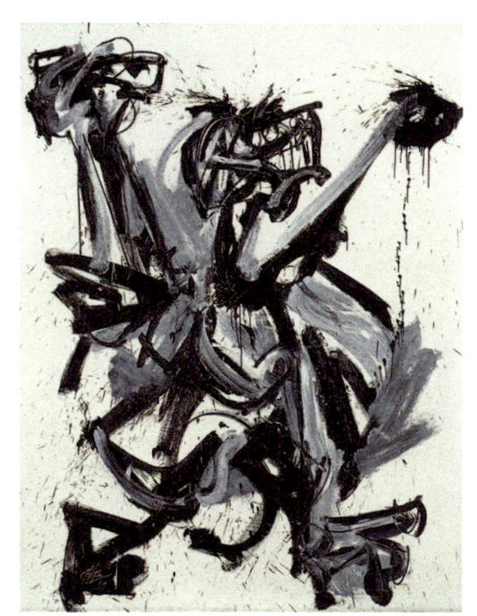

Fig. 10

Fig. 6
Théodore Géricault
Portrait of a Woman Suffering from Obsessive Envy, 1819–22
Musee des Beaux-Arts de Lyon

Fig. 7
Théodore Géricault
The Woman with a Gambling Mania, 1819–22
Musée du Louvre, Paris

Fig. 8
Théodore Géricault
Portrait of a Kleptomaniac, c. 1820
Museum of Fine Arts, Gent

Fig. 9
Caius Gabriel Cibber
Raving Madness, sculpture at the Bethlem Royal Hospital, London, 1676
Bethlem Museum of the Mind, London

Fig. 10
Antonio Saura
Grito n.º 7, 1959
Museo Reina Sofía, Madrid

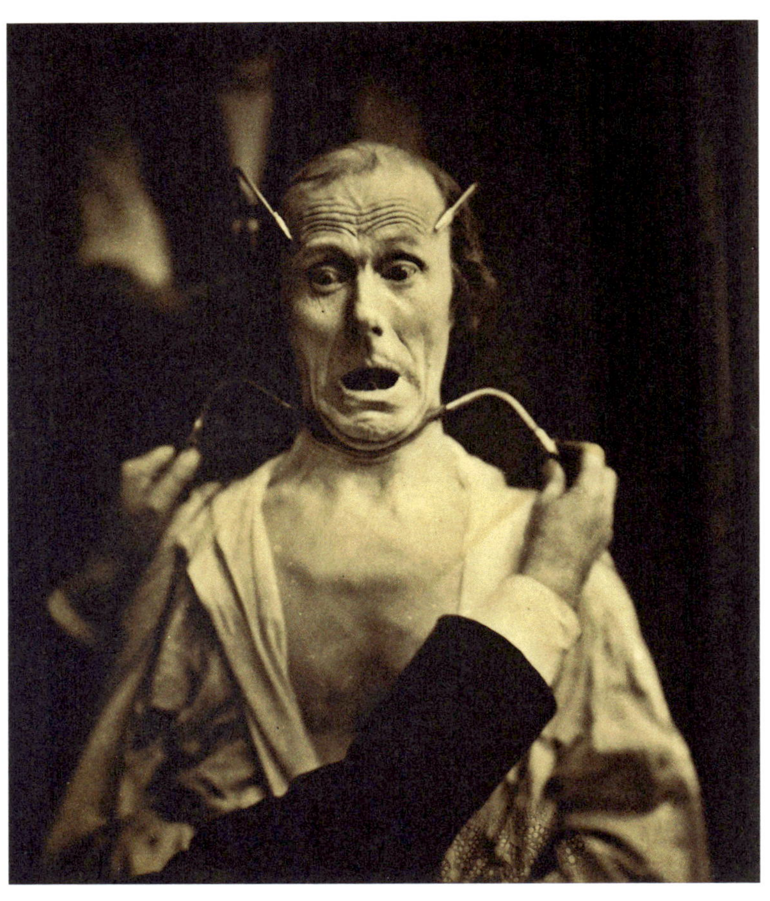

Fig.11

It is relevant that he started creating these works some one hundred years before Charles Darwin would publish *The Expression of the Emotions in Man and Animals* (1872, once intended as a chapter of *The Descent of Man*, but eventually a book in its own right), which contains various illustrations and, innovatively, photographs by Duchenne de Boulogne (fig. 11), showcasing experiments into facial expressions and muscles, conducted using electrical probes, which look like odes to Messerschmidt's *Heads*. Darwin contended, as the *Heads* also arguably do, that expressions were a collective dialect, common acts, shared across cultures, and even species, serving a link to our animal ancestry. It was not until the 1960s and 1970s that the American psychologist Paul Ekman, influentially, formalised notions of universality, writing that disparate humans, from all around the world, could reliably infer emotional states from expressions.

Today our thinking remains in line with this notion of a smile or a frown as a lingua franca. Today Microsoft and Amazon offer algorithms engineered to detect a person's emotions from their face. These are useful for companies keen to better understand their consumer—their needs,

Fig. 11
Duchenne de Boulogne
Terror, 1854–56
Museum of Fine Arts, Houston, Texas

Fig. 12
After Franz Xaver Messerschmidt
A Lecherous and Careworn Fop, before 1923
Belvedere, Vienna

Fig. 13
After Franz Xaver Messerschmidt
A Grievously Wounded Man, before 1923
Belvedere, Vienna

Fig. 14
After Franz Xaver Messerschmidt
The Enraged and Vengeful Gypsy, before 1923
Belvedere, Vienna

their hopes, their dreams. They want to look into your eyes, read your lips, know how you feel, what moves you, what shakes you, who you are. Their goals are likely not far from those attributed to Messerschmidt, in a much-debated essay by Franz Strunz on the occasion of the exhibition of the *Heads* in 1793; Messerschmidt and others, he said, could 'exclusively on the basis of someone's features ... explore, judge, and depict their character and their passions.'[3]

3
Franz Strunz, *Merwürdige Lebensgeschichte des Franz Xaver Messerschmidt, k. k. öffentlichen Lehrer der Bildhauerkunst* (Vienna, 1794), pp. 3–4; translation from Maria Pötzl-Malikova, *Franz Xaver Messerschmidt, 1736–1783*, translated by Otmar Binder (Weitra, 2015), p. 118.

It was Strunz who named the heads, calling some after characters (*An Arch-Rascal, A Hypocrite and a Slanderer*), or professions (*A Scholar, Poet),* others after mental or physical states (*The Troubled Man*, *The Vexed Man),* and others after physiological reactions (*The Sneezer*, *Just Rescued from Drowning*). Strunz's impulse to classify, to explain, is important when thinking about the lineage of Messerschmidt's *Heads*, and the critical response to them and to him as an artist; the drive to diagnose, to brand, is a process that has continued within contemporary medicine and culture today, shaping how artists have treated and depicted the mentally ill and the different. (It is relevant that Messerschmidt worked and lived during a period of European history marked by a rush of confinement; a drive to control the insane, to physically separate them into institutions, to assert boundaries and labels.)

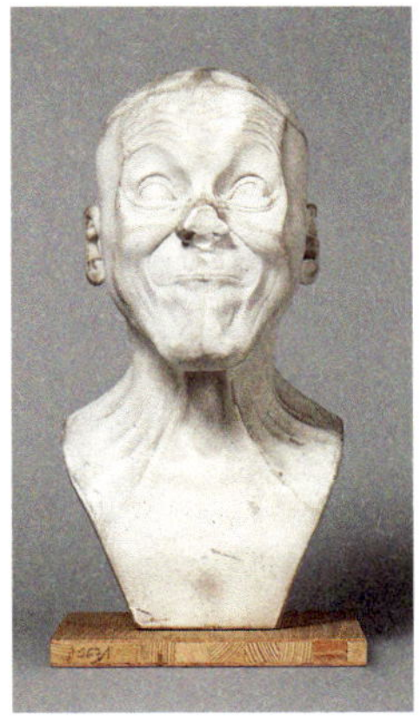

Fig.12

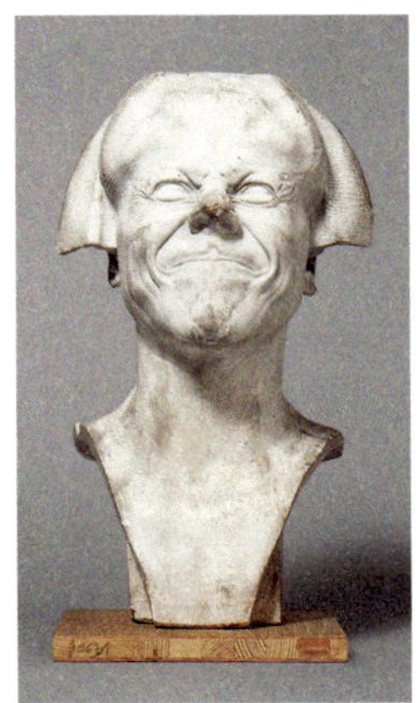

Fig.13

How can art show madness without objectifying or categorising or othering? Potentially, asking that question is a problem in itself, due to the implicit idea that the mentally ill are there to be depicted, made subject and viewing matter—recalling those tourists paying a few coins to enter the gates of Bethlem (or 'Bedlam', as it became known) to gawp and judge—rather than to create and contribute. For far too long, and even today, there has been a deficit of interest in art produced by the unwell, those in intuitions or those with diagnoses. Indeed, when, in 1945, the French painter Jean Dubuffet toured Swiss asylums and institutions, collecting works by inpatients to bring

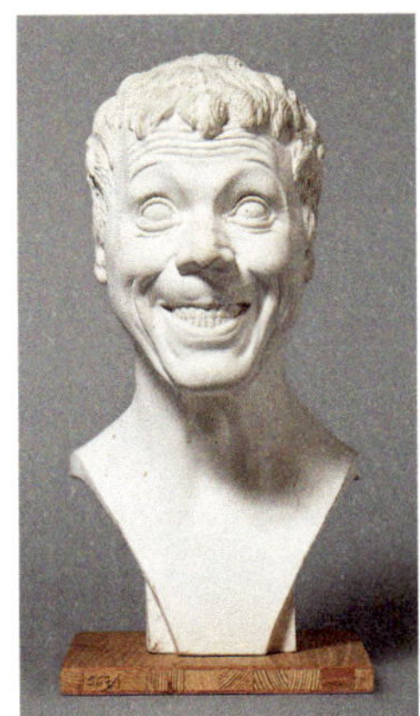

Fig.14

4
Kay Redfield Jamison, *Touched with Fire: Manic-Depressive Illness and the Artistic Temperament* (New York, 1993).

5
Nicolai 2010 (see note 1).

back to Paris, stunning in their vibrancy, the genuineness of the expression, he received very limited interest and little uptake from galleries, salons, and collectors. These works, and the ambivalence to them, led to Dubuffet's *The Art Brut Manifesto* (1947), which laid out the depth and beauty he believed was overlooked by the mainstream art world. Where does Messerschmidt sit within these definitions? Brut? Mainstream?

There exists a shared idea that art can provoke madness, that art can stir and ignite and unbalance. Indeed, in most hospitals it is accepted, when it comes to décor, that abstract art, or particularly emotive art, could somehow disturb or rile or upset the patients and that the muted, the nature-themed is safe. Art and the artist, whether aspiring or successful, are both dangerous and in danger.

Indeed, it is commonly accepted that artists are well positioned to descend into madness, given the nature of their role; the solitude, the internal searching, the pressure of trying to capture or explain. The research is shaky, but a 1993 book by Kay Redfield Jamison, professor of psychiatry at the Johns Hopkins University School of Medicine in Baltimore, noted that distinguished artists tend to have depressive illnesses at a rate of about ten to thirty times higher than the population at large.[4]

'A healthy strong man, working in a sitting position, living consistently alone and celibate while constantly straining his imagination, must experience some bodily consequences as a result of insufficient circulation', wrote Nicolai of Messerschmidt. 'Nervous palpitations combined with a lively imagination and his favourite prejudices surely will produce all manner of spirits that, although conjured up from within, may well manifest seemingly from the outside.'[5] To Nicolai, the art was born from the madness, while also causing it.

And yet, the correlation between great artist and madman—in fits of feeling, barely responsible for actions or choices, propelled by the strength of his vision—has become almost a cliché; a habit for tolerating and justifying male ego, abuse, poor behaviour. Again, where do we see Messerschmidt in relation to this?

Sometimes it is best to take things as they are presented: face value. Look: the *Character Heads* are a balance of the strange and the familiar. Like the expressions and conditions they depict, they offer opportunities for empathy and connection.

They continue to inspire, both artists and viewers, specifically because of the familiarity of what they show; the sequences embedded within them, of contractions, twitches, stretches, conducted back then and to this day. The expressions are a biography of all of us, a record of muscles that have, at different times for each of us, moved in the same way; a group dance, performed worldwide, constantly, alone, and in the round. They are a reminder of the common nature of many of our afflictions and troubles. To look at some is to confront an unfamiliar abyss—and perhaps be drawn towards it, the start of the slippery slope—but the majority ask us simply to gaze into a mirror, to a reality that is already here, reflecting us back at ourselves, hesitant and awed.

Franz Xaver Messerschmidt and His Heads

Georg Lechner

Franz Xaver Messerschmidt presumably started working on the pieces that were later to become known as his *Character Heads* (fig. 1) and to become highly popular back in 1771.[1] At that time, he was in his mid-thirties and could be considered to have 'made it'. He had completed major works commissioned by the Ducal family of Liechtenstein and the Imperial Court, owned a house in what is today Vienna's Third District, and had been designated to succeed Jakob Christoph Schletterer (1699–1774) as Professor of Sculpture at the academy in Vienna. However, when Schletterer died in 1774, things turned out very differently: Messerschmidt was ignored when the prestigious post was filled, with his mental stability being cited as the key argument against him.

In 1775 a very ill Messerschmidt left Vienna first for Munich and then travelled on to his hometown of Wiesensteig. There, he spent a longer period of time completely withdrawn from society and worked on his *Heads*, and after the months of isolation resolved to relocate to the then fast-growing city of Pressburg (now Bratislava), where from 1777 onwards he lived with his brother, Johann Adam (1738–94), in the latter's spacious residence, before later buying his own house. He does not seem to have wanted to live a life of luxury and evidently earned his living by making small portrait medals, preferentially from alabaster, of which a few have survived in the collections of various European museums.[2]

Despite having received bids from prospective buyers, he did not want to part company with his *Heads* collection. He made them from alabaster as well as from alloys consisting of differing ratios of lead and tin. In the eighteenth century, lead was a somewhat valuable material as it was required for various everyday purposes. That said, sculptors had also discovered the material, and in Vienna particularly its refined dark qualities were held in high esteem. The best-known examples include the Providentia Fountain by Georg Raphael Donner, which

1
The biographical data in the present article are adopted from those given in Maria Pötzl-Malikova's monograph on Franz Xaver Messerschmidt (Maria Pötzl-Malikova, *Franz Xaver Messerschmidt, 1736–1783* Belvedere Werkverzeichnisse, vol. 4 [Vienna, 2015]).

2
See Pötzl-Malikova 2015 (see note 1), pp. 259–72 and 276–8.

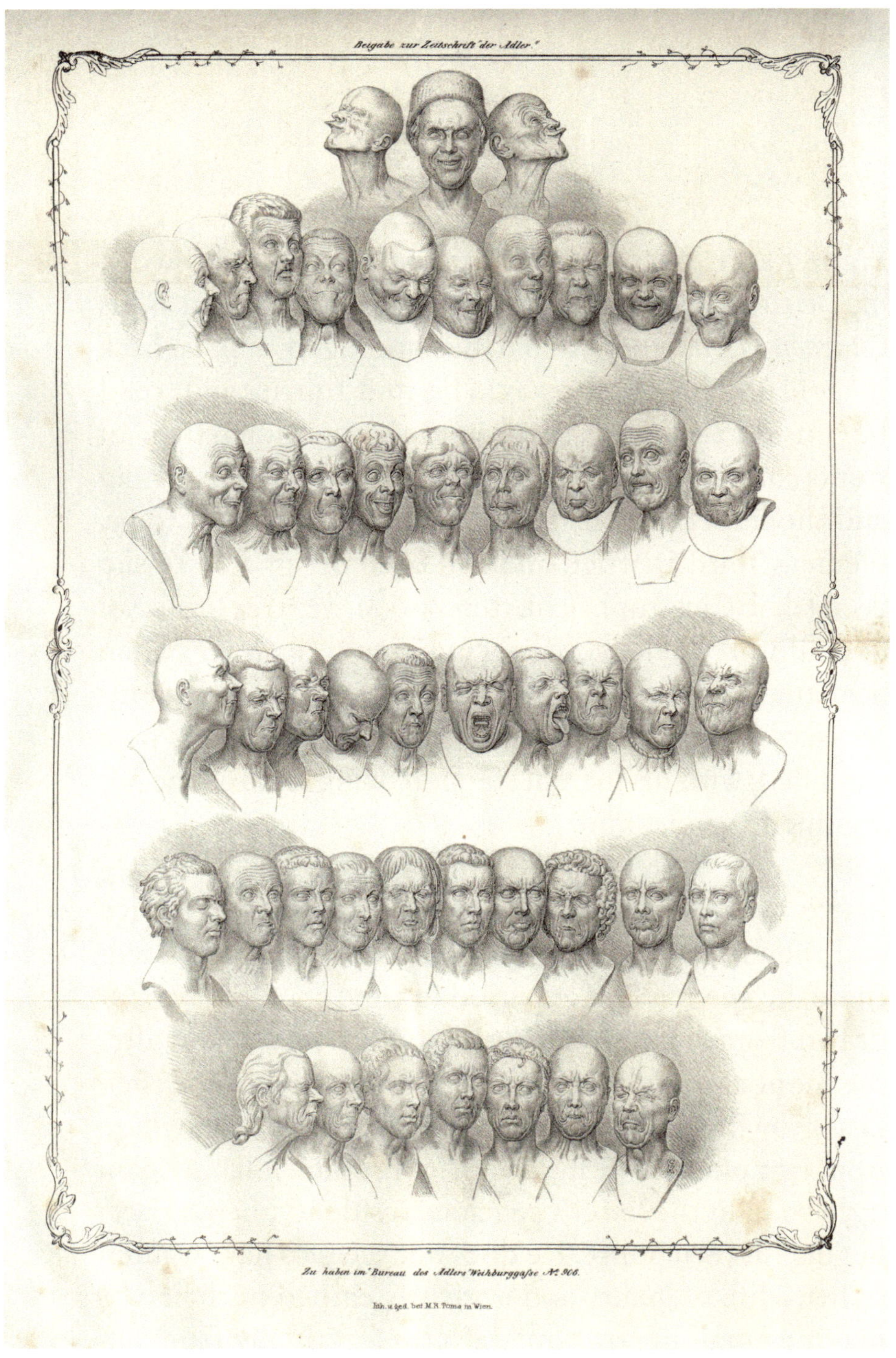

Fig. 1

was completed in 1739. Donner died aged only forty-seven, presumably also as a result of working with this toxic metal. To what extent Messerschmidt was also affected by the toxicity is hard to judge. He probably had the requisite technical skills to work it, having started out in life as a mould-cutter in the Imperial Arsenal, where he worked on and decorated cannons.

For a long time, in the relevant literature Messerschmidt was described as mentally infirm, and the at times bizarre *Heads* were considered the logical consequence of that fact.

Fig. 1
Matthias Rudolph Toma
Messerschmidt's 'Character Heads',
1839
Austrian National Library, Vienna

Fig. 2
Franz Xaver Messerschmidt
Franz Anton Mesmer, 1770
Belvedere, Vienna
(on permanent loan from private owner)

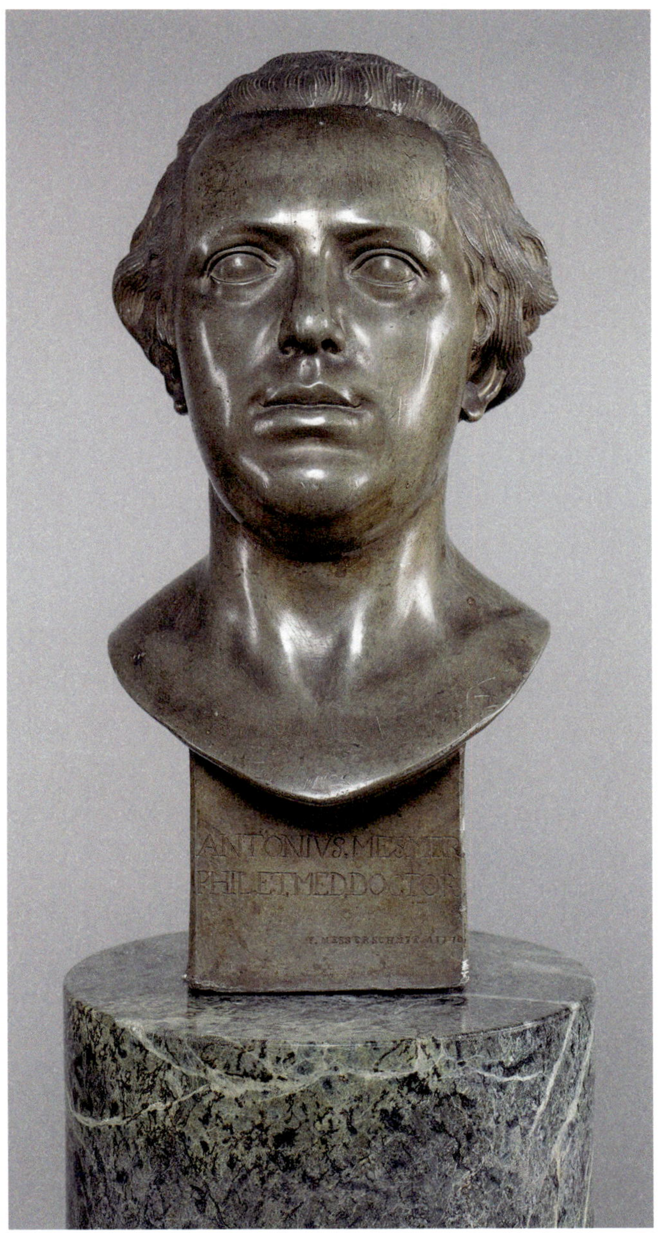

Fig. 2

The treatise published by art historian Ernst Kris (1900–57) in 1932 seems especially controversial in this regard; back then, Kris was exploring the potential of psychoanalysis, which was a key topic precisely in Vienna, and suggested that Messerschmidt had suffered from schizophrenia.[3] Such assessments seem problematic to the extent that contemporary source materials were by no means extensive and hardly allow such conclusions to be drawn.

3
Ernst Kris, 'Die Charakterköpfe des Franz Xaver Messerschmidt: Versuch einer historischen und psychologischen Deutung', in *Jahrbuch der Kunsthistorischen Sammlungen in Wien*, new series 6 (1932), pp. 169–228.

A very good idea of Messerschmidt's actual state is given in the report by Friedrich Nicolai (1733–1811), who visited the artist in Pressburg. By way of introduction, he summarises Messerschmidt's life and works as follows: 'In his art, an extraordinary genius; in his customary life, a slight tendency to be odd, which mainly stemmed from his love of independence.'[4] Nicolai goes on to describe how Messerschmidt pinched himself and pulled faces in the mirror—both devices serving as the basis for his work on his *Heads*.[5] Nicolai also mentions that the artist was terrorised by ghosts. All in all, it seems to have been a pleasant and insightful conversation between two gentlemen, who liked each other.

If we do not believe that Messerschmidt was suffering from schizophrenia, then how was it he came to make the extraordinary series of so-called *Character Heads*? In his time, Albert Ilg (1847–96) suggested one should not ignore the influence of medical doctor and magnetiser Franz Anton Mesmer (1734–1815).[6] Michael Krapf also took up this idea and viewed the *Heads* as documentation of the therapies that Mesmer had conducted.[7] In other words, he published a hypothesis that was not to go unopposed.[8] It is hard to judge to what extent Mesmer's teachings influenced the artist. The two men at any rate knew each other because Messerschmidt created fountain figures for Mesmer's garden that have sadly not survived, and produced a bust of the doctor (private collection, on permanent loan to Belvedere, fig. 2).[9]

In the most recent past, Czech psychiatrist Michal Maršálek focussed on the genesis of these remarkable artworks and suggests that Messerschmidt may have suffered from dystonia. He reaches this conclusion on the basis of the artist's behaviour as reported in contemporary sources, as well as the strangely distorted faces that can be associated with the cramps from which people with dystonia suffer.[10]

Messerschmidt died in August 1783—purportedly from pneumonia—and the *Heads* thereafter became the possession of his brother. The *Heads* subsequently changed owner several times, their status degraded to the level of fair-time attractions on the Prater, and then came their dispersal. Finally, it was architect Camillo Sitte (1843–1903)

4
Friedrich Nicolai, *Beschreibung einer Reise durch Deutschland und die Schweiz im Jahre 1781*, vol. 6 (Berlin/Stettin, 1785), p. 401.

5
Nicolai 1785 (see note 4), pp. 413–14.

6
Albert Ilg, *Franz Xaver Messerschmidts Leben und Werke: Mit urkundlichen Beiträgen von Johann Batka* (Vienna/Leipzig, 1885), pp. 18–20.

7
Michael Krapf, 'Die Auftraggeber und der Freundeskreis', in Krapf, ed., *Franz Xaver Messerschmidt, 1736–1783*, exh. cat., Unteres Belvedere, Vienna (Ostfildern-Ruit, 2002), pp. 65–76, here: pp. 69–72.

8
Claudia Maué, 'Franz Xaver Messerschmidt 1736–1783', *Frühneuzeit-Info* 13, no. 1 (2003), pp. 169–78, here: pp. 171–78. Maria Pötzl-Malikova, 'Zur aktuellen Situation in der Messerschmidt-Forschung: Anmerkungen zu einer Präsentation', *Österreichische Zeitschrift für Kunst und Denkmalpflege* 57, no. 2 (2003), pp. 253–64, here: pp. 263–4.

9
See on this Pötzl-Malikova 2015 (see note 1), pp. 233–4, 247–8.

10
Michal Maršálek, 'Dystonia in Art: The Impact of Psychiatric and Neurological Disease on the Work of the Sculptor F. X. Messerschmidt', in Petr Kanovsky, Kallash P. Bhatia, and Raymond Rosales, eds., *Dystonia and Dystonic Syndromes* (Vienna, 2015), pp. 227–44.

dispersal. Finally, it was architect Camillo Sitte (1843–1903) who noticed these extraordinary artworks and had ten of the *Heads* acquired for the State College of Commerce (Staatsgewerbeschule). They were then forgotten for a few years, until in 1907 eight of them were presented at the twenty-second Hagebund Exhibition alongside pieces by living artists. From there, they moved on to Vienna's Museum of Applied Arts and then to the Belvedere, where they became increasingly popular with visitors and today count as what they are, namely the incomparable works of a brilliant artist.

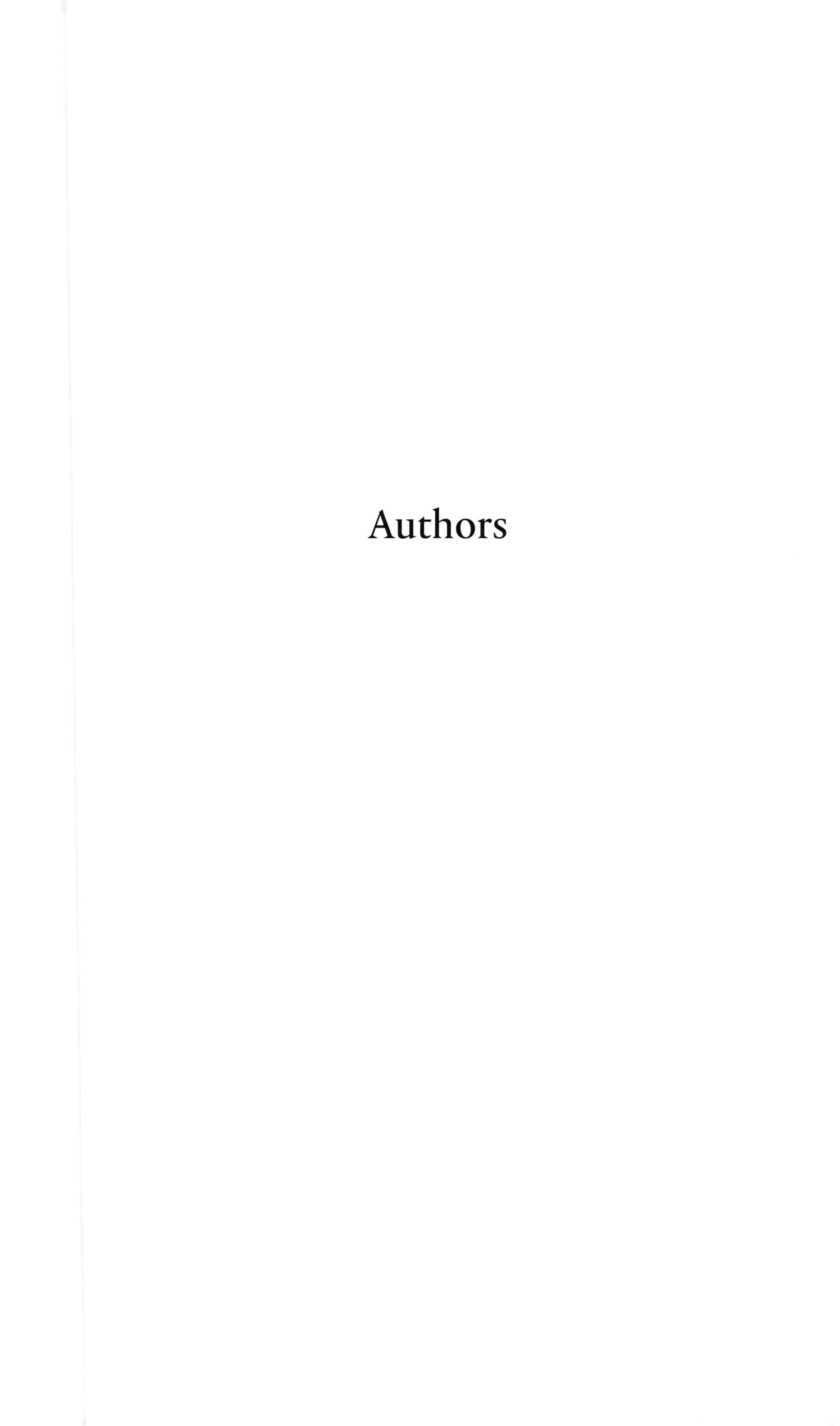

Authors

Georg Lechner studied art history at the University of Vienna. Since 2009 he has worked in the Baroque Collection at the Belvedere. The focus of his research and publications includes Austrian Baroque painting in general, as well as portrait art, the reciprocity between paintings and prints, and the history of the Belvedere and its collections. Lechner recently curated the following exhibitions at the Belvedere: *Martin van Meytens the Younger* (2014–15), *Heavenly! The Baroque Sculptor Johann Georg Pinsel* (2016–17, with Maike Hohn), *Maria Theresa and the Arts* (2017), *Kremser Schmidt: On His 300th Birthday* (2018), and *Johann Jakob Hartmann* (2021).

Cat Marnell is a New York City–based writer and editor. Her 2017 memoir, *How to Murder Your Life* (Simon & Schuster, Ebury), was an instant New York Times Best Seller. She is a former Condé Nast beauty editor and a founding editor of xoJane.com. She wrote the 'Amphetamine Logic' column for *VICE*. Her new column, *Beautyshambles*, is exclusively on Patreon.

Stella Rollig has been CEO and artistic director of the Belvedere since January 2017. She studied German and art history at the University of Vienna and later worked as an arts journalist (for ORF, *Der Standard*, and others). From 1994 to 1996, Rollig was the Austrian Federal Curator for the Fine Arts; during this time, she also founded the discussion platform *Depot, Kunst und Diskussion* at MuseumsQuartier Wien in Vienna. From 2004 to 2016, she was artistic director of the Lentos Kunstmuseum in Linz, and from 2011 also director of Nordico Stadtmuseum Linz. In addition to her curatorial roles, Rollig has taught at numerous institutions.

Lou Stoppard is a British writer and curator. She has written for *The Financial Times*, *Aperture*, *The New York Times*, and *The New Yorker*. She has curated a variety of exhibitions including *North: Fashioning Identity*, at Open Eye Gallery, Liverpool, and Somerset House, London; and *The Hoodie*, at Het Nieuwe Instituut, Rotterdam. Her books include a survey of the work of street photographer Shirley Baker, published by Mack in 2019; *Fashion Together*, an exploration of collaboration, published by Rizzoli in 2017; and *Pools*, an exploration of swimming in photography, published by Rizzoli in 2020.

Tim Smith-Laing is a writer and critic based in London. A former lecturer in literature at Jesus College, Oxford, he is a regular guest speaker at the Royal Academy of Arts and writes widely on art and literature for publications including *Apollo*, *Frieze*, and *The Daily Telegraph*. He holds a doctorate in early modern literature and mythography from Merton College, Oxford, and has published on subjects ranging from Hieronymus Bosch to The Monkees. Among his current projects is a novel based on the lives of Franz Xaver Messerschmidt and his contemporary Franz Anton Mesmer.

The following images are direct reproductions from Marc Quinn's archival scrapbooks from the years 1994 to 1995.

Die folgenden Reproduktionen stammen aus Marc Quinns Fotoarchiv-Alben aus den Jahren 1994 und 1995.

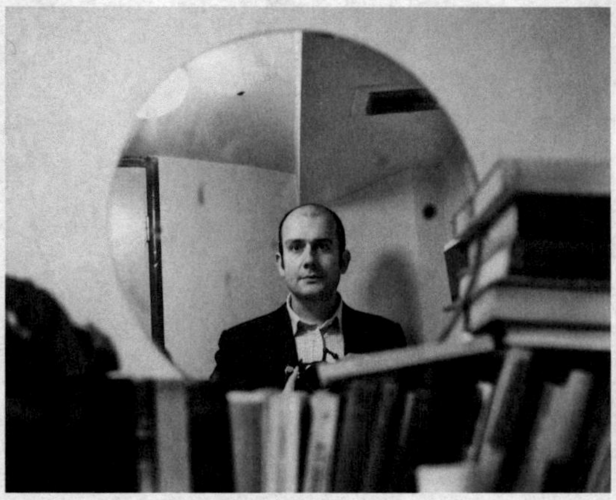

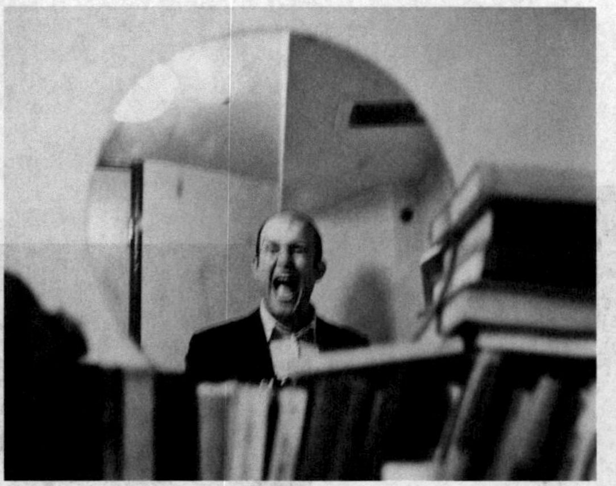

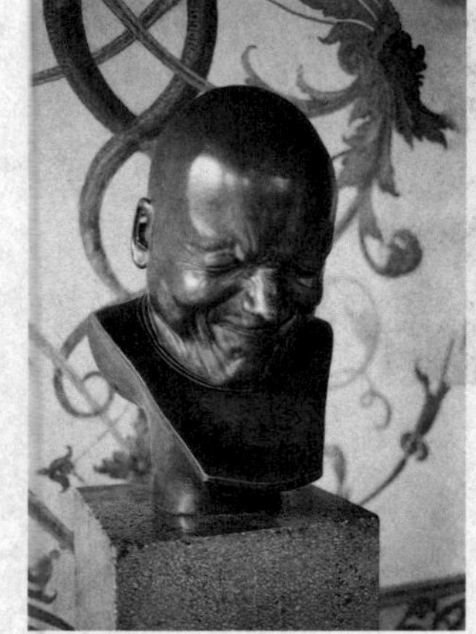

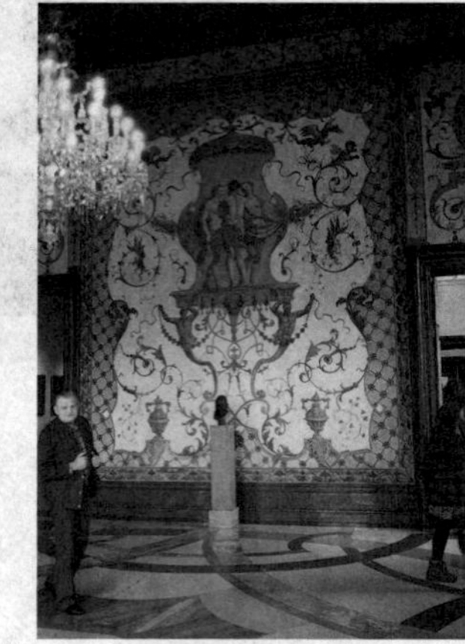

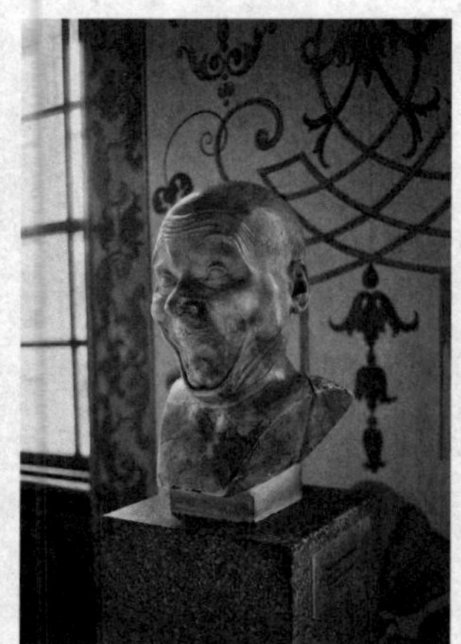

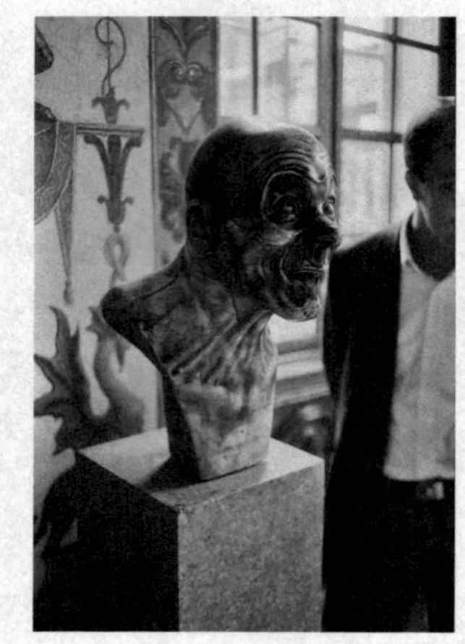

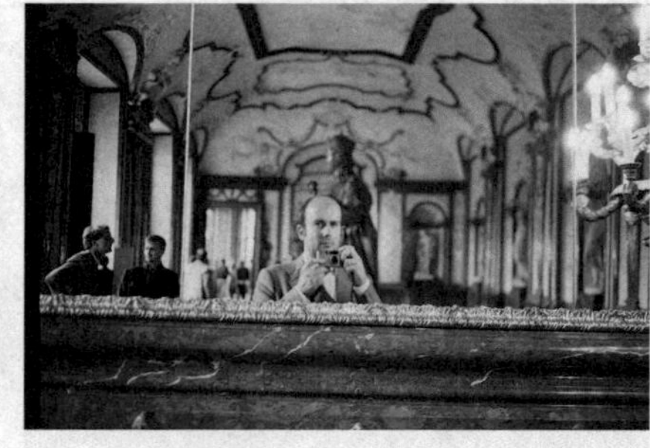

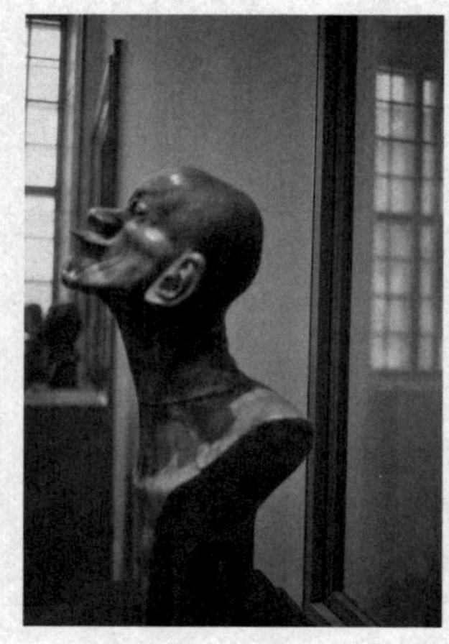

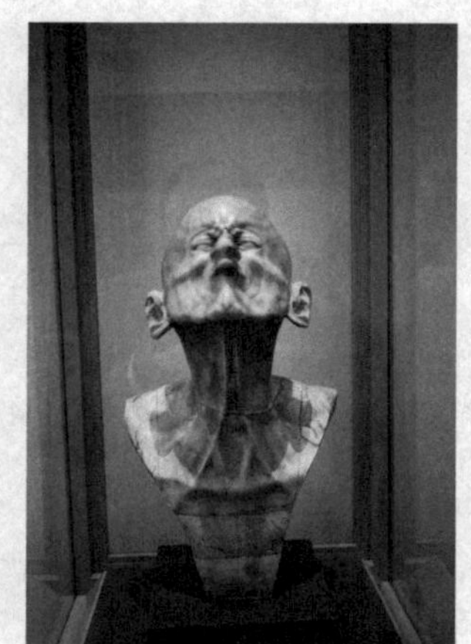

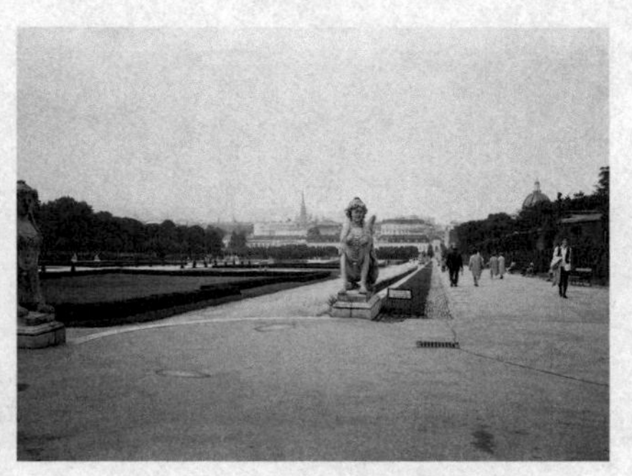

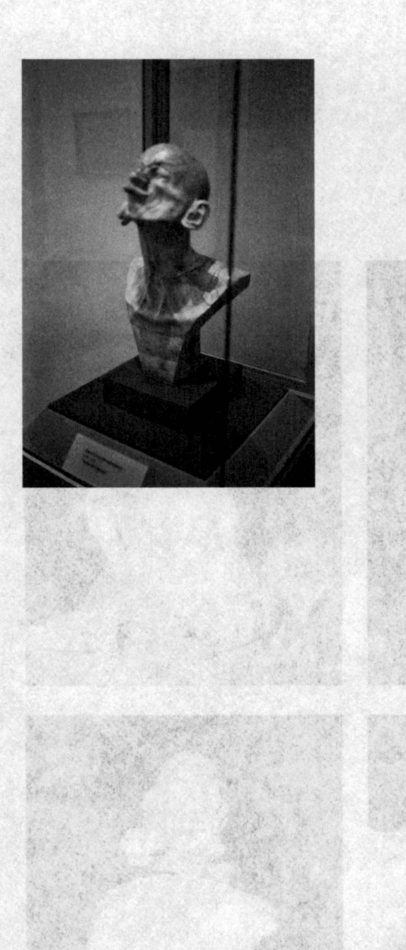

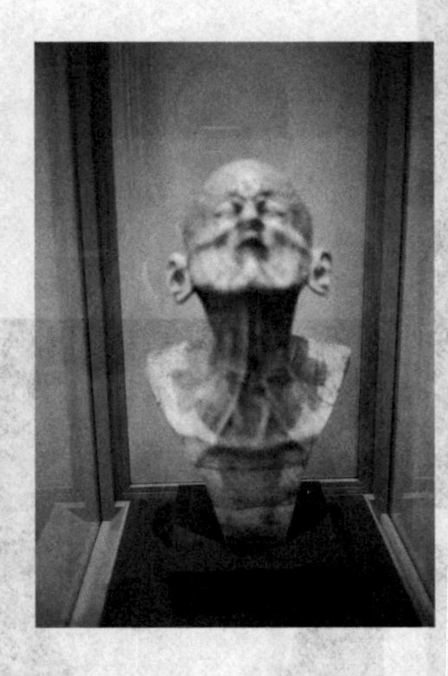

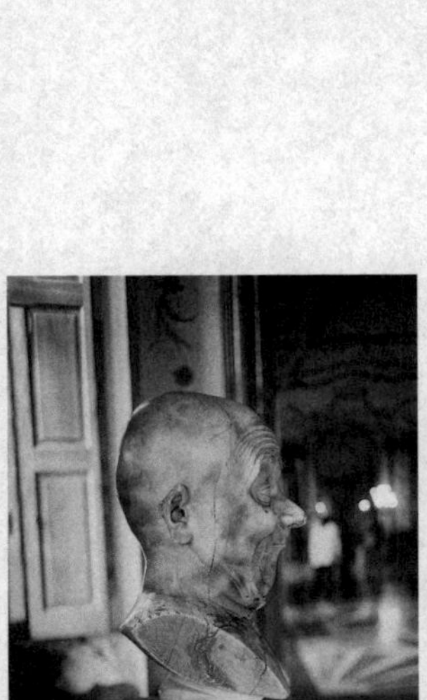

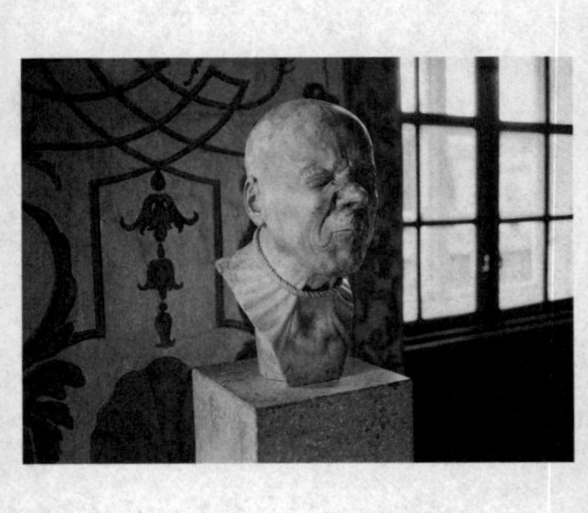

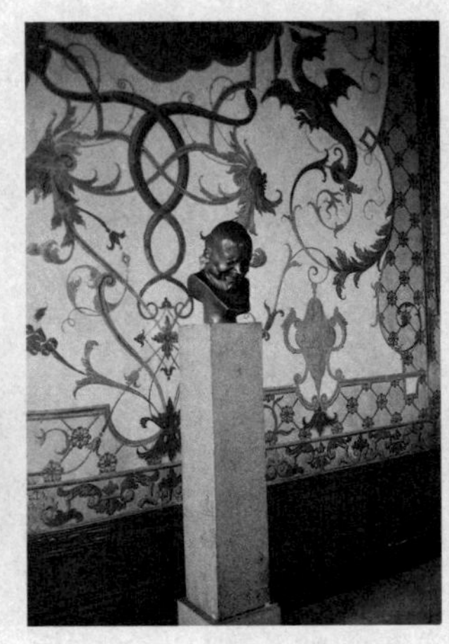

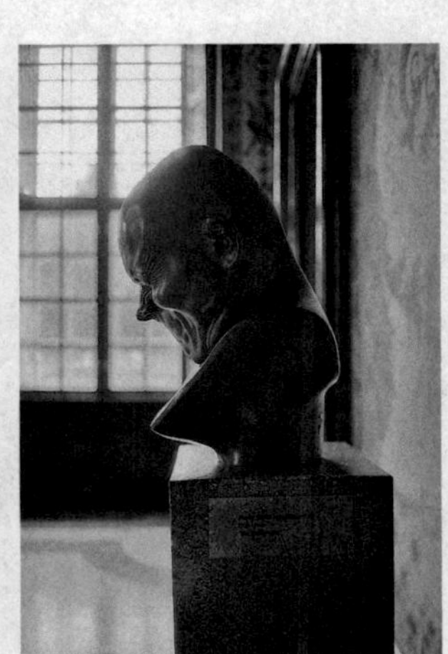

Belvedere Vienna 17 September 1995

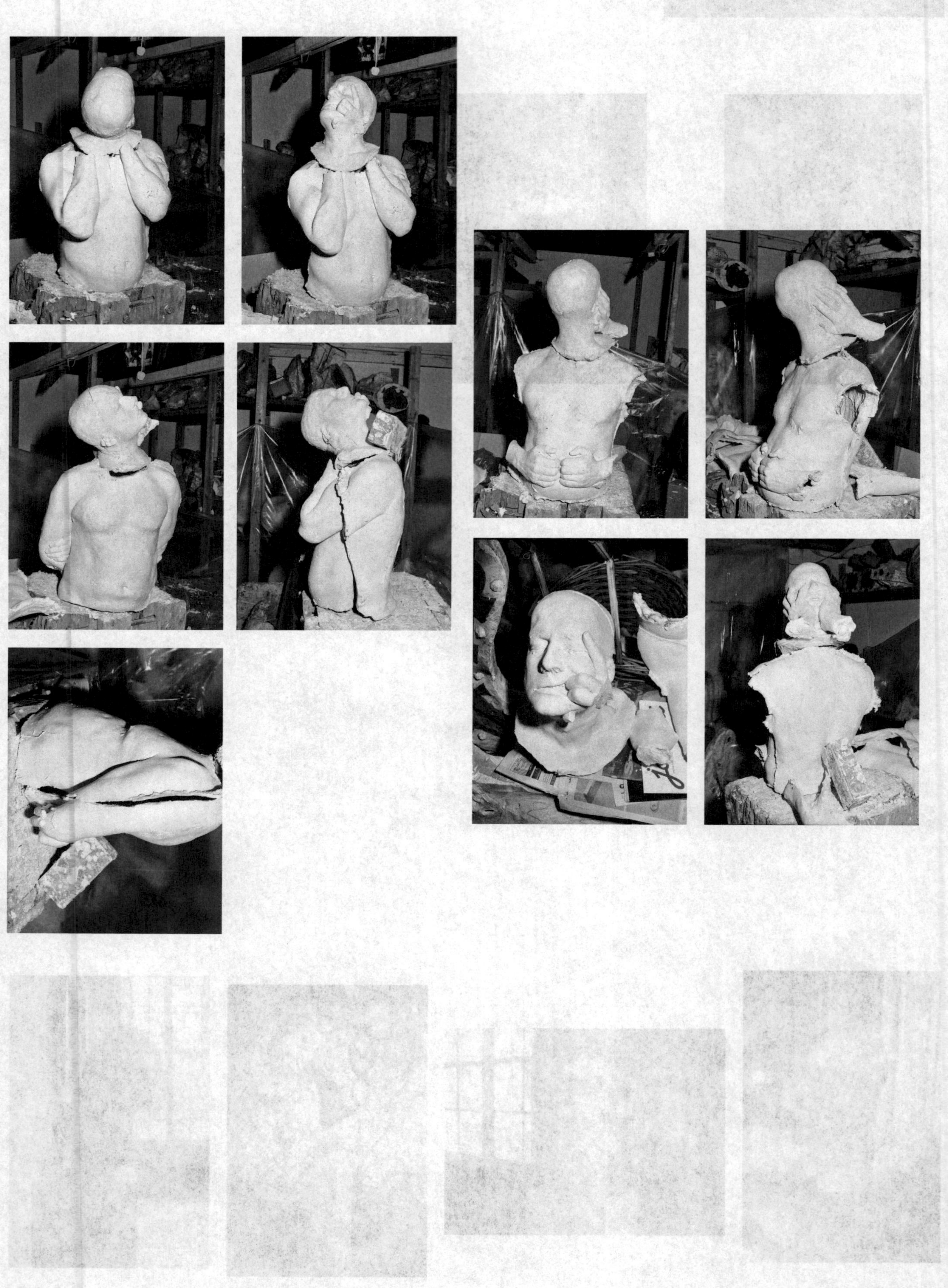

Working works for *Emotional Detox* August 1994

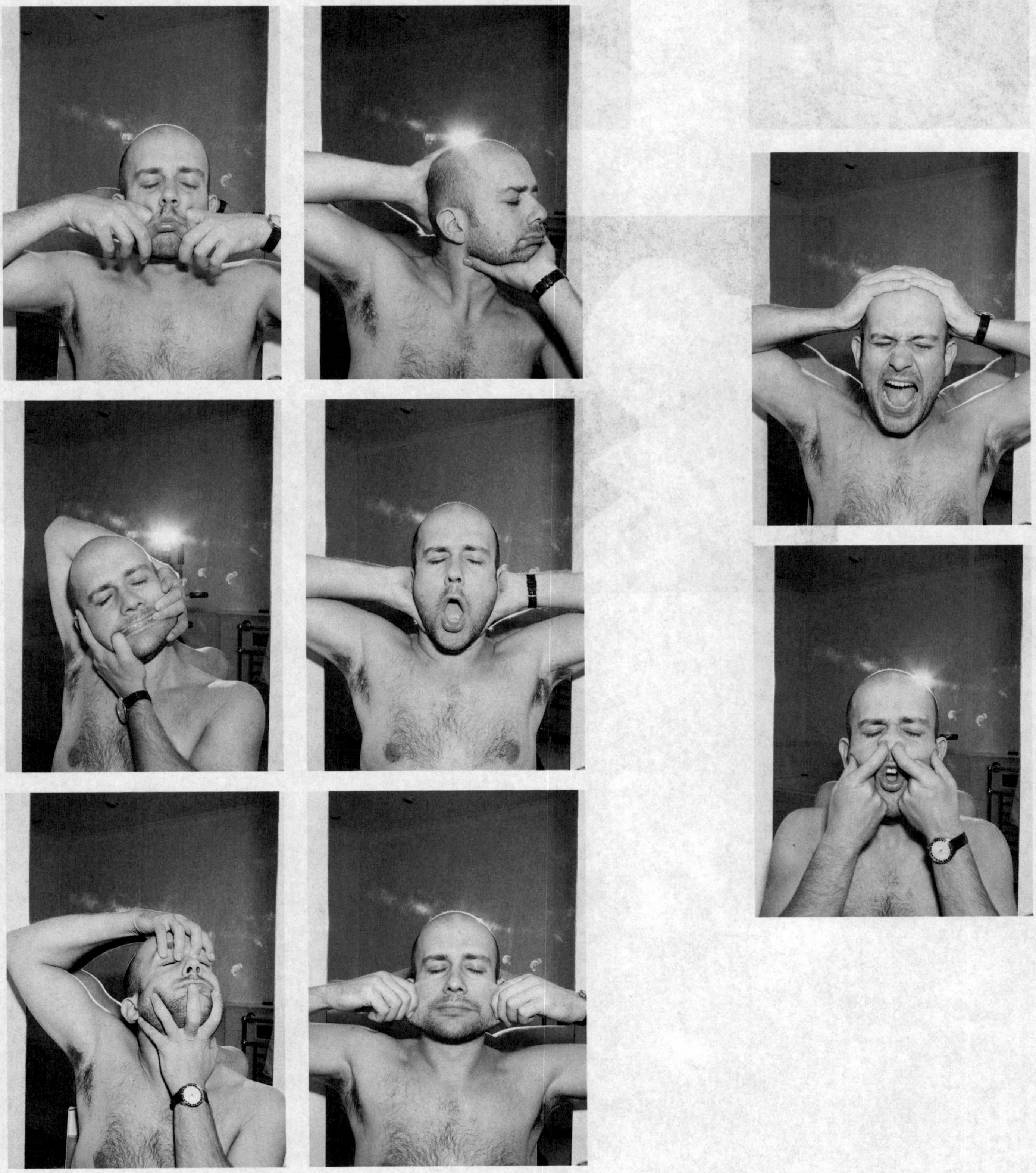

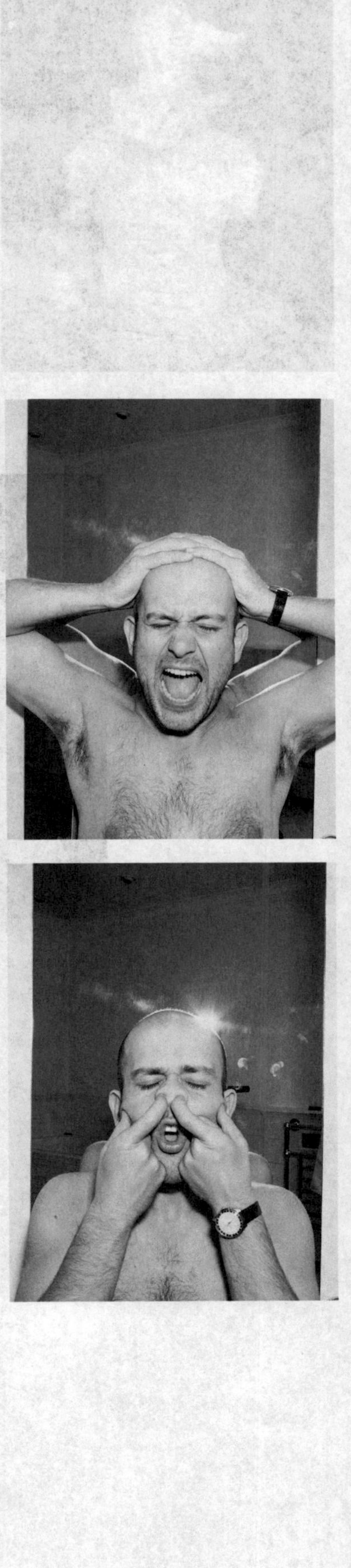

Test expressions for *Emotional Detox* September 1994

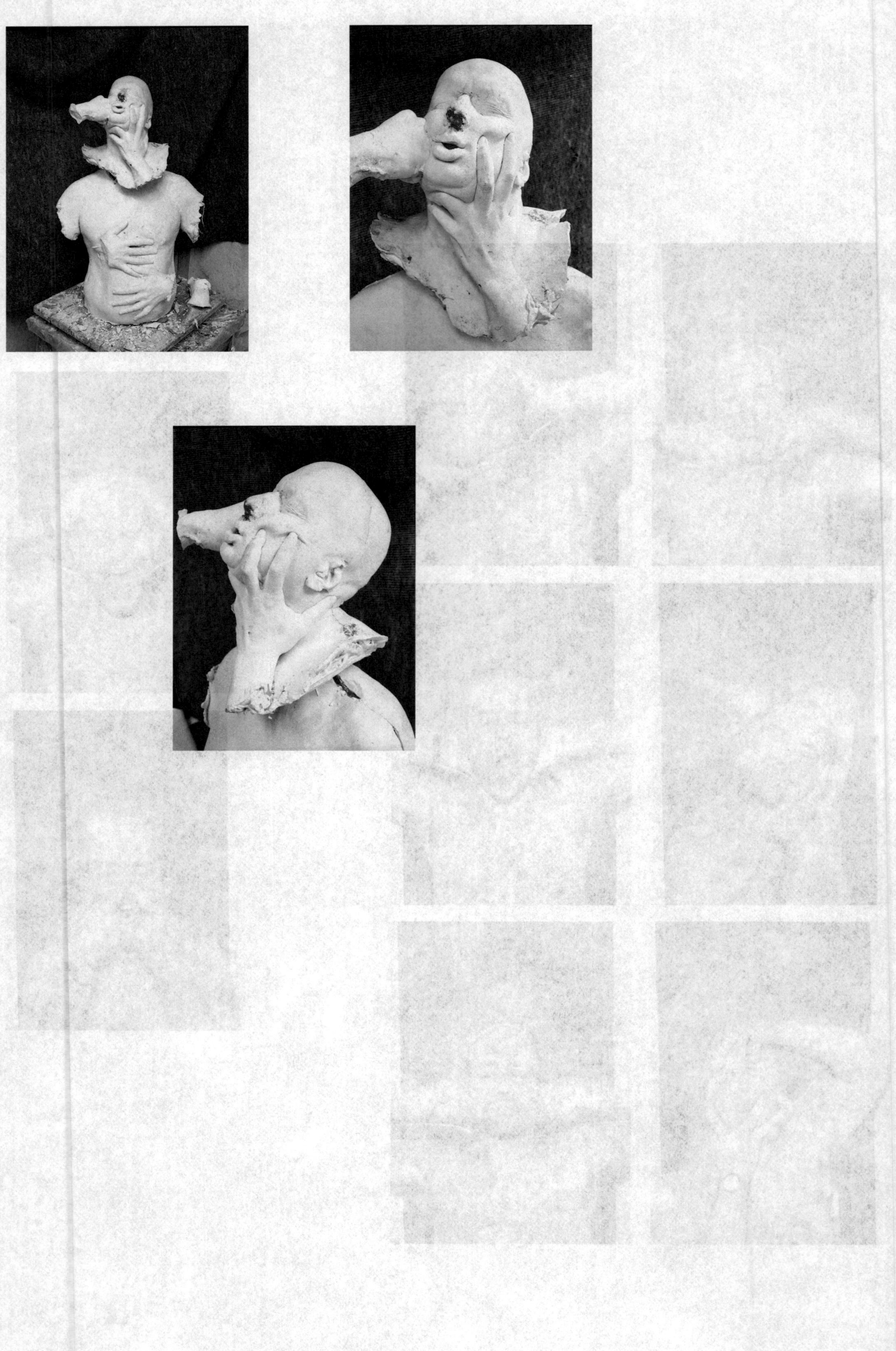

VI

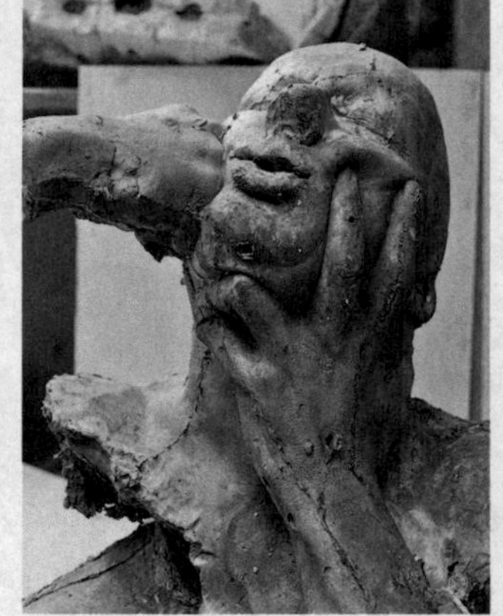

Patney *Emotional Detox VI* late April 1995

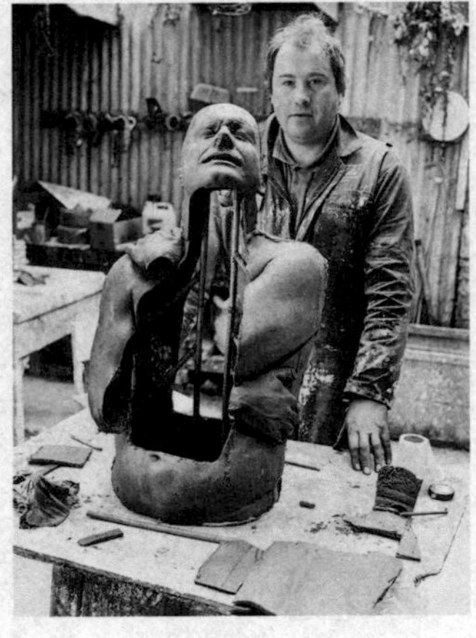
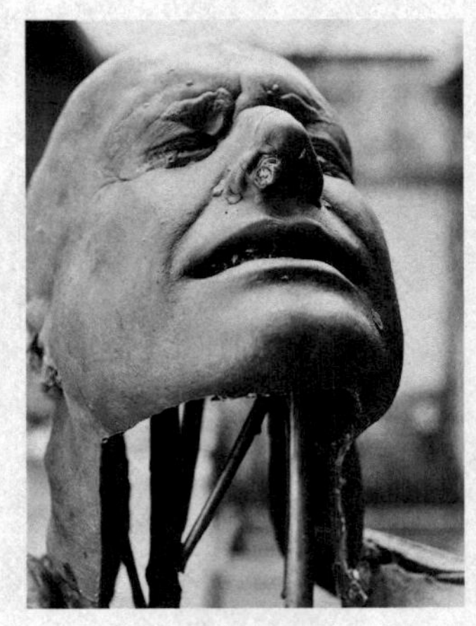
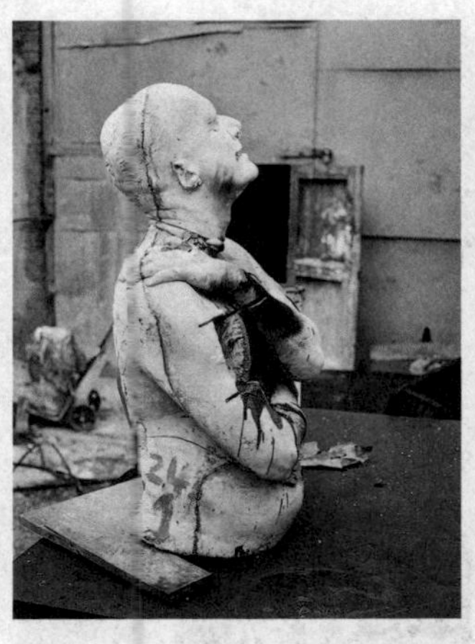
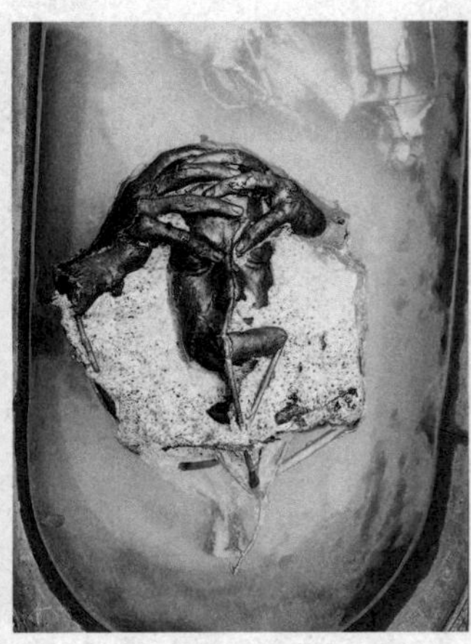
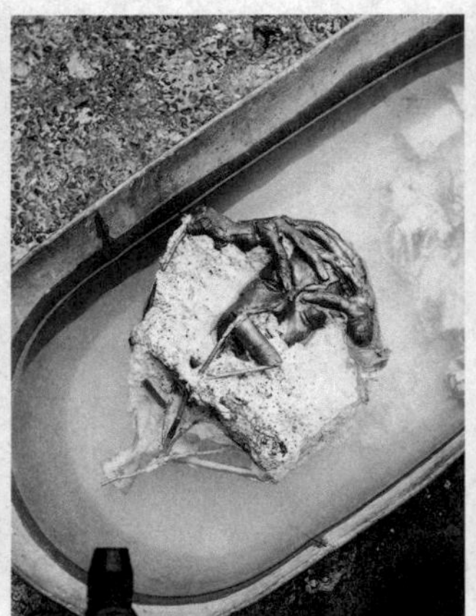
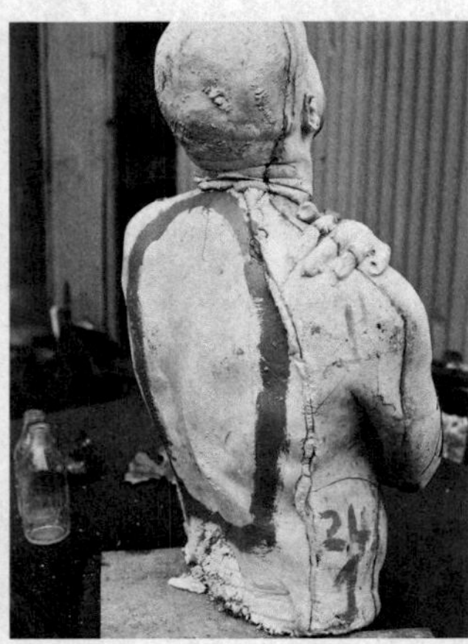

Working model

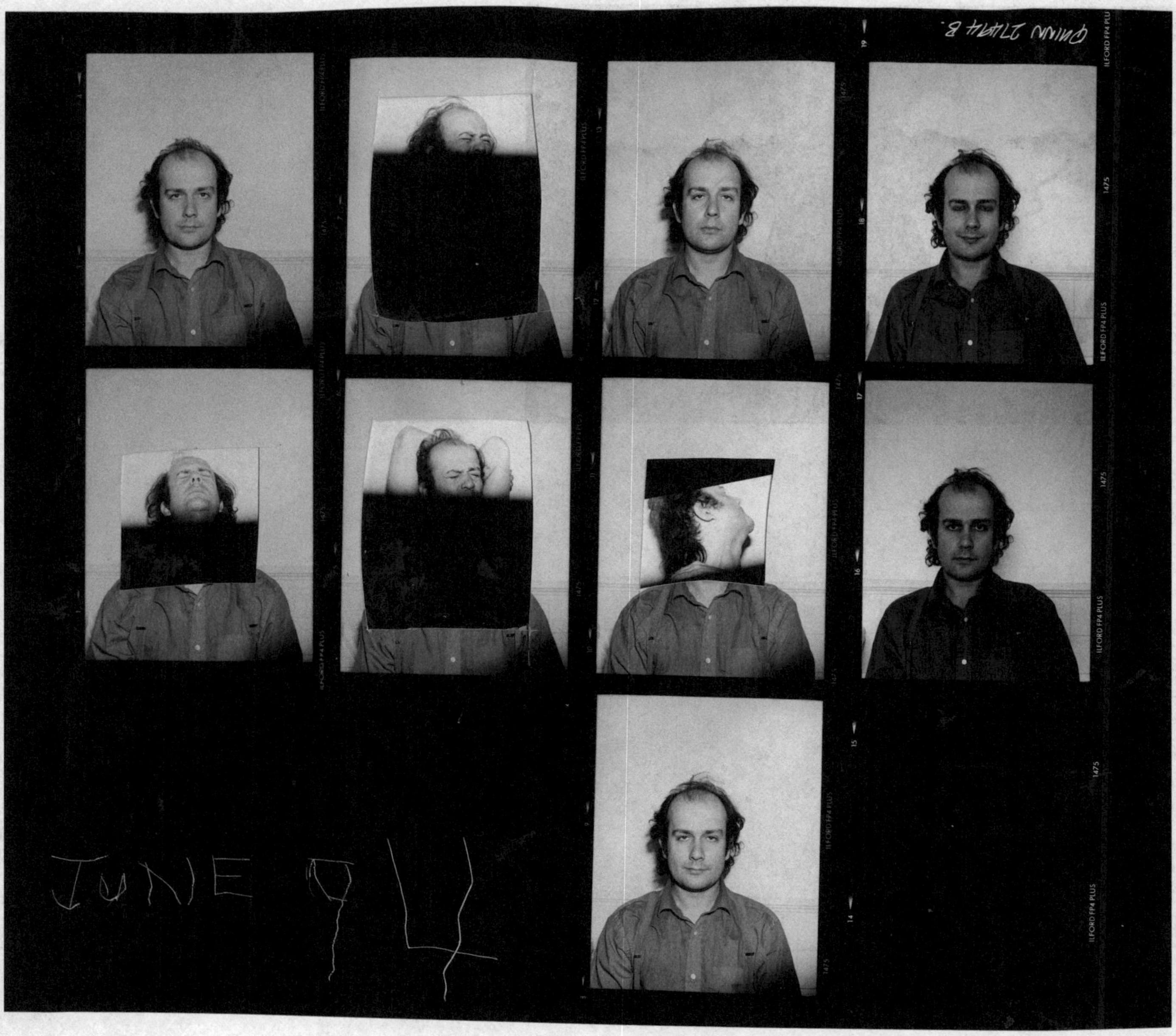

From passport photos mixed with *Emotional Detox* Traits with wrong shutter synchronisation

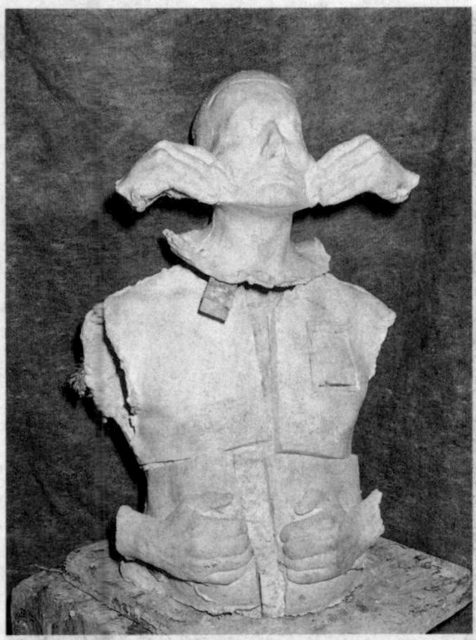

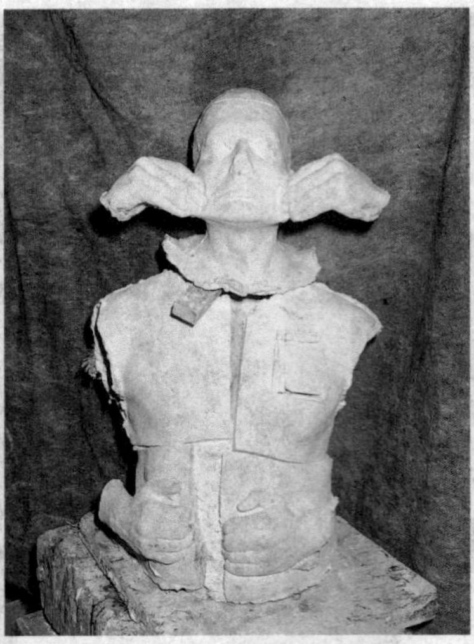

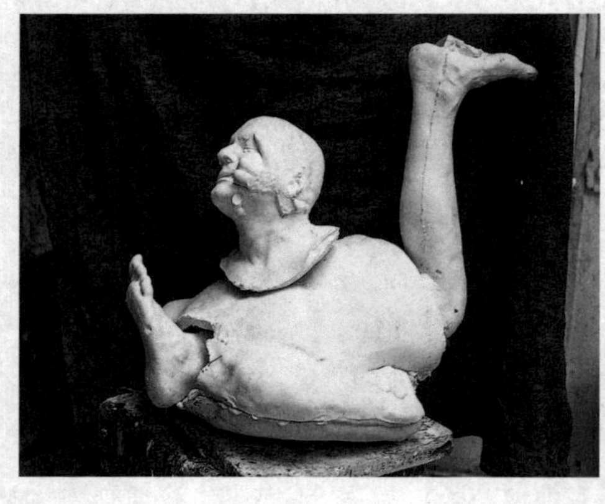

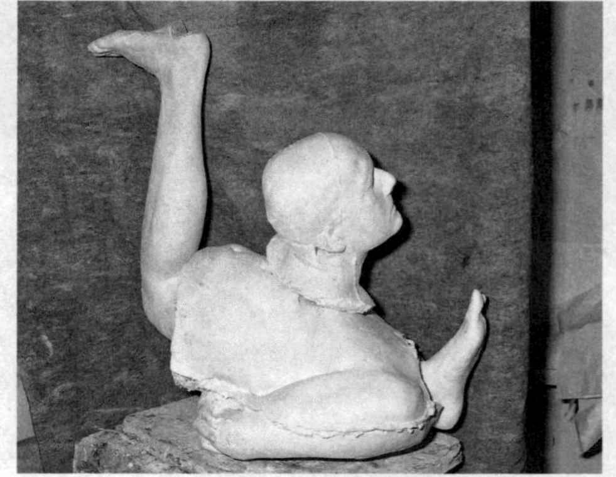

Foundry The mold January 1995

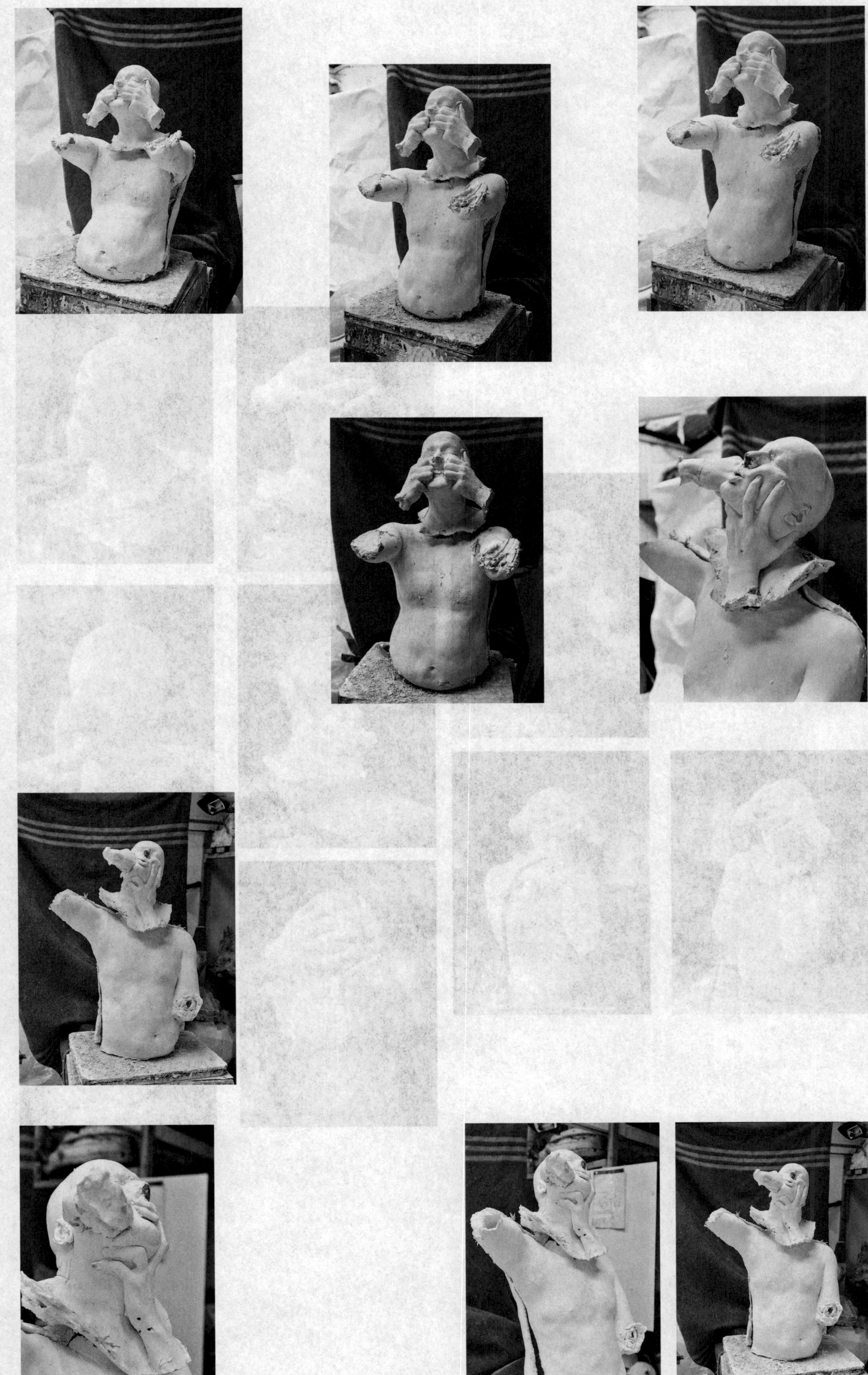

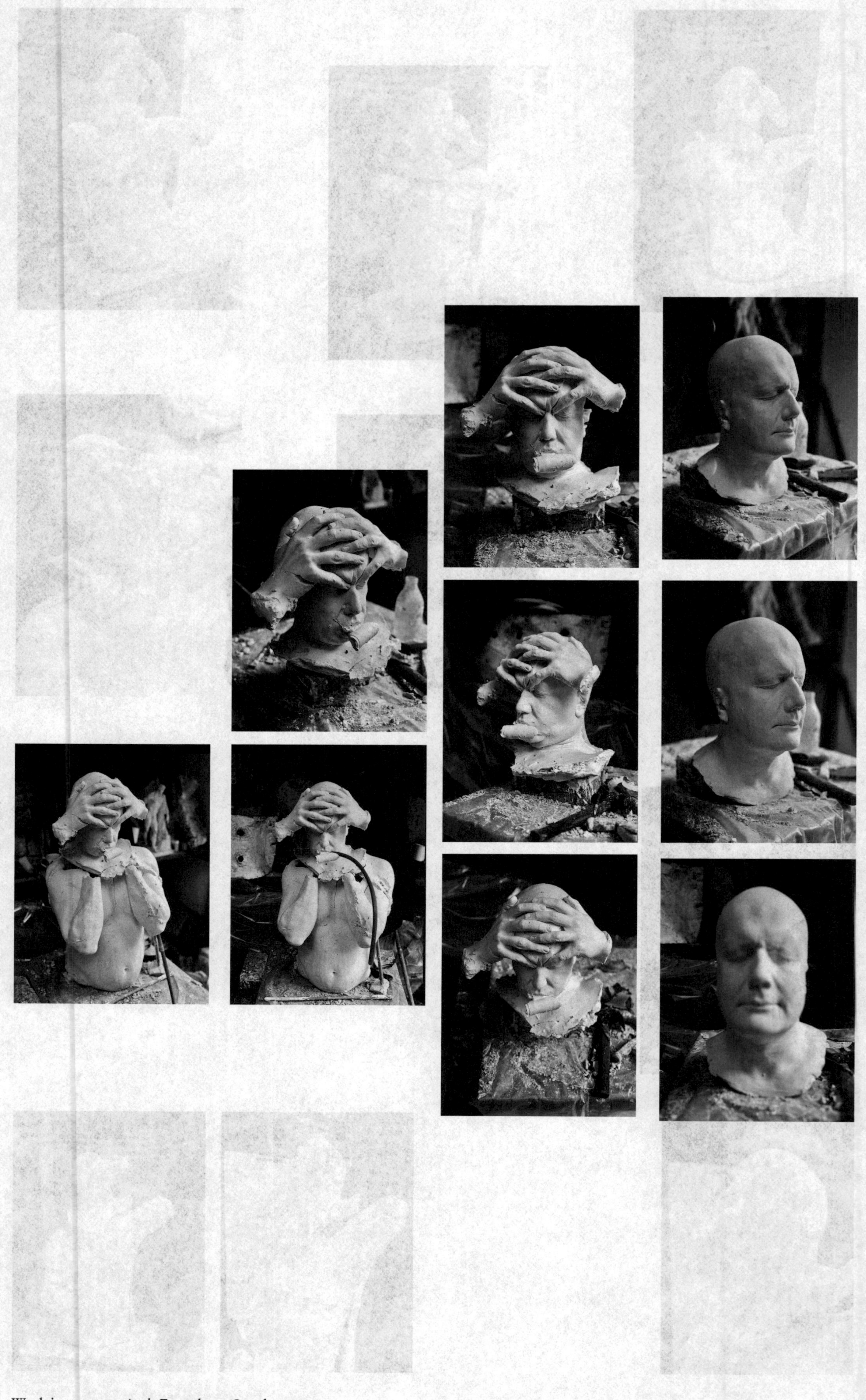

Work in progress Arch Foundry   October 1994

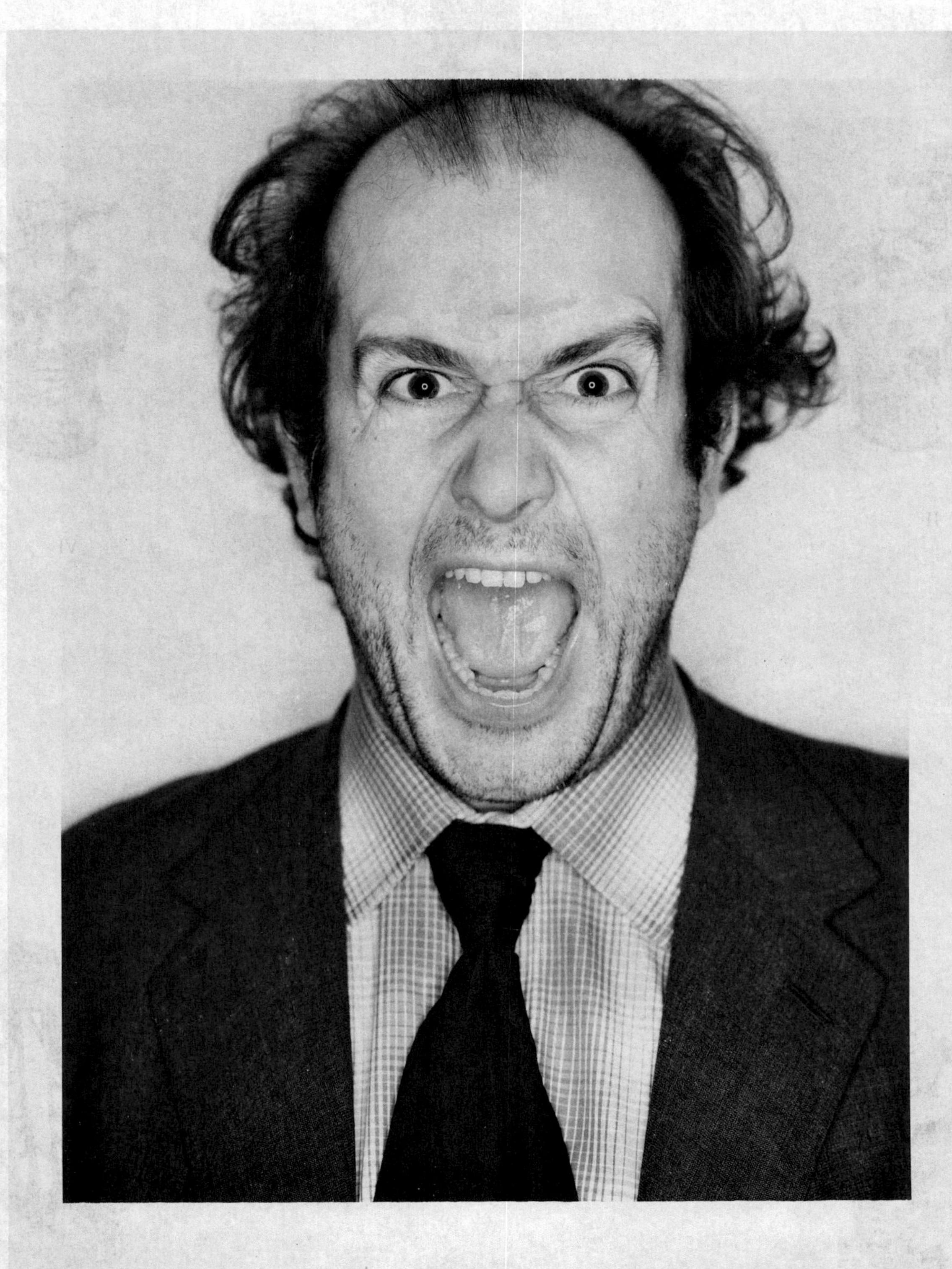

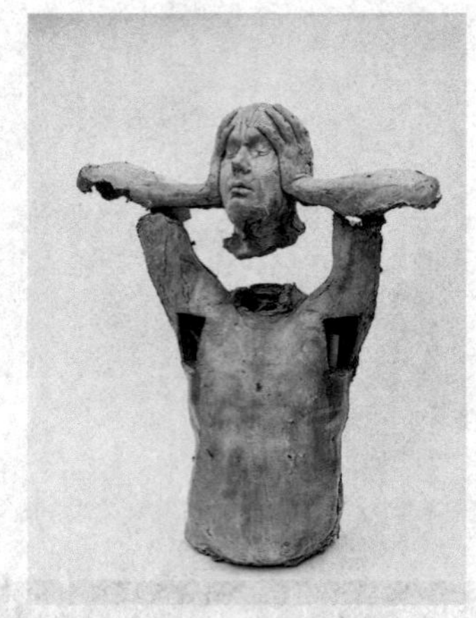

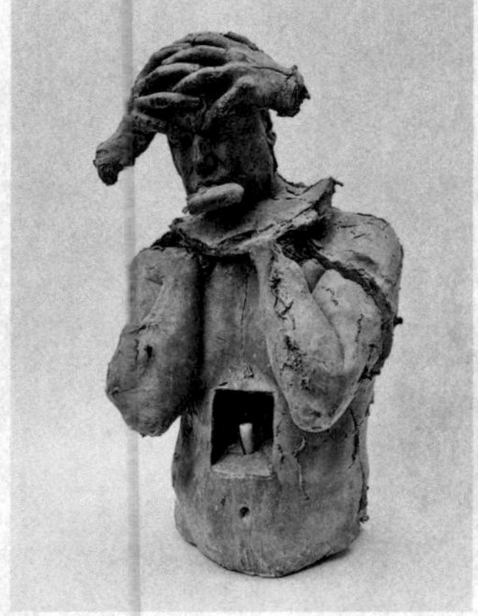

II

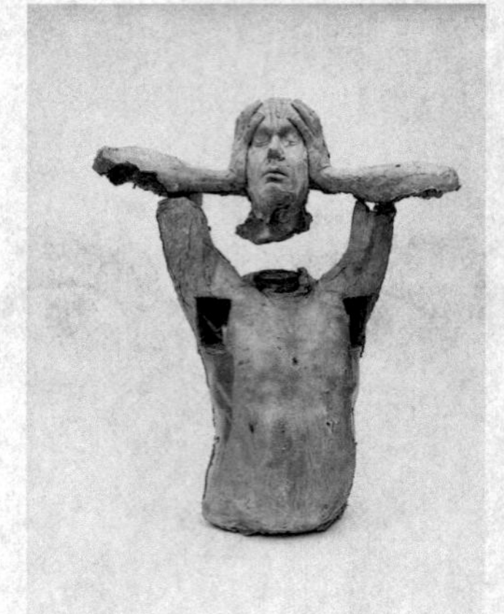

IV

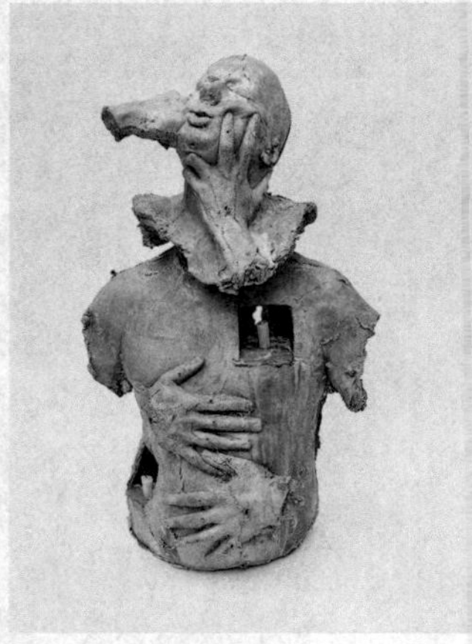

VI

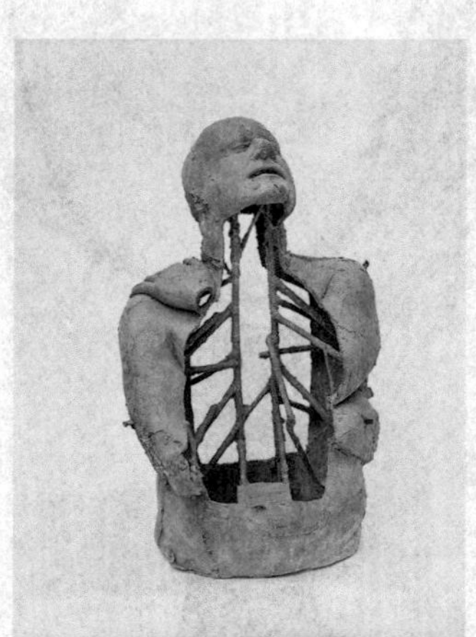

Fever of Fever

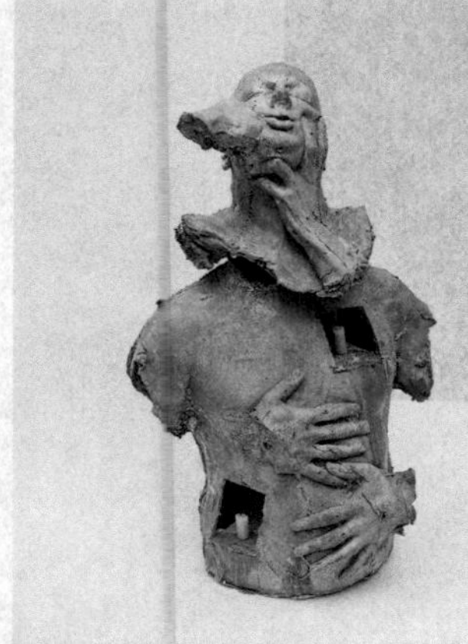

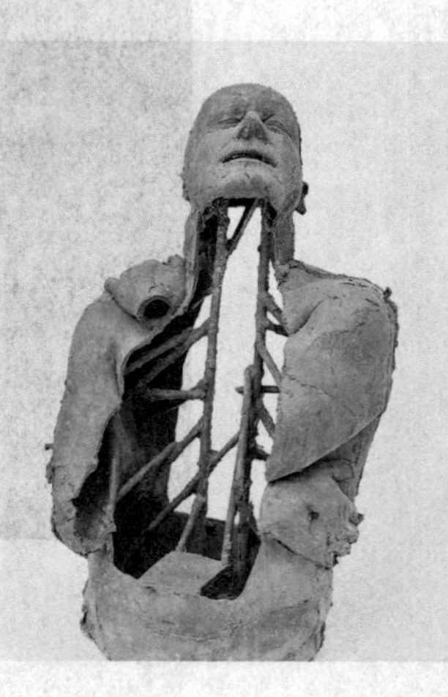

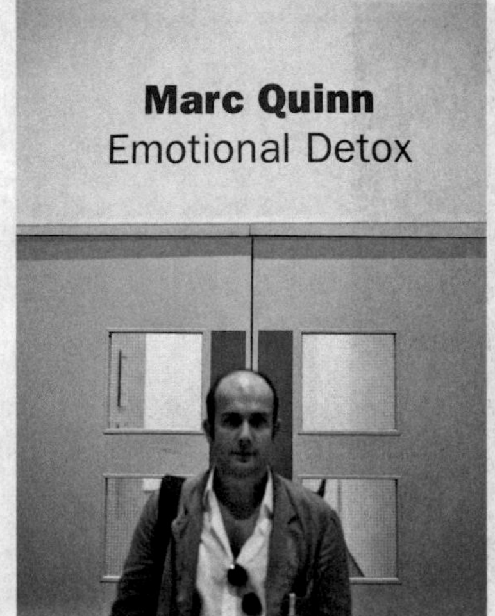

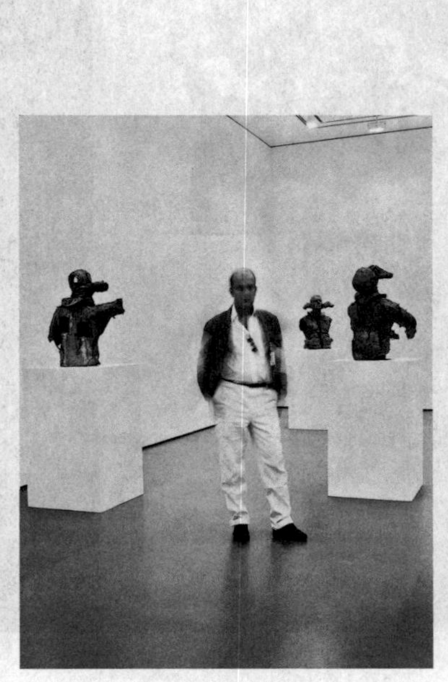

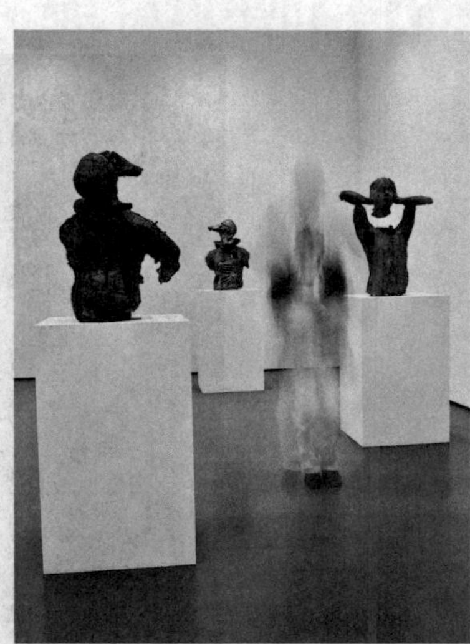

Tate Britain *Emotional Detox* 1995

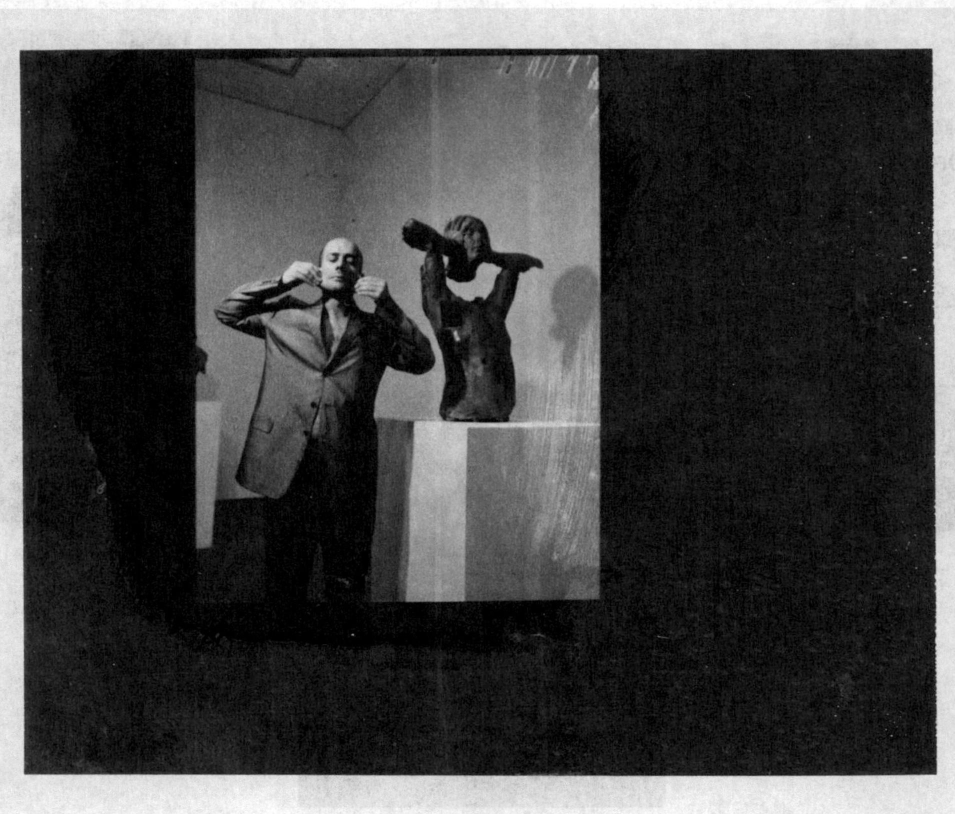

Tate Britain Polaroid by Manuela Panerosa for Italian *Vogue* 12 July 1995

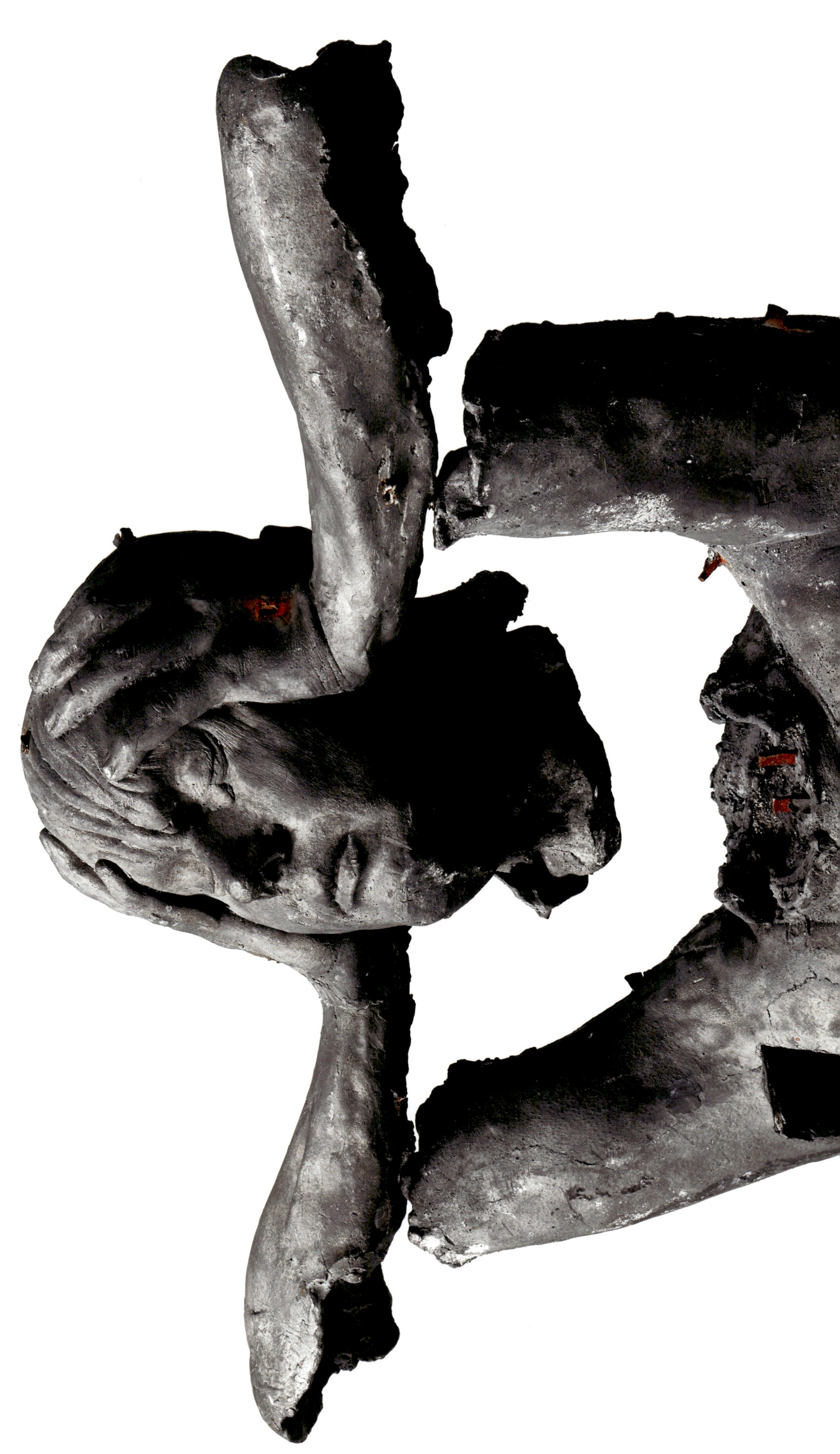

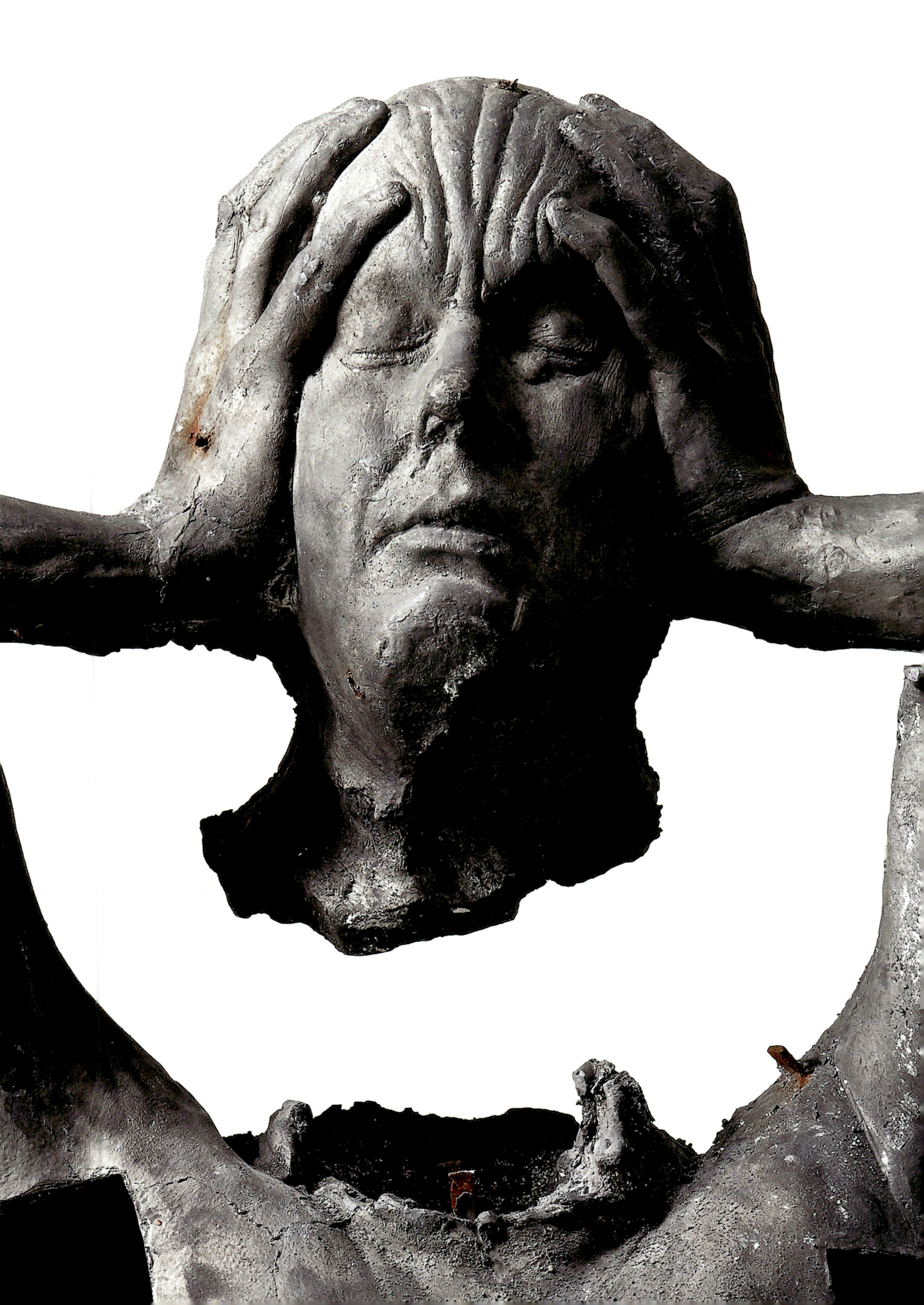

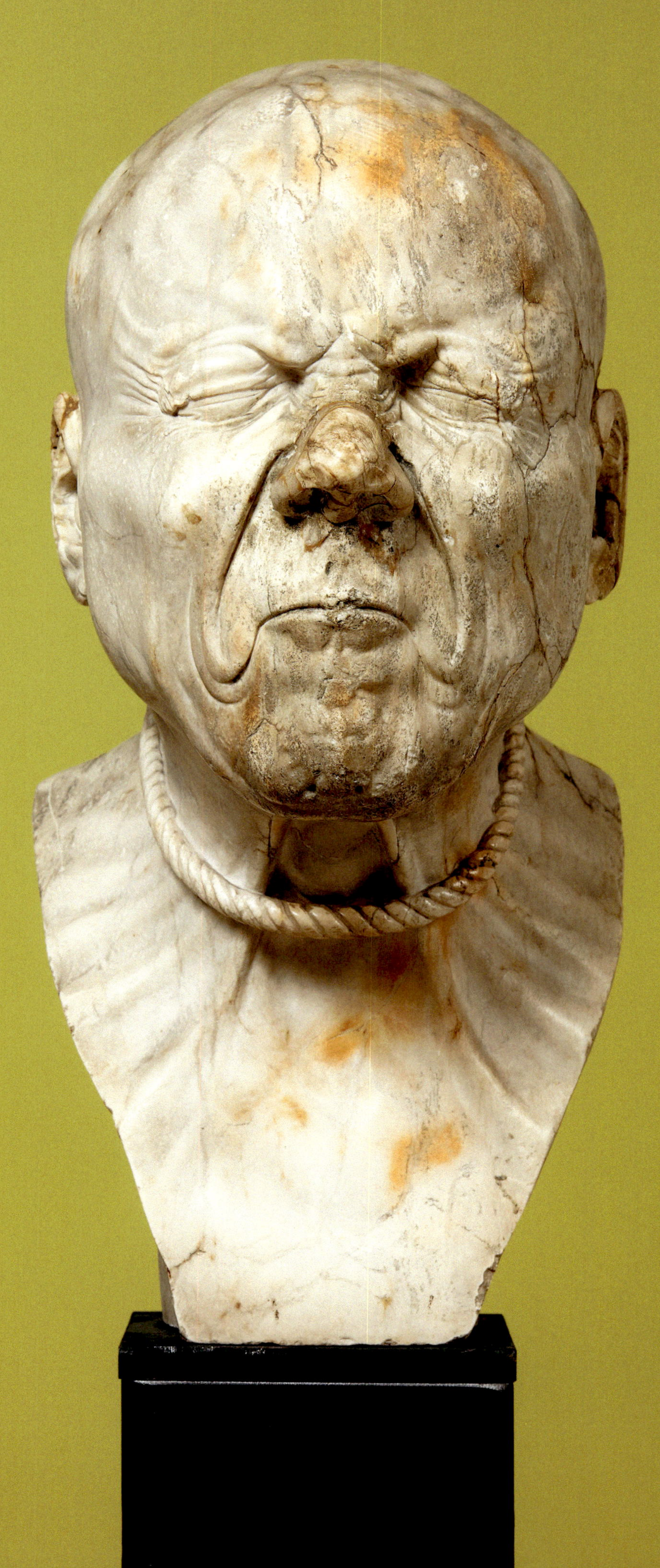

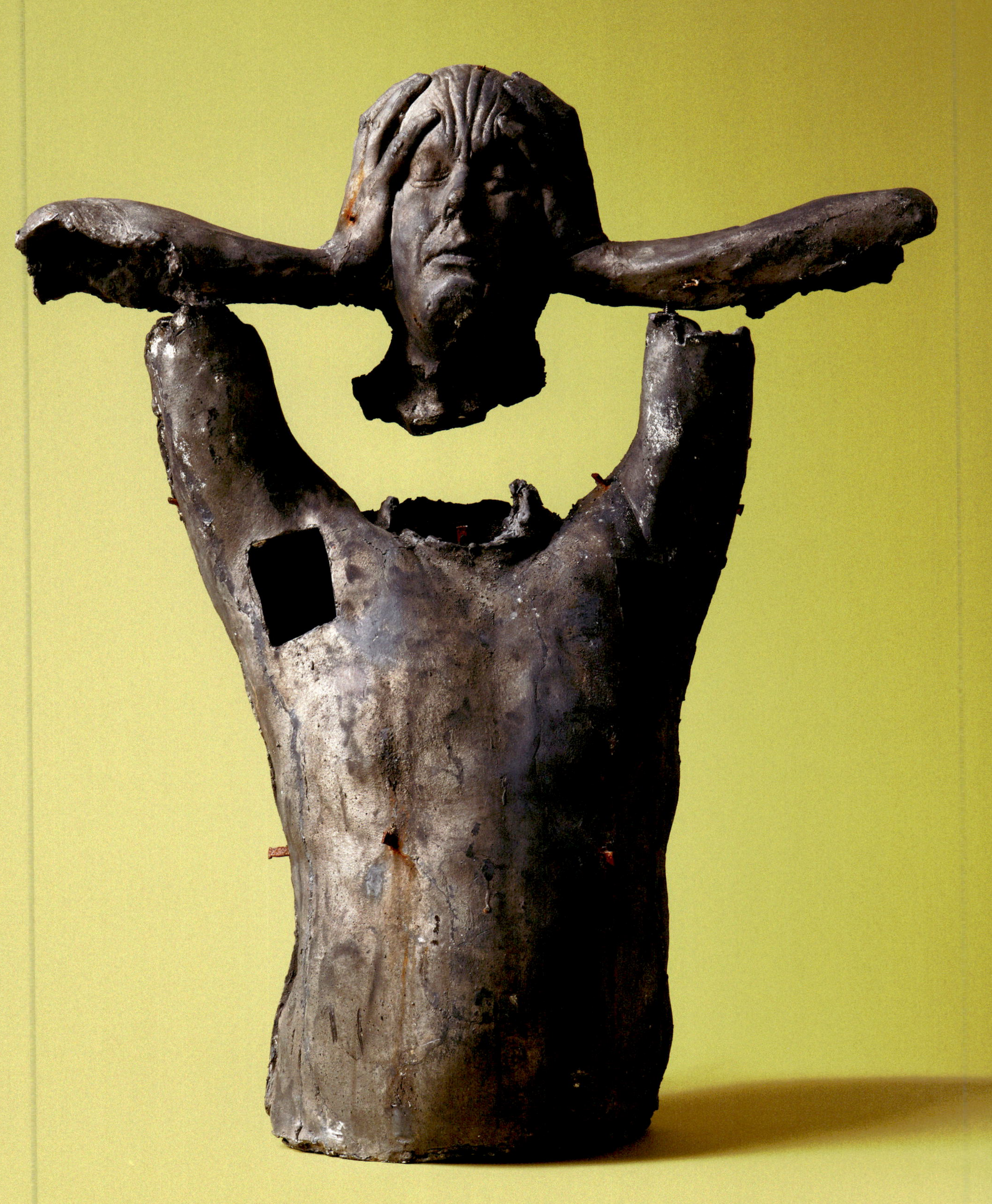

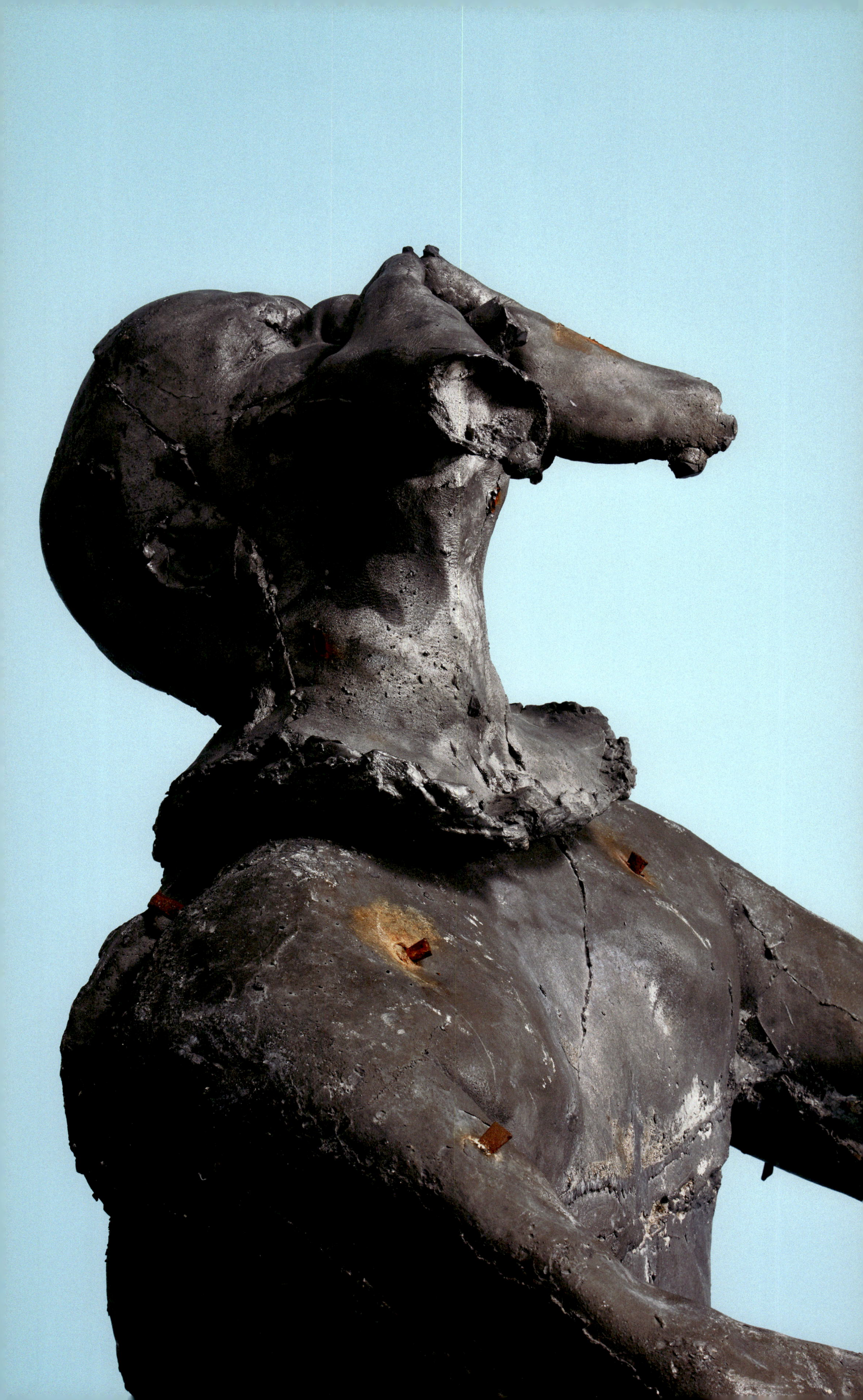

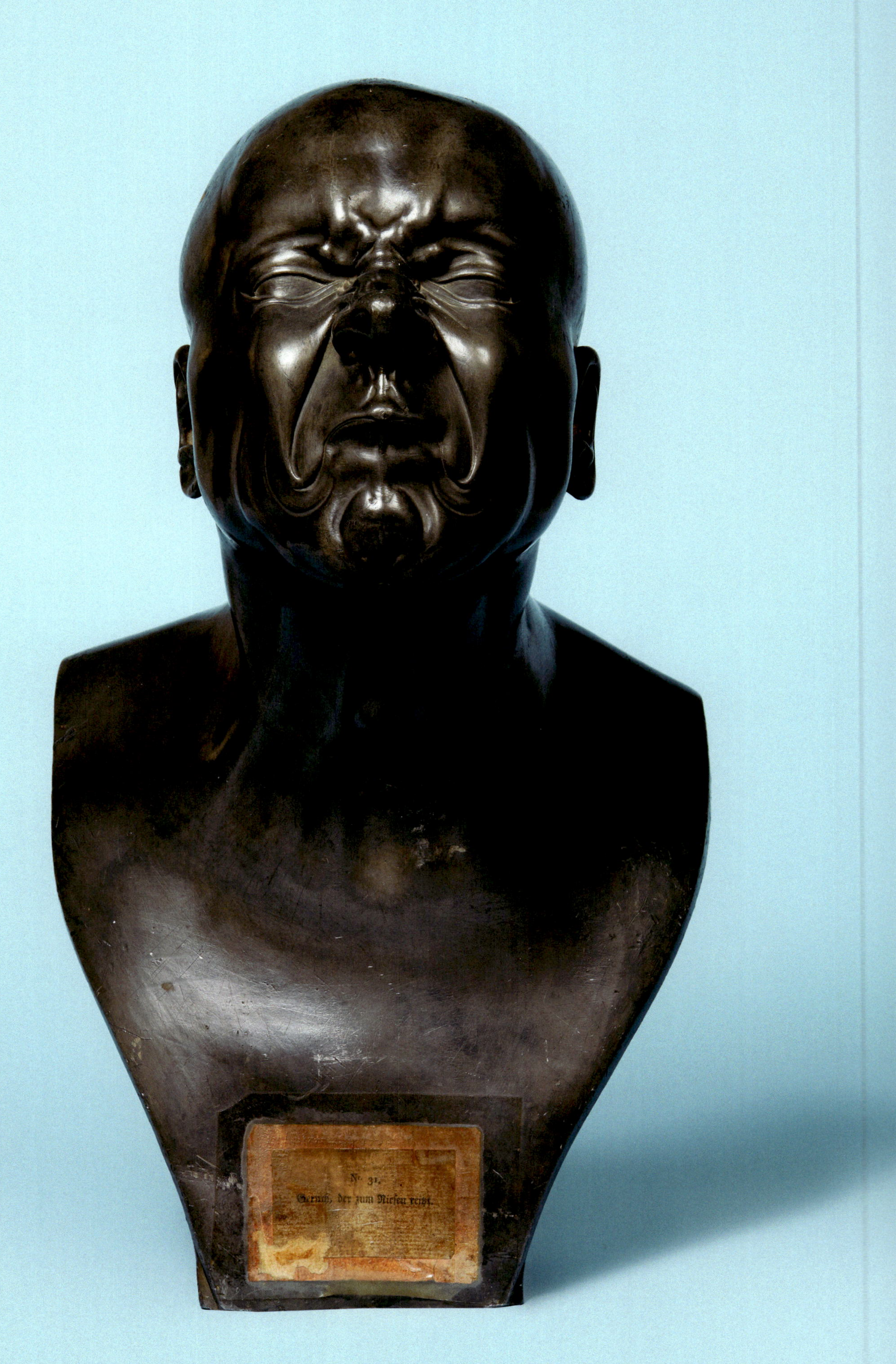
Nr. 31.
Geruch, der zum Niesen reizt.

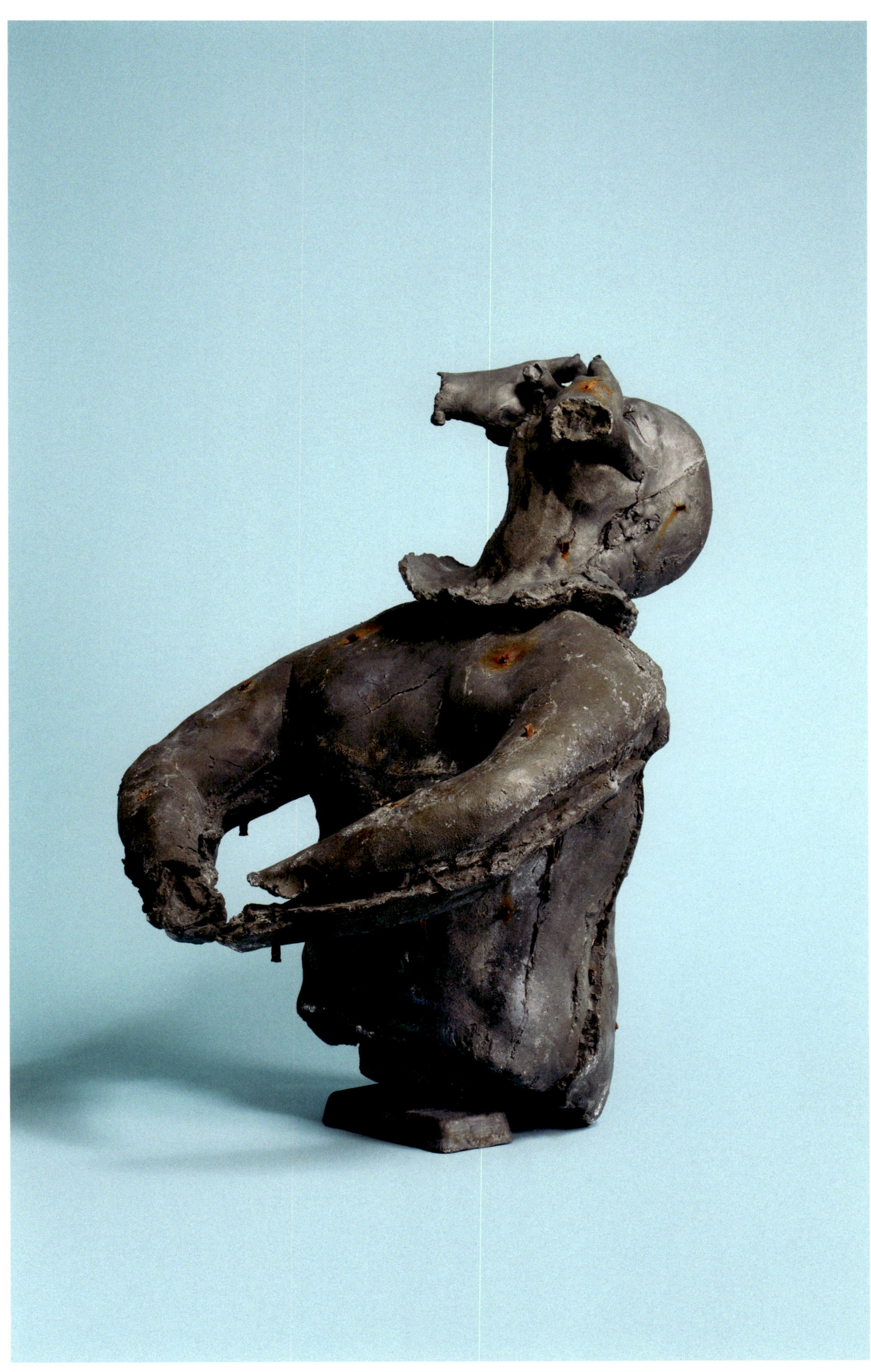

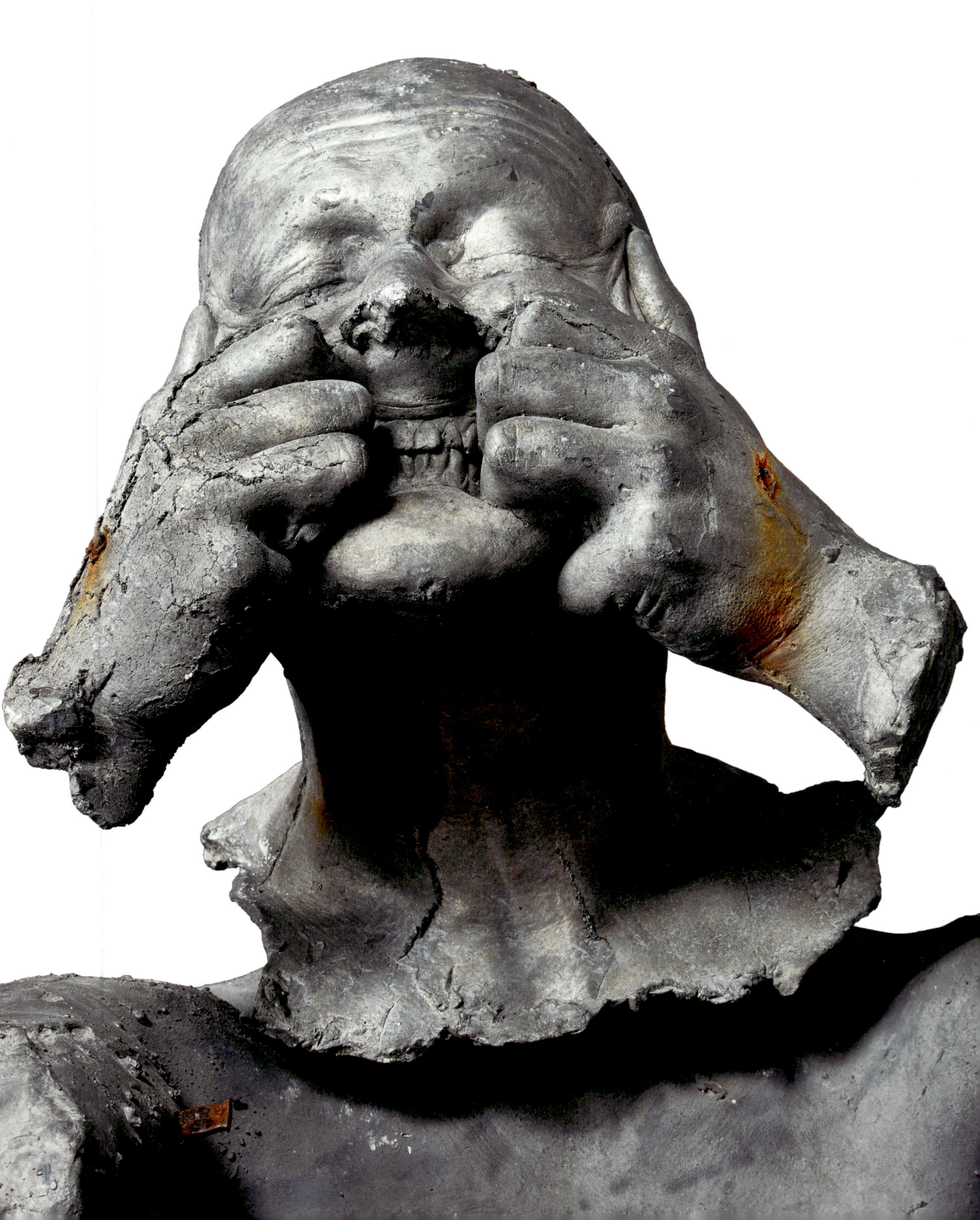

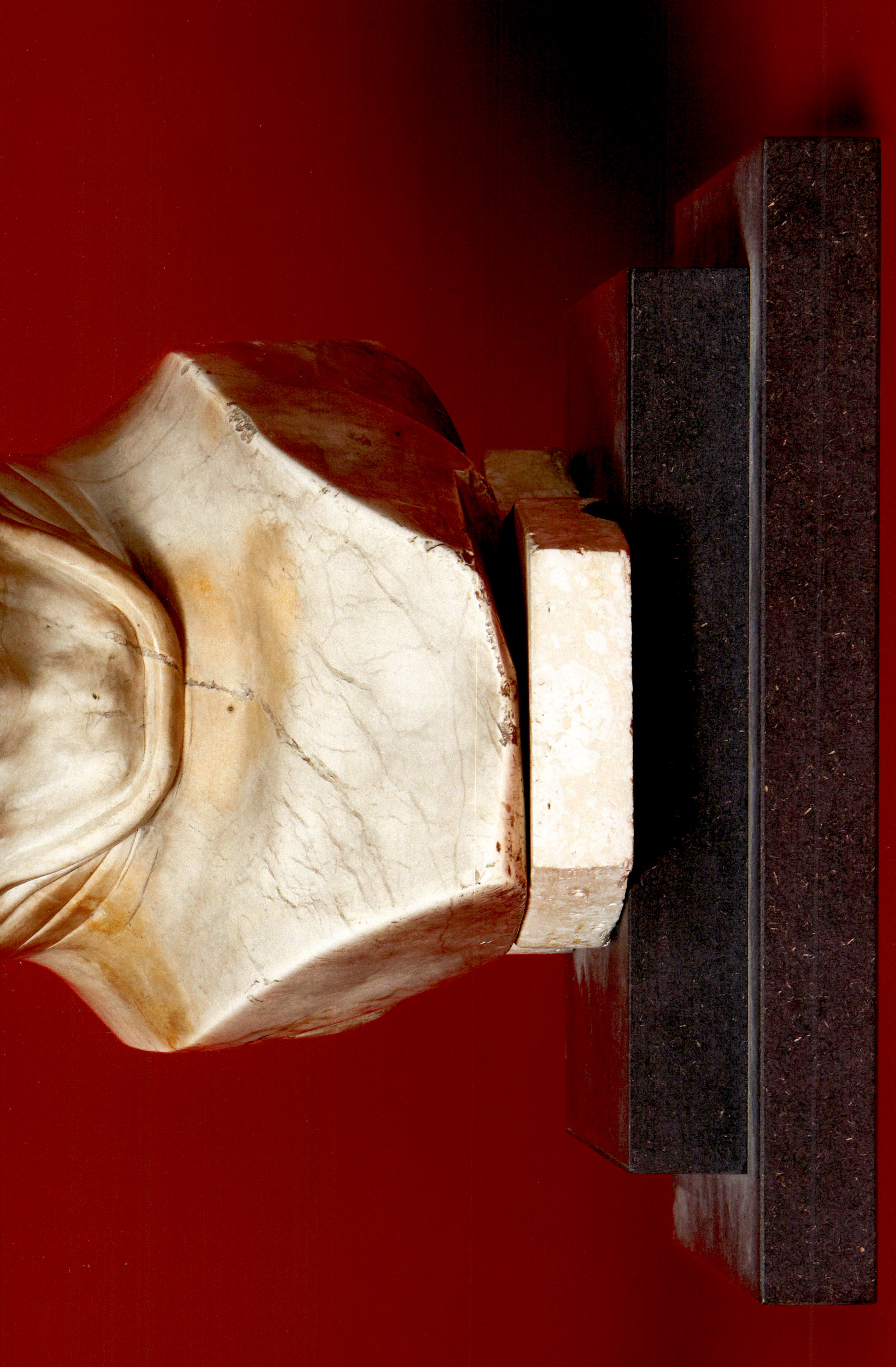

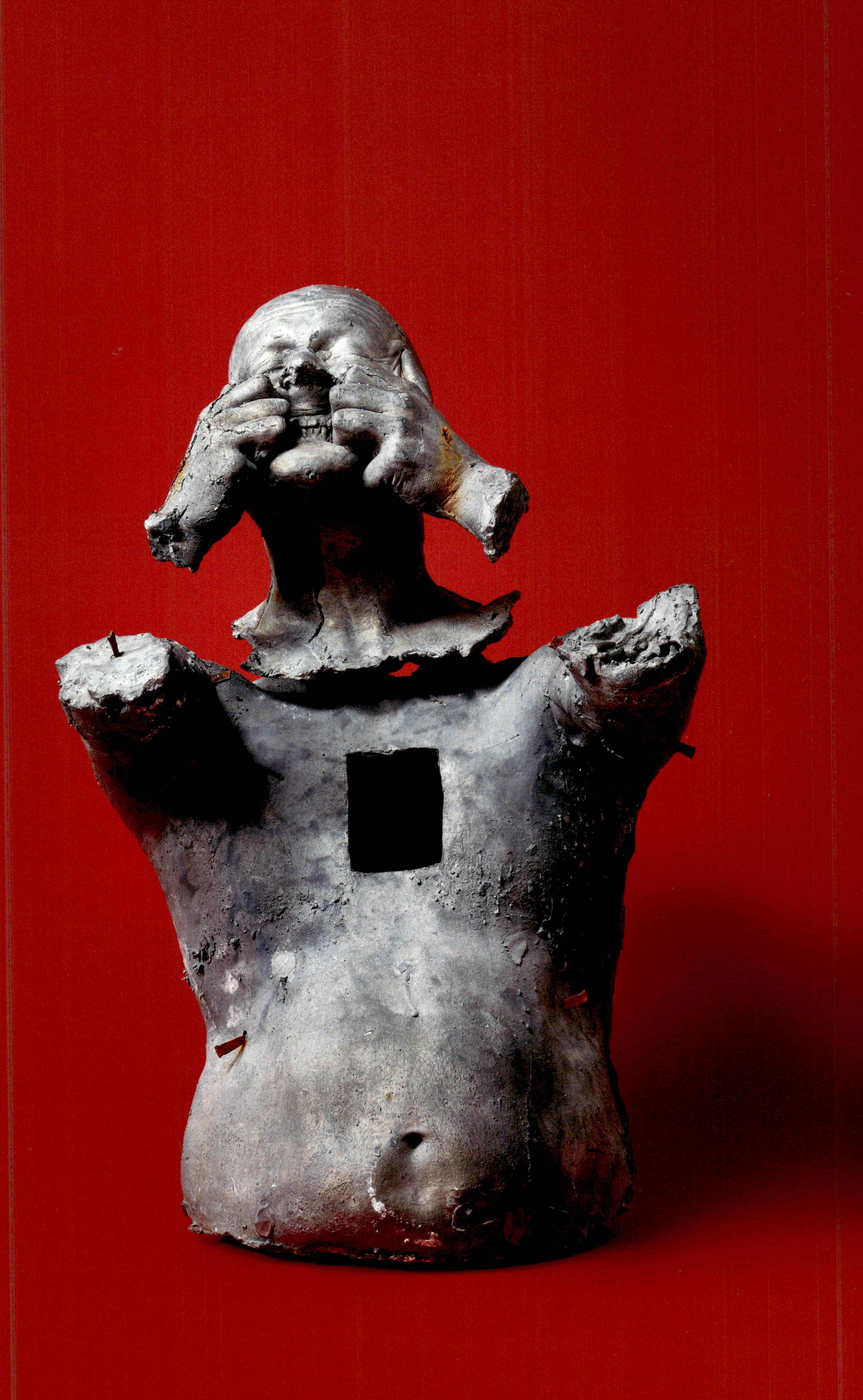

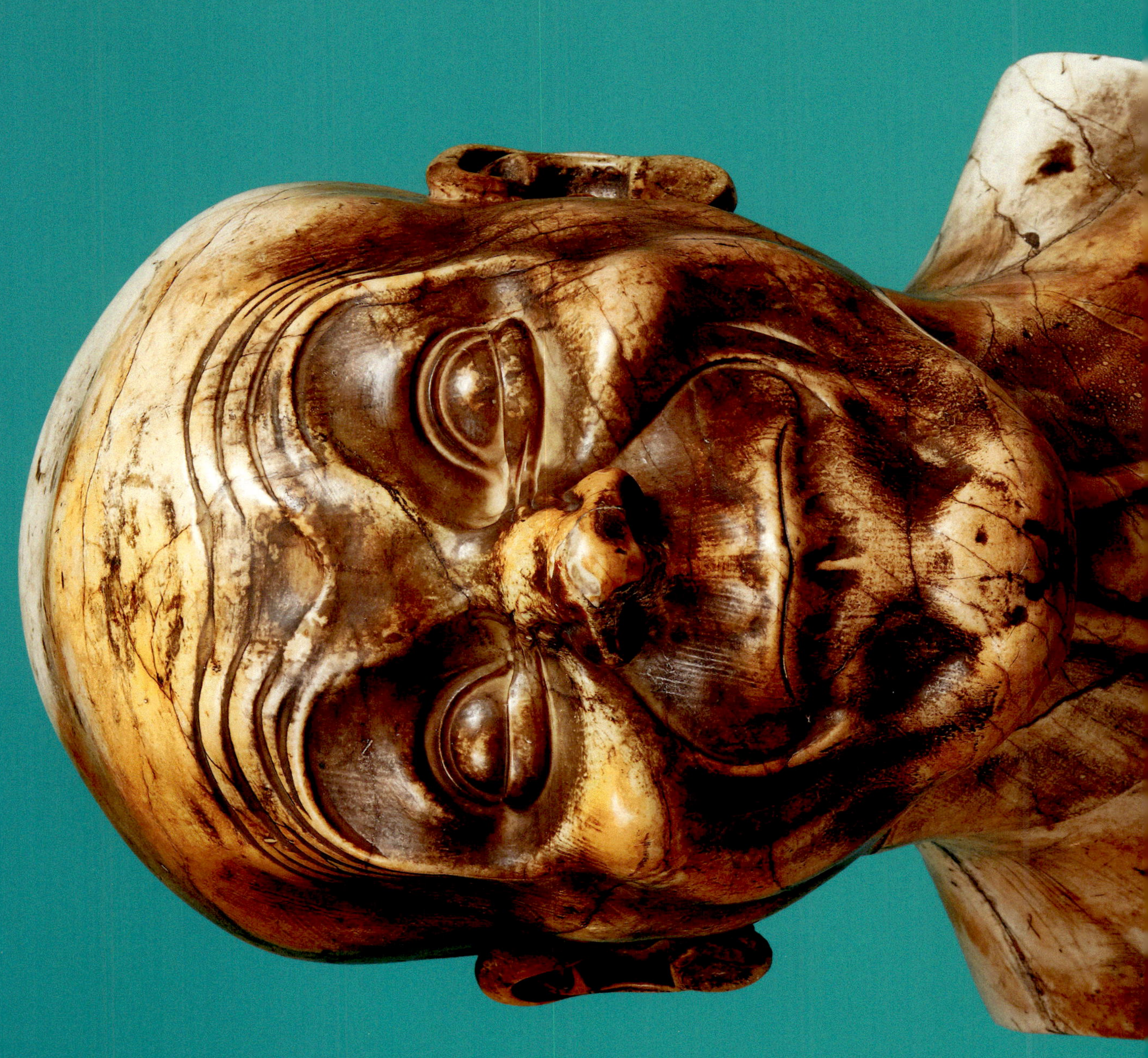

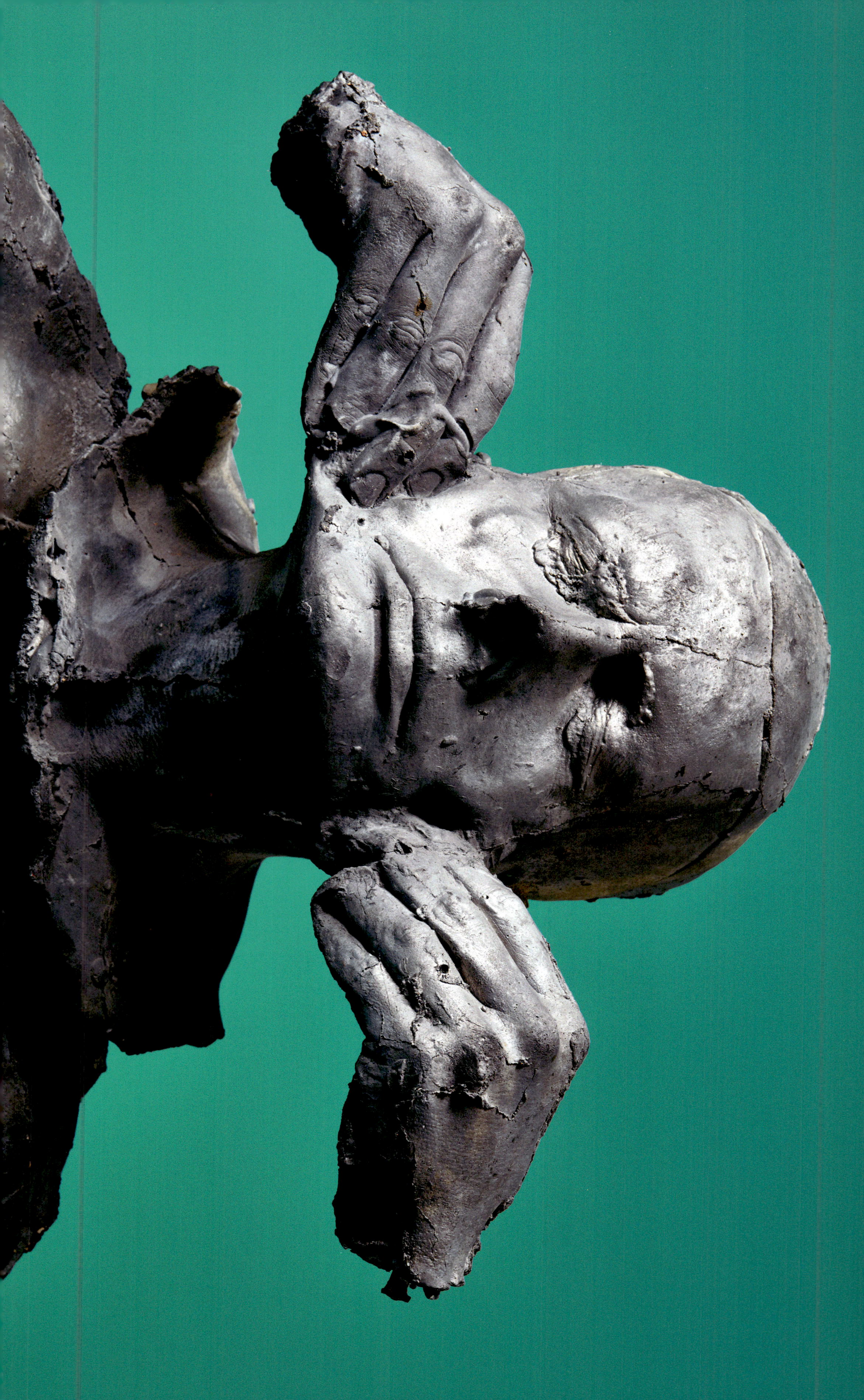

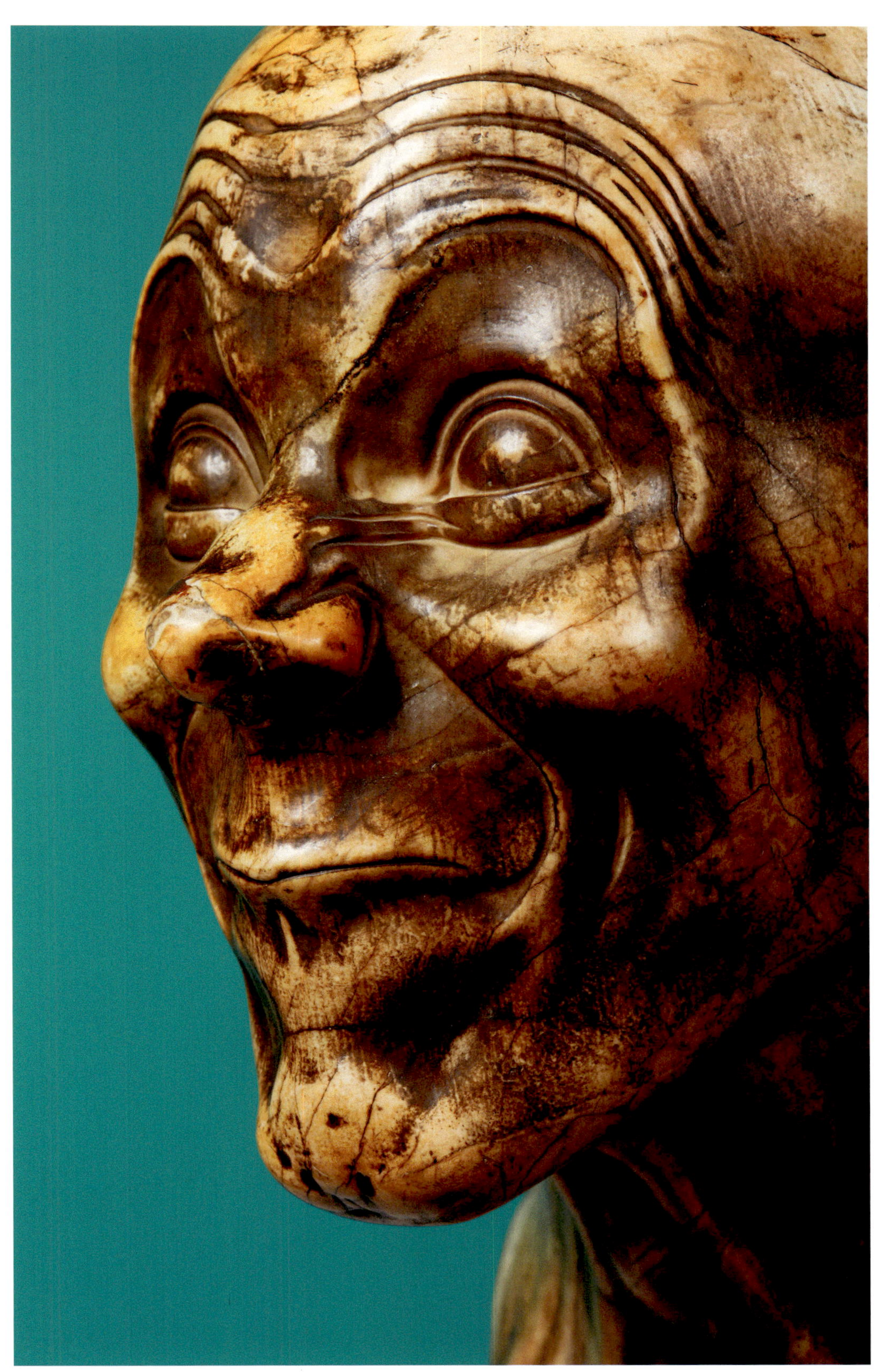

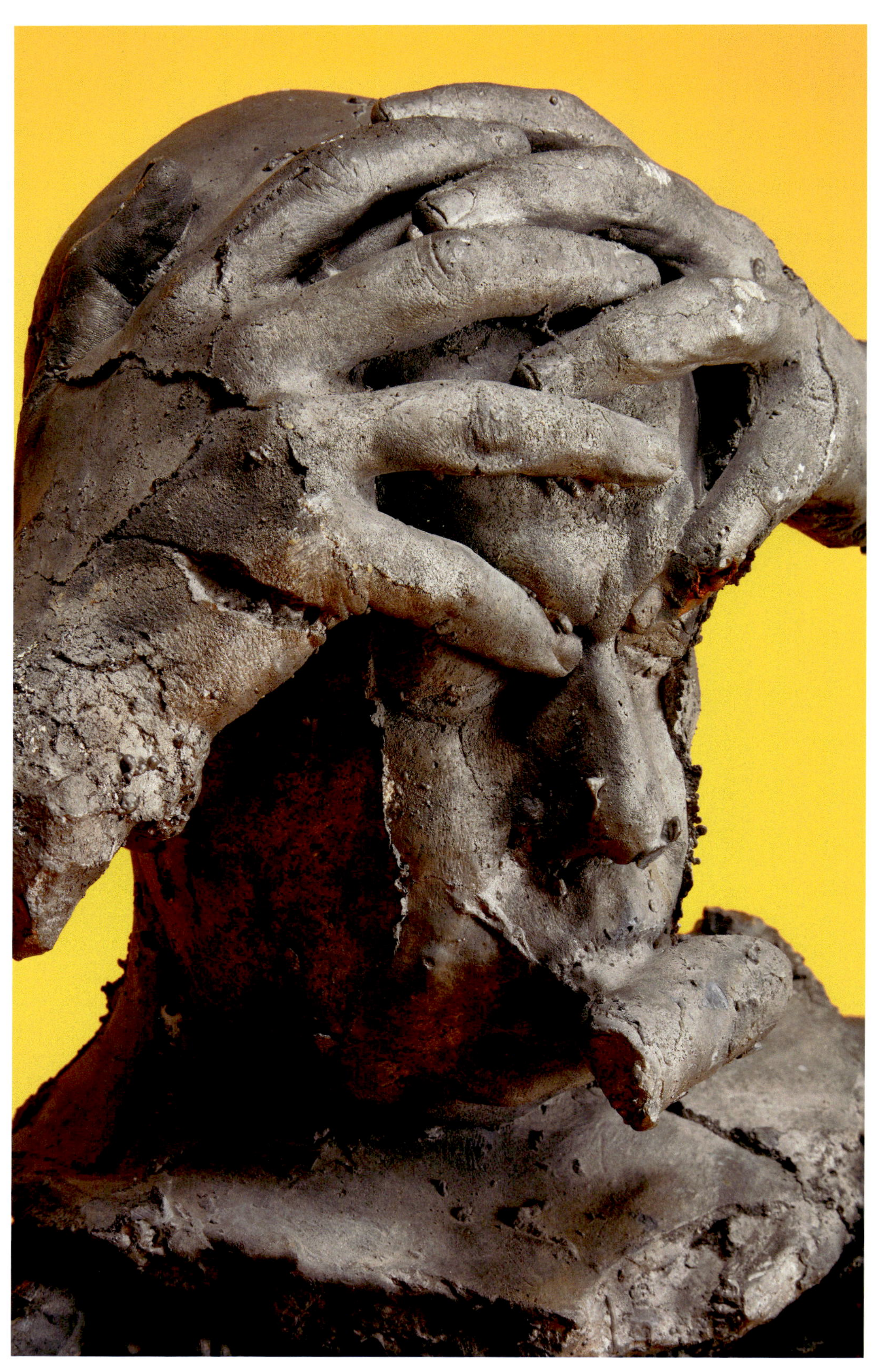

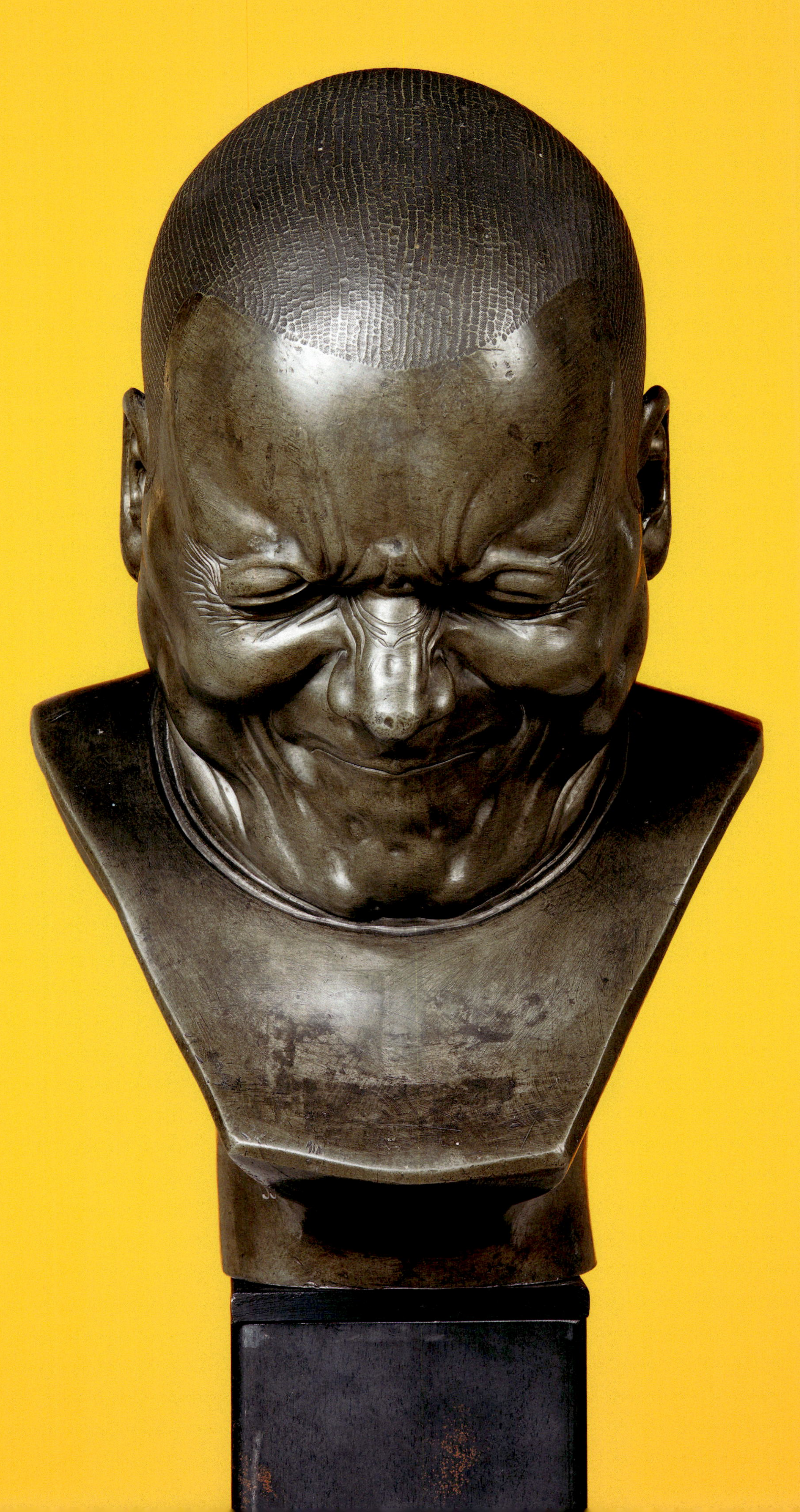

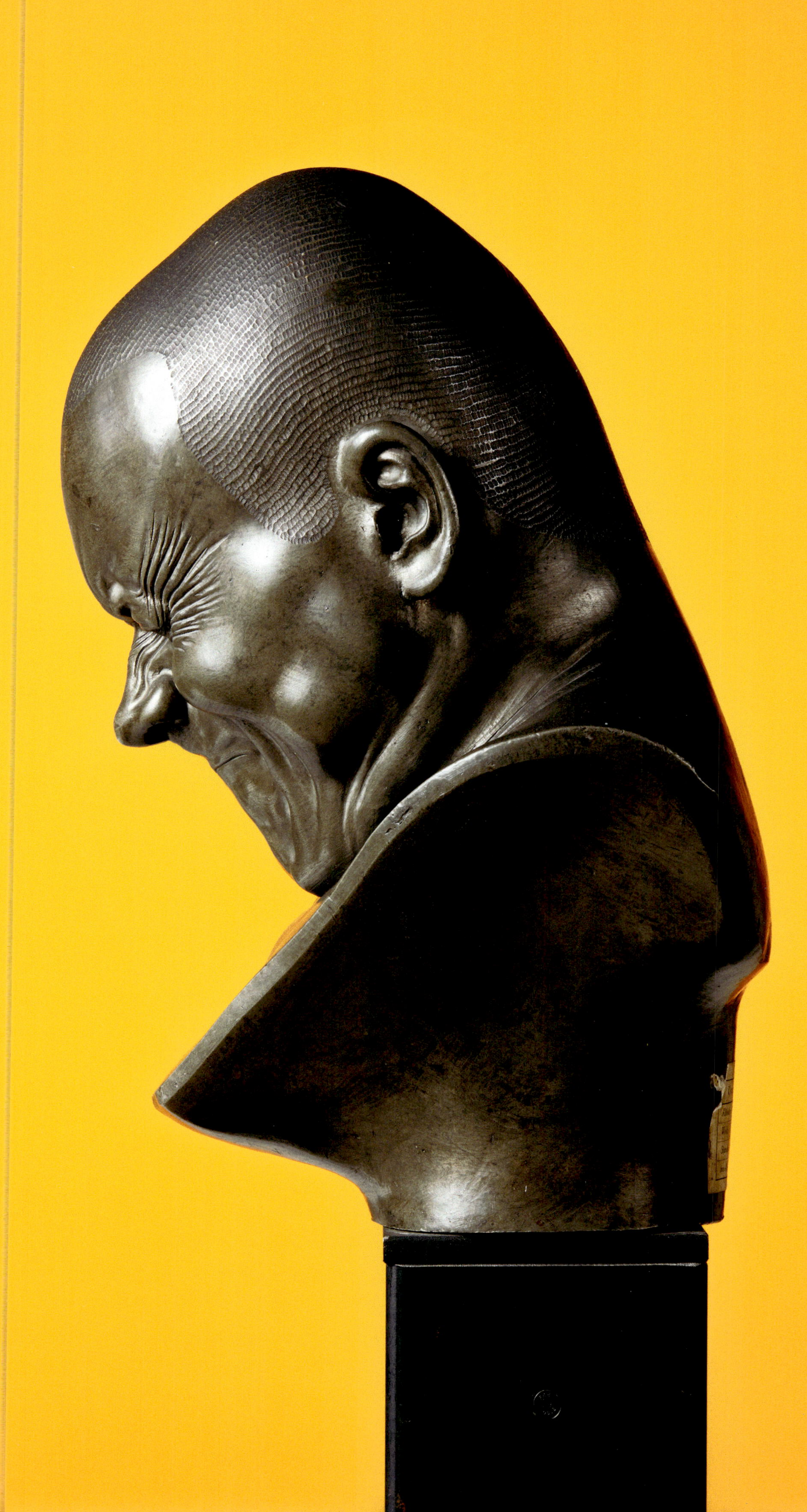

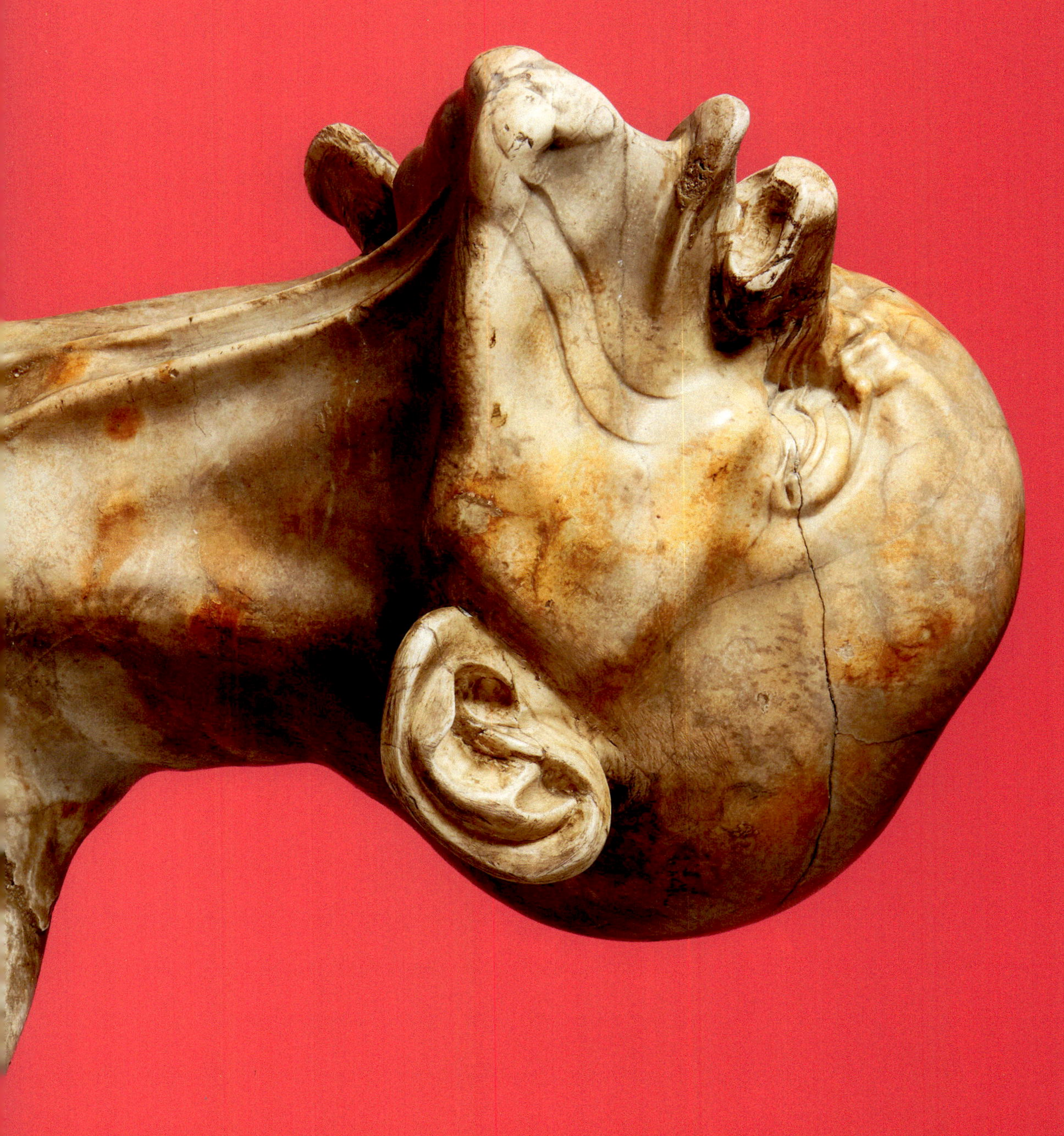

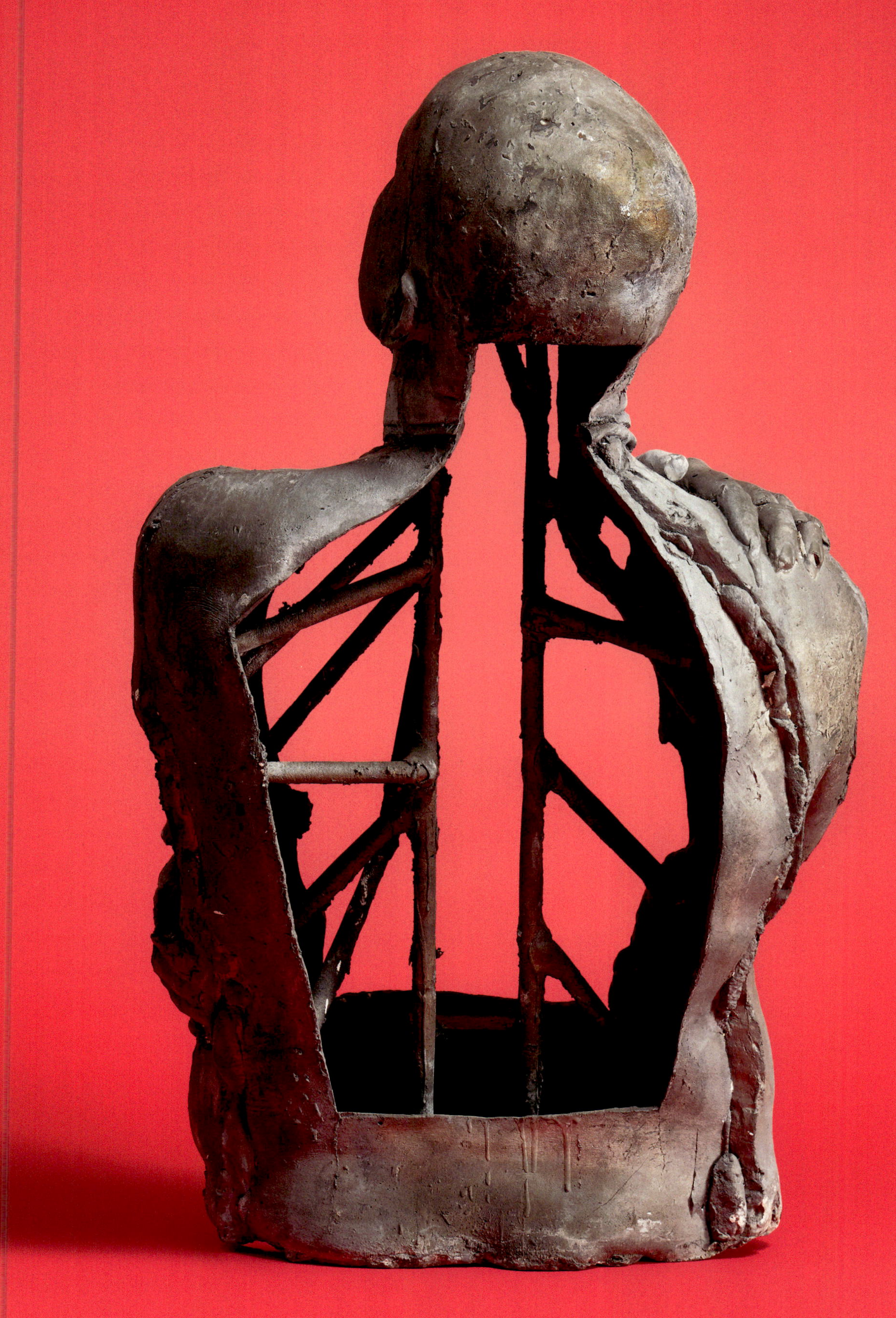

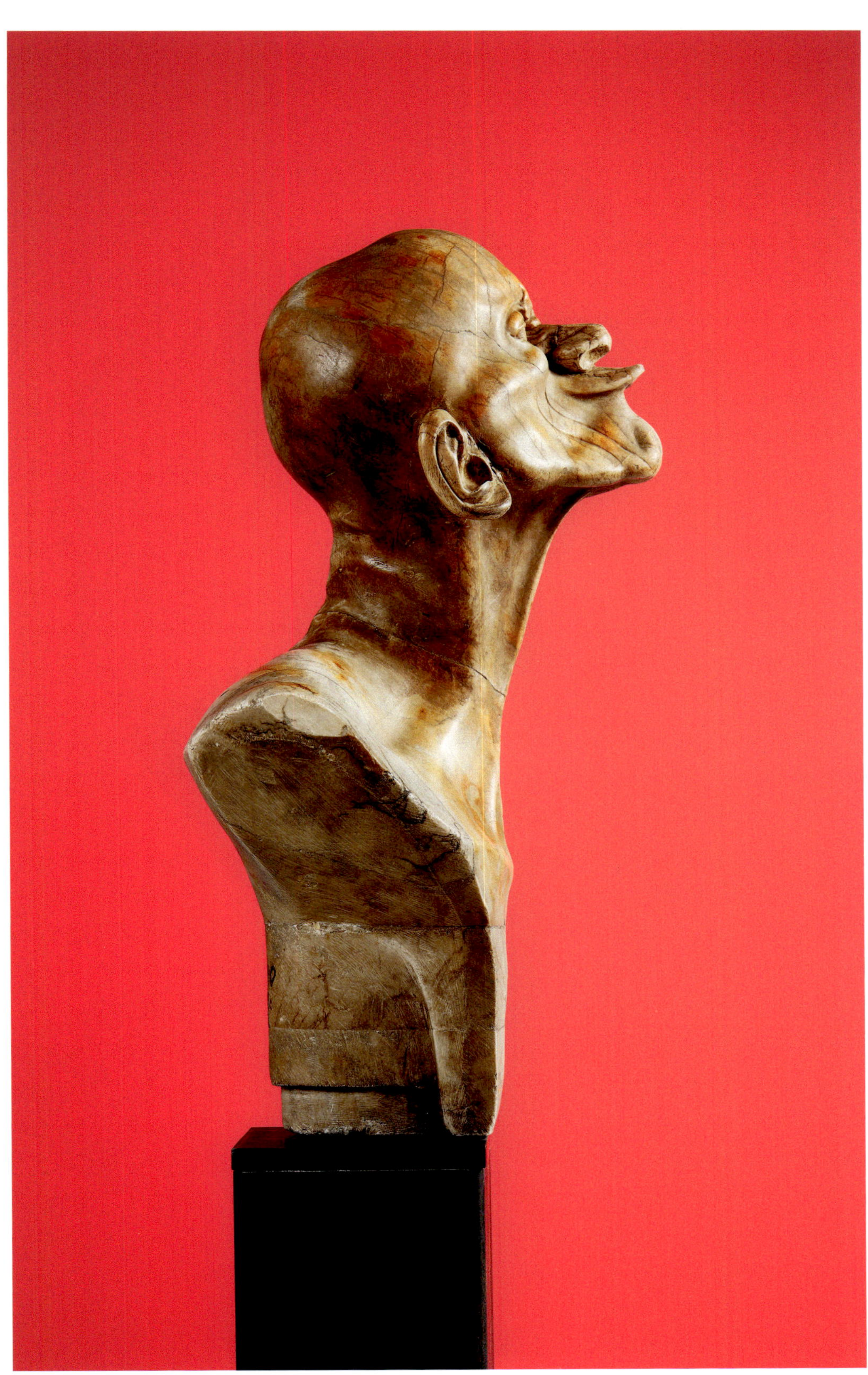

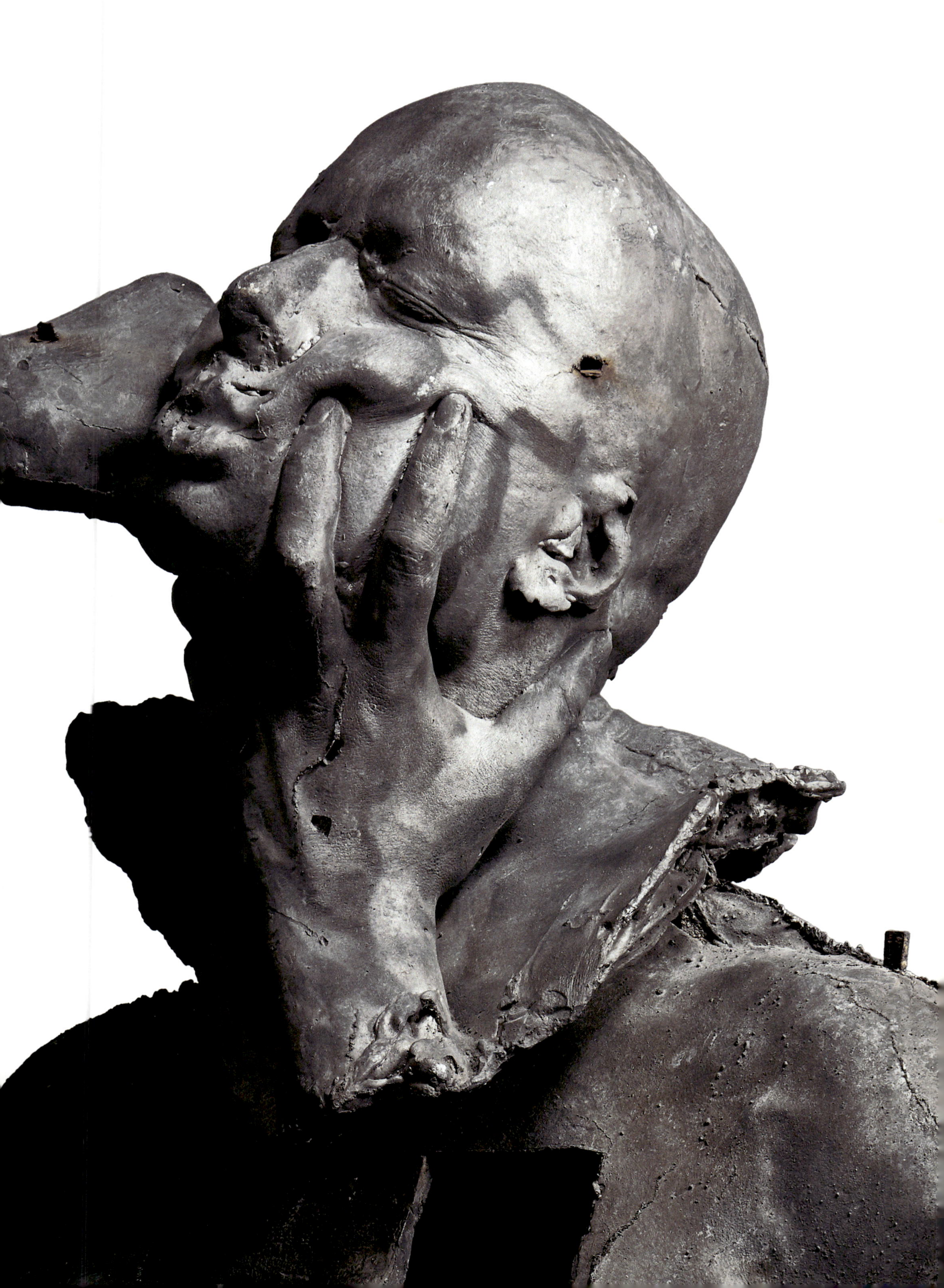

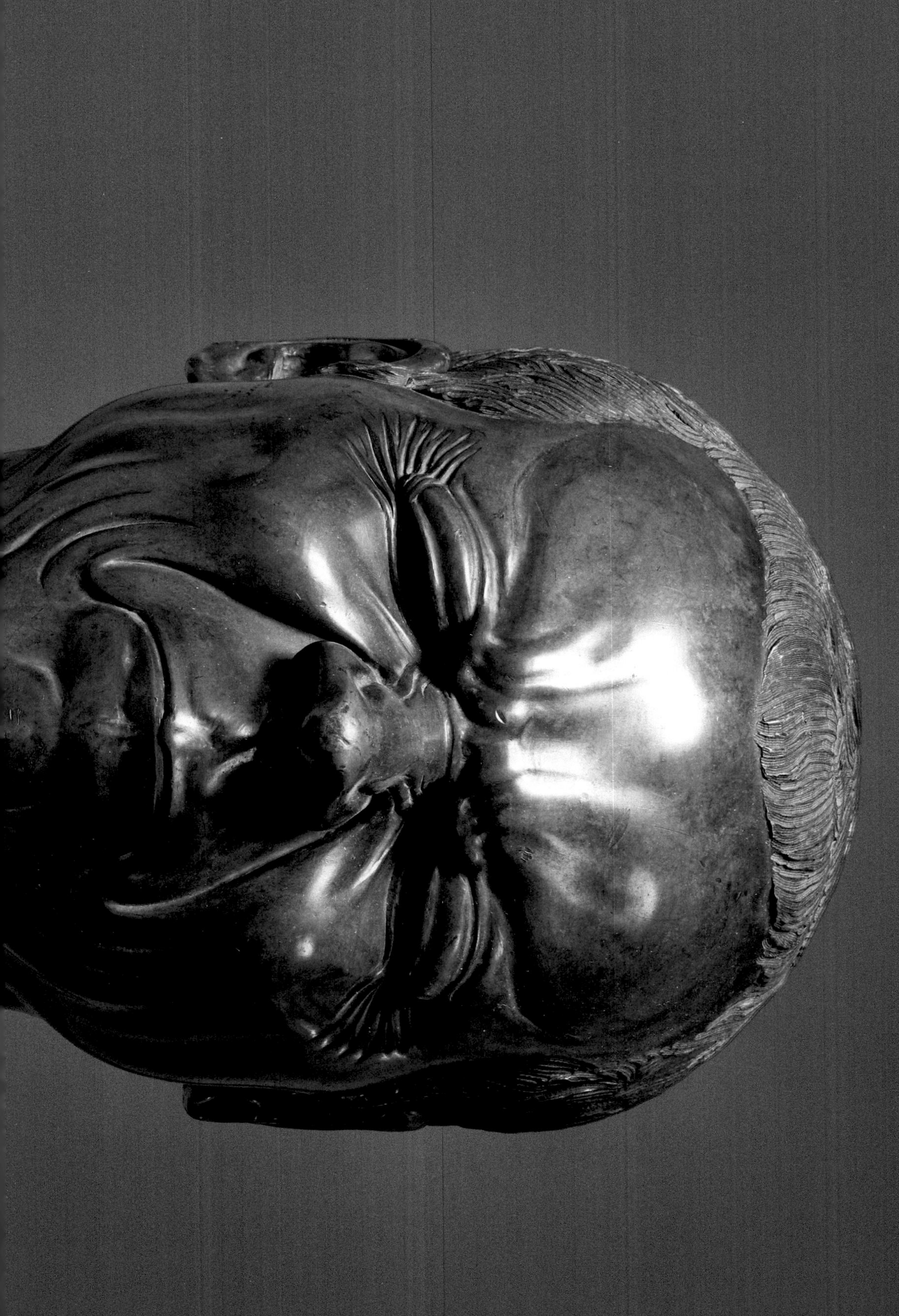

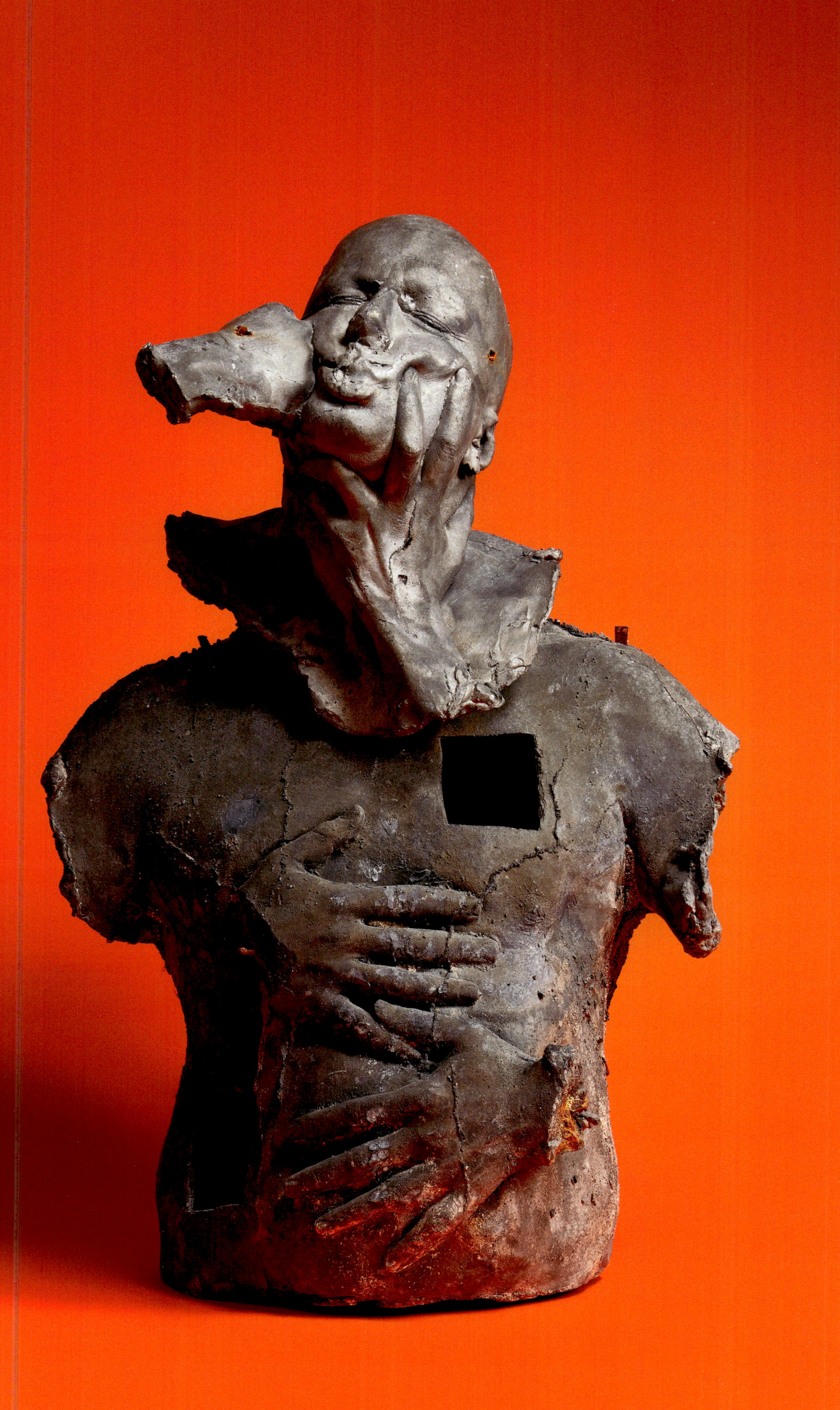

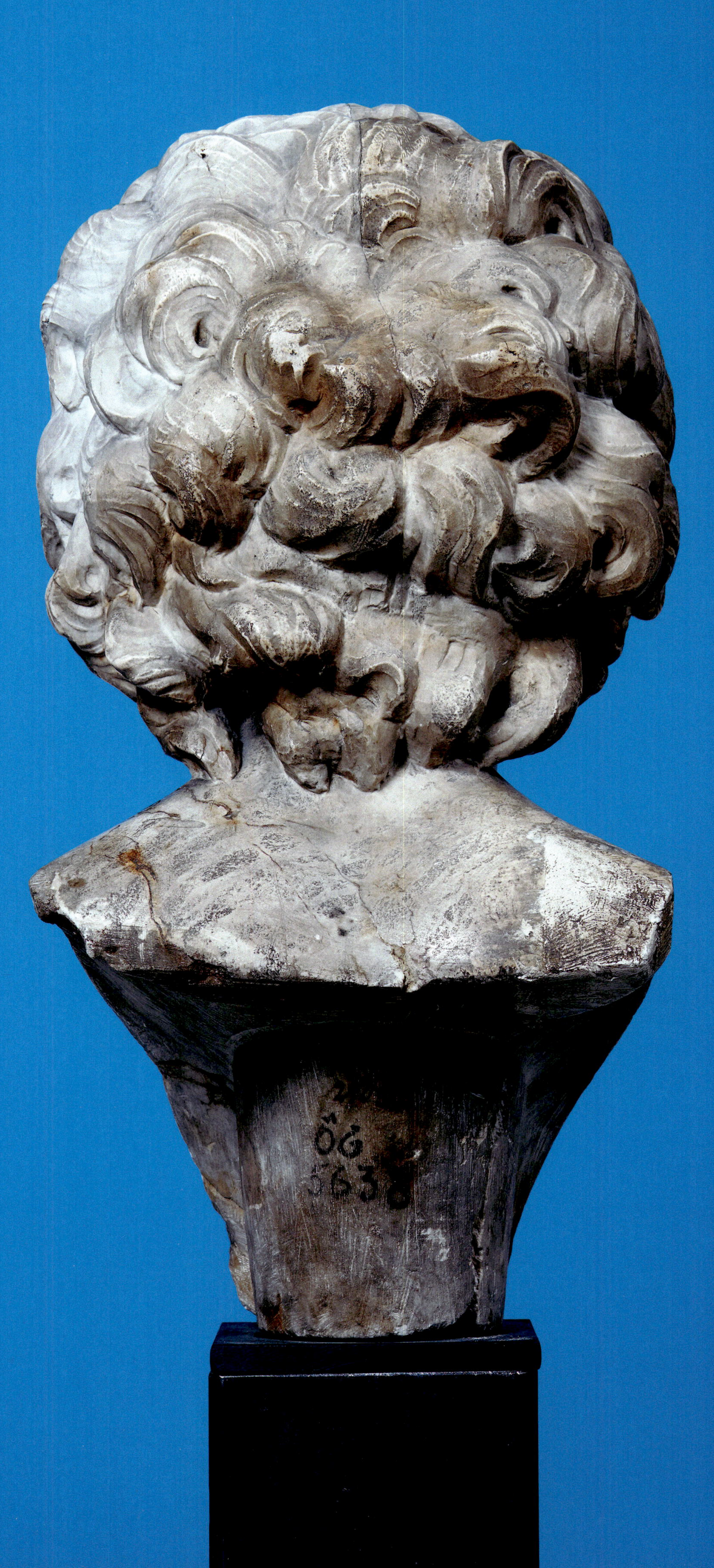

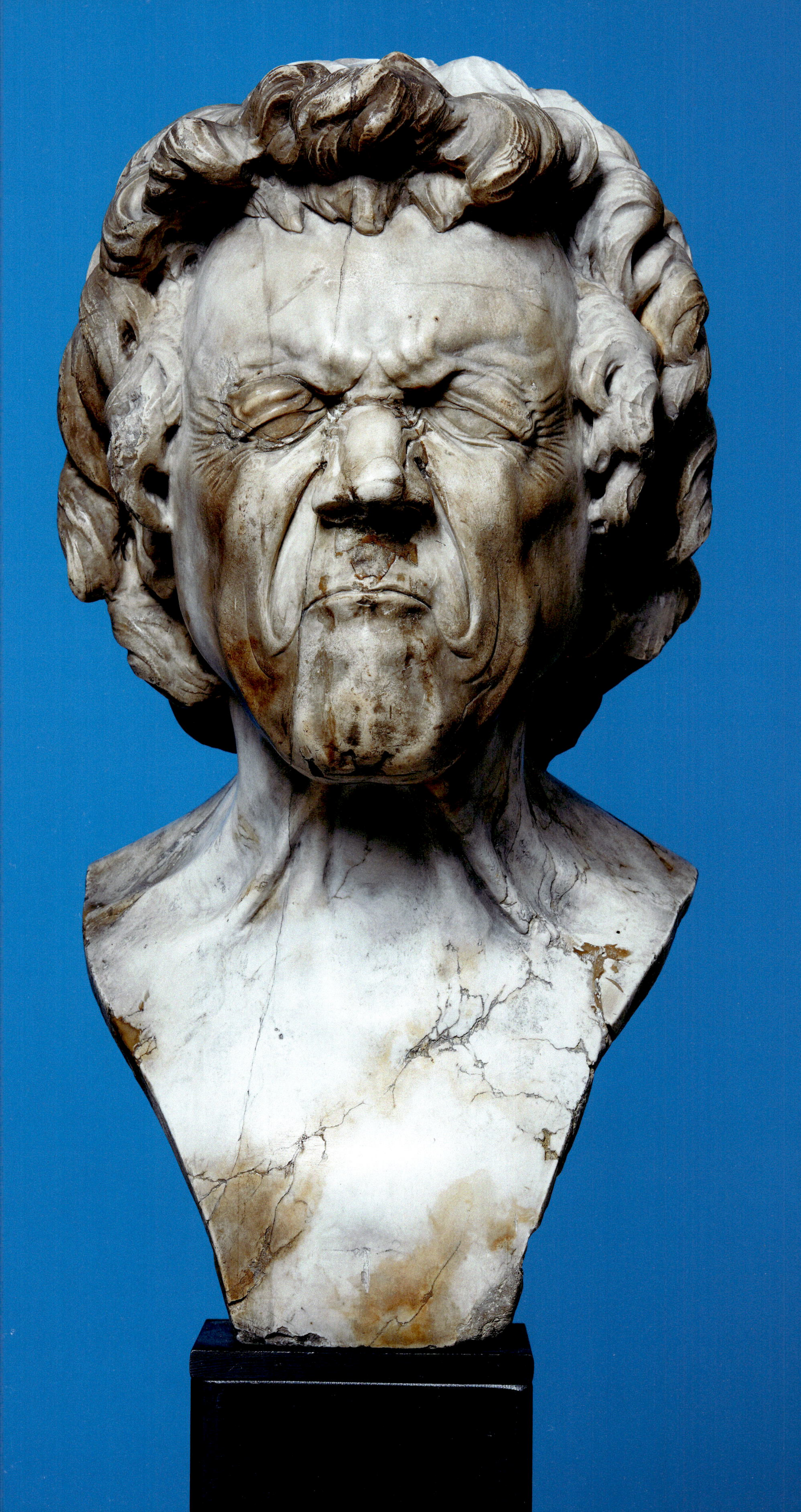

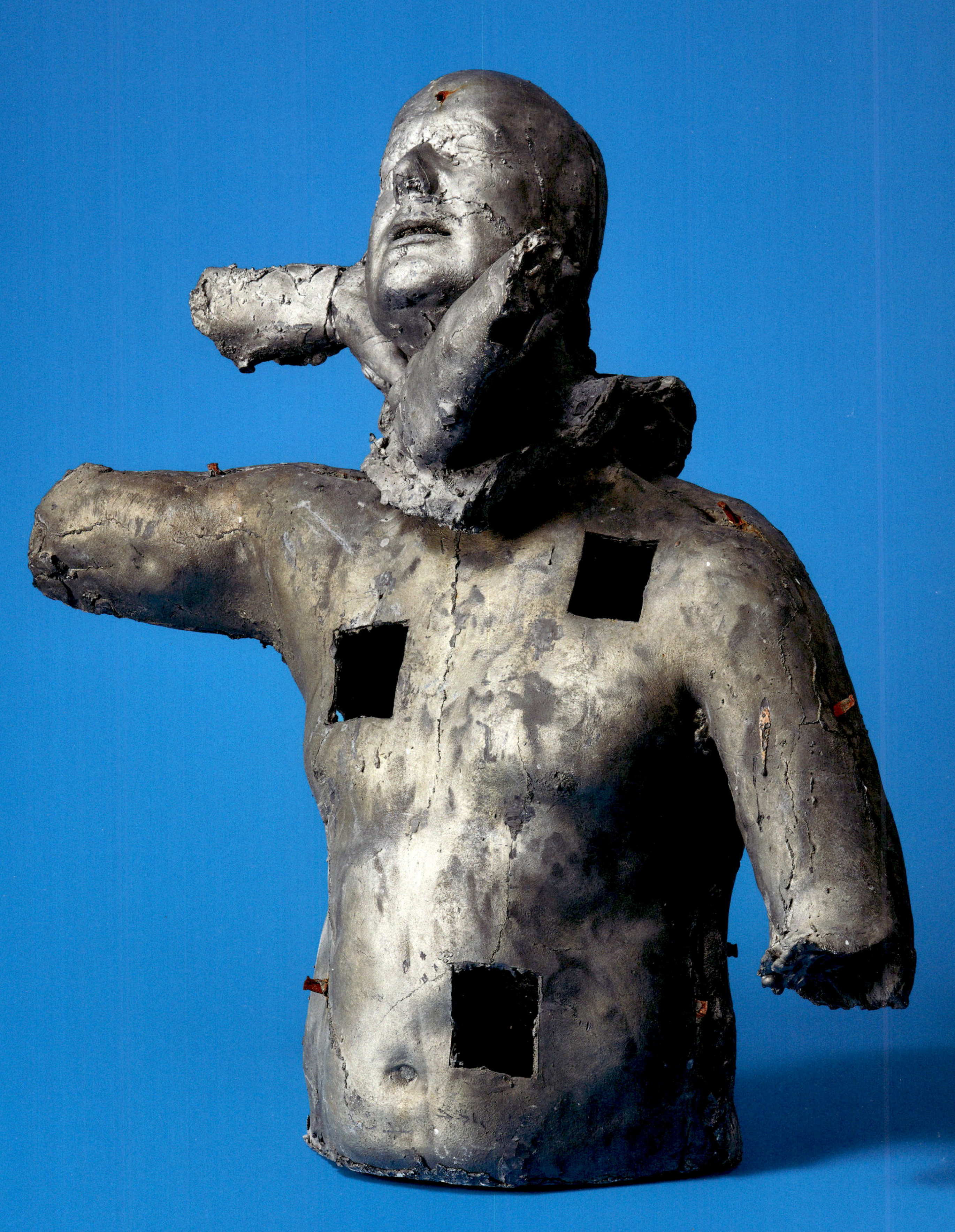

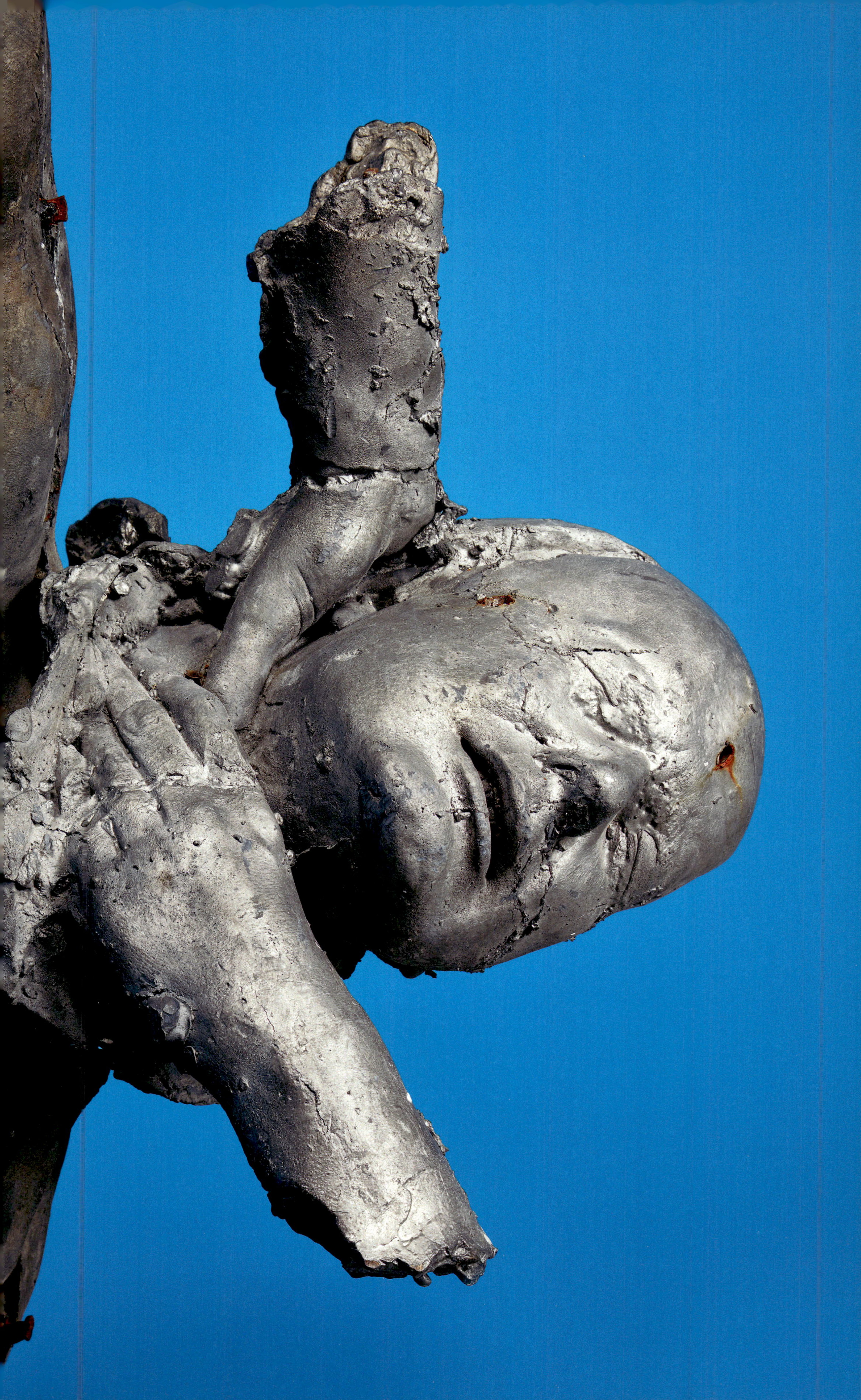

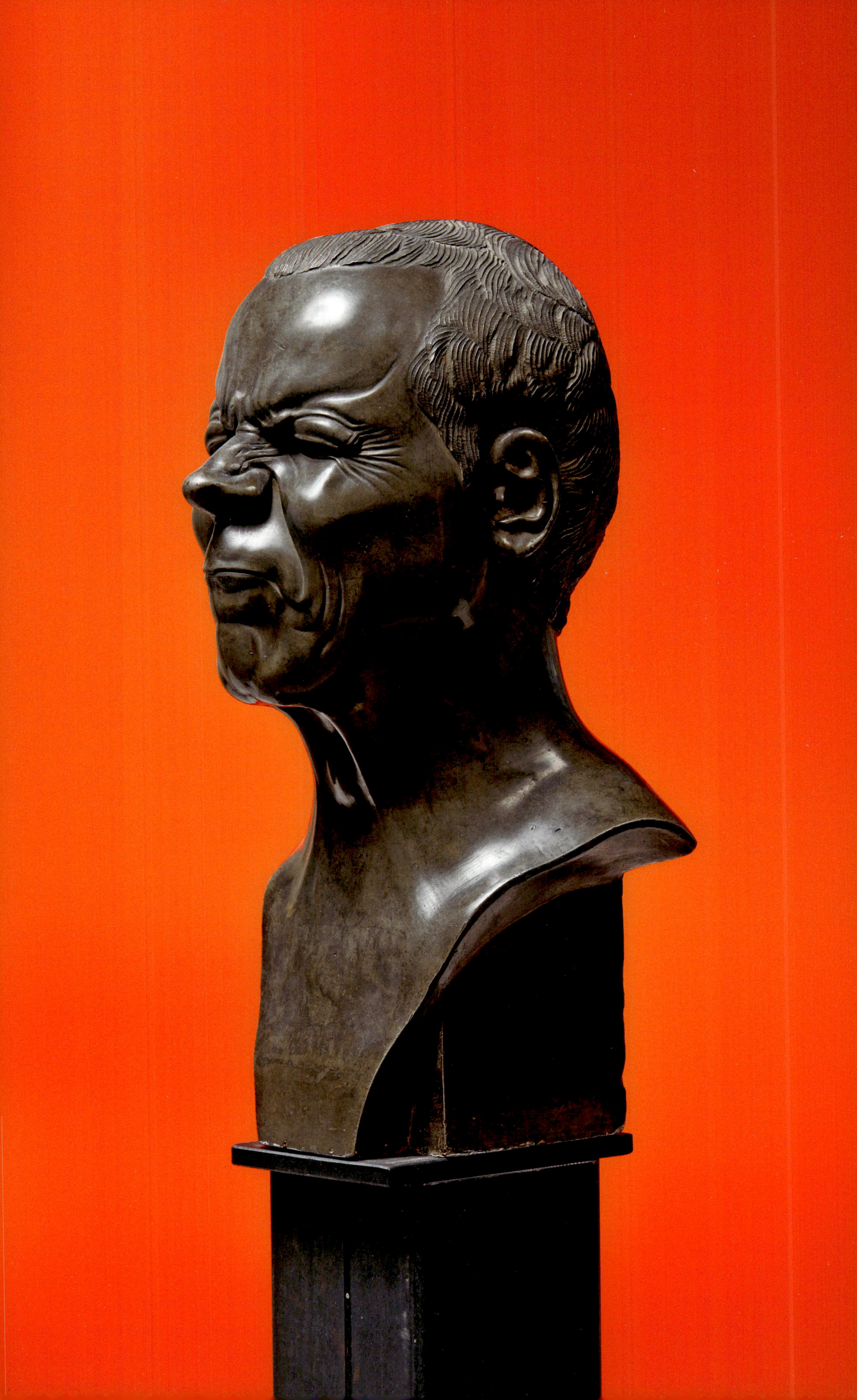

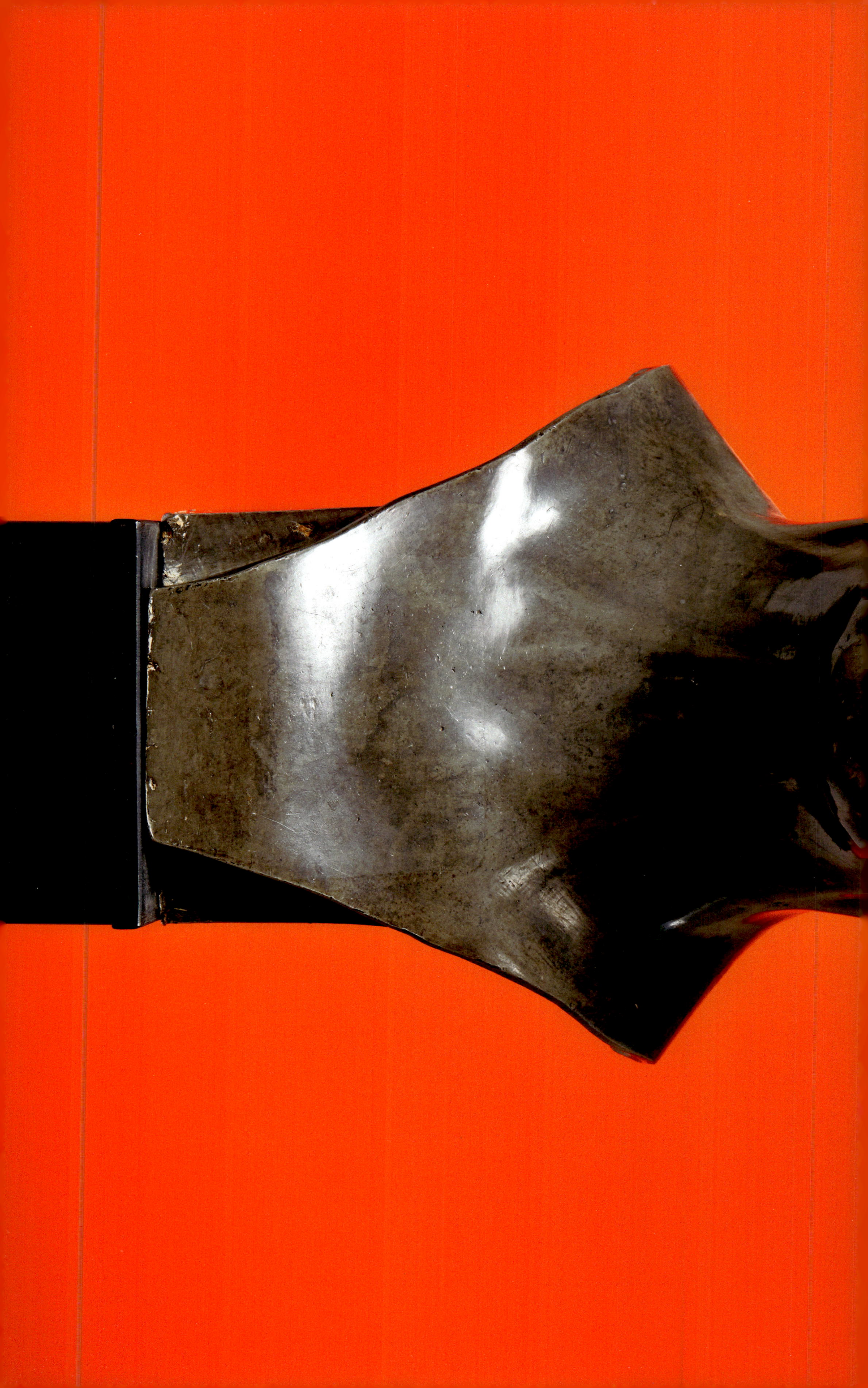

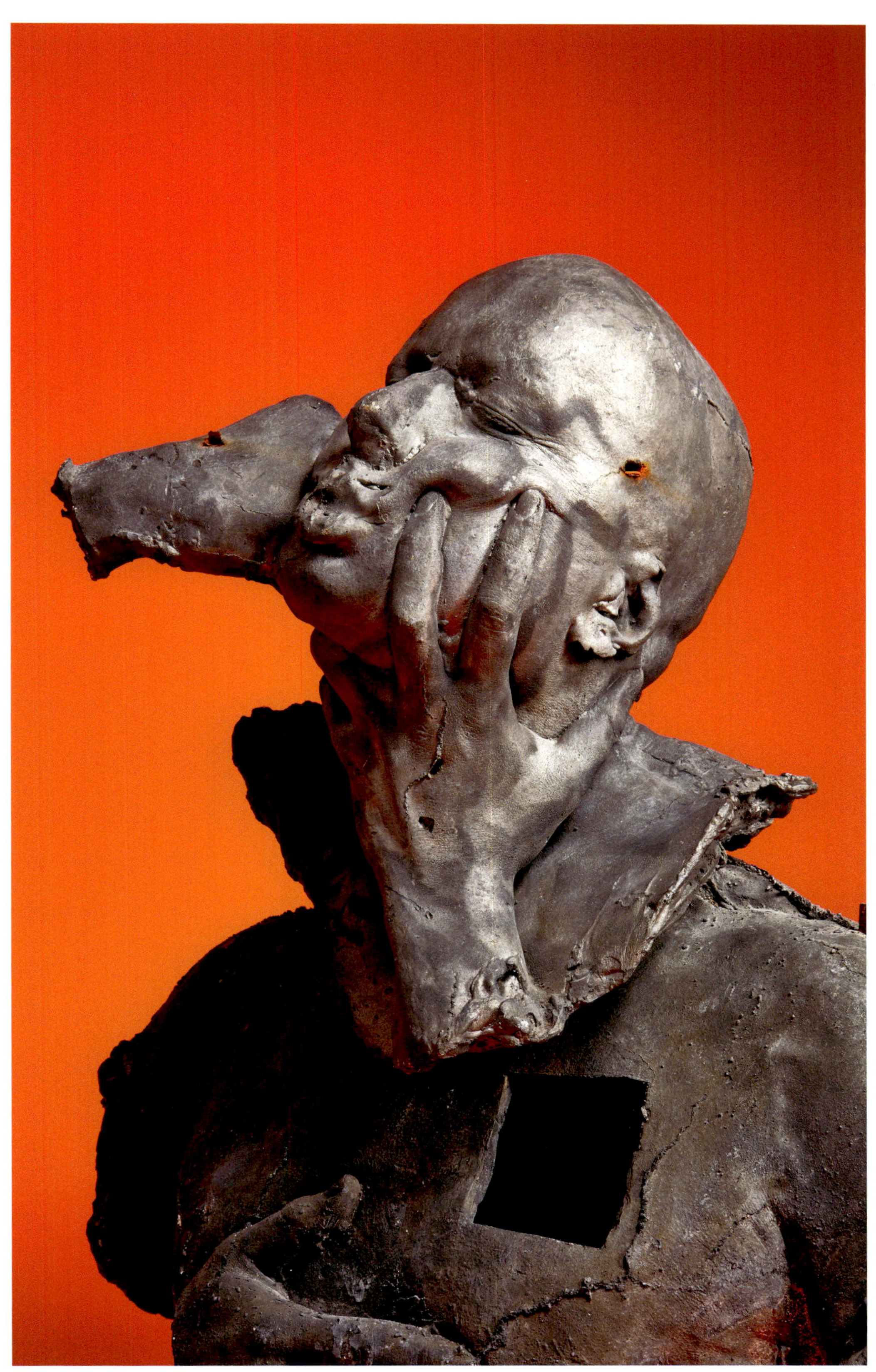

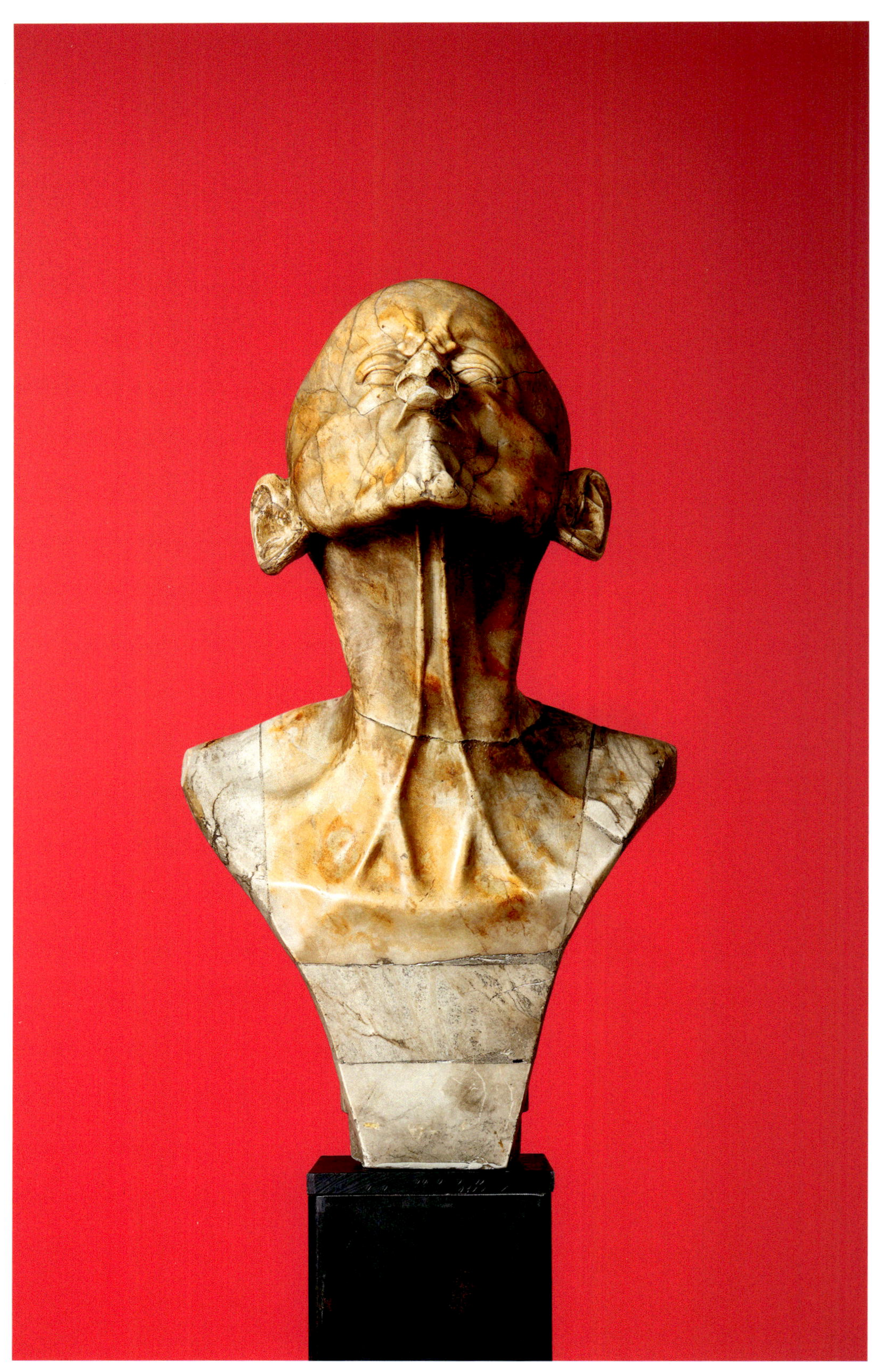

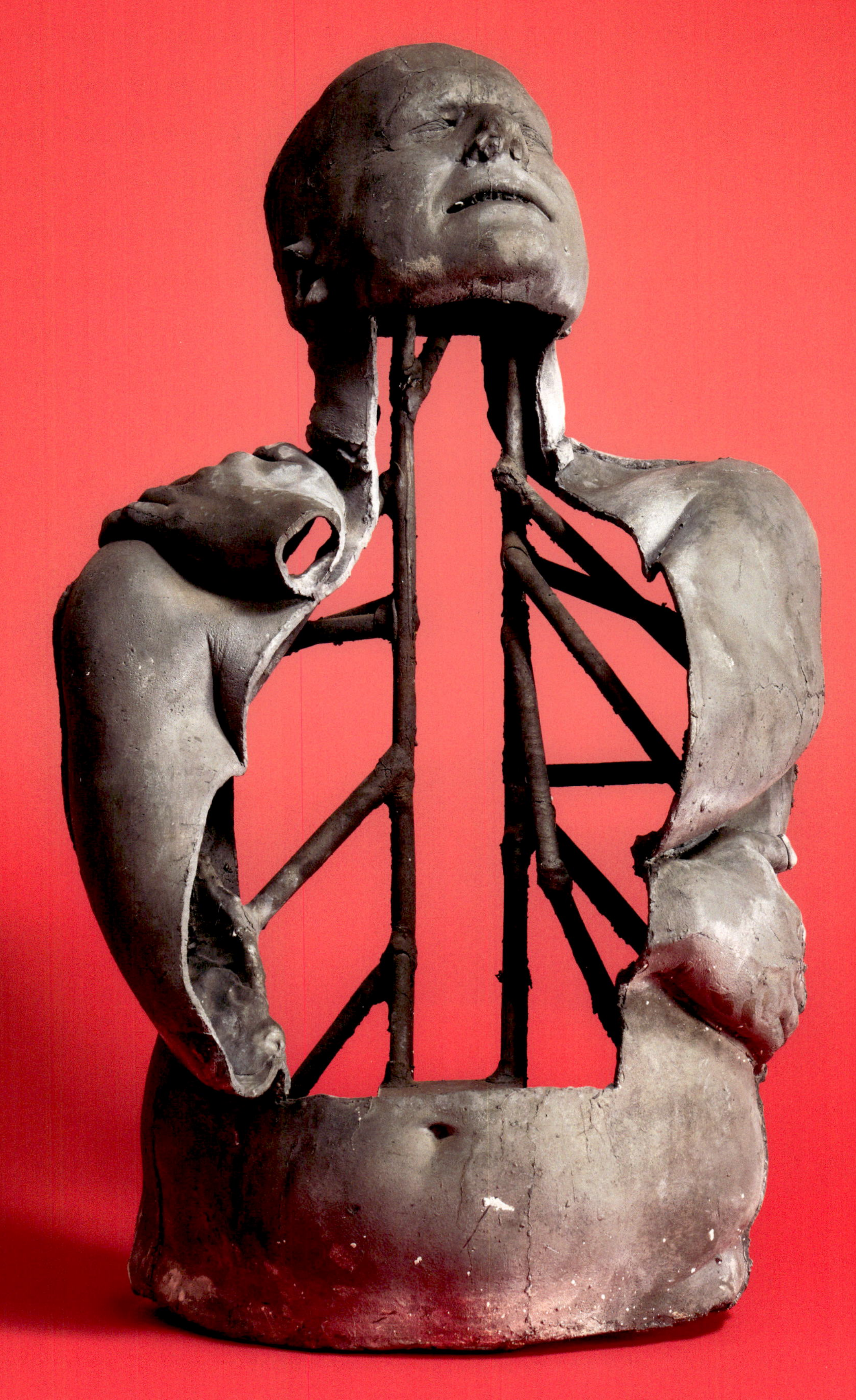

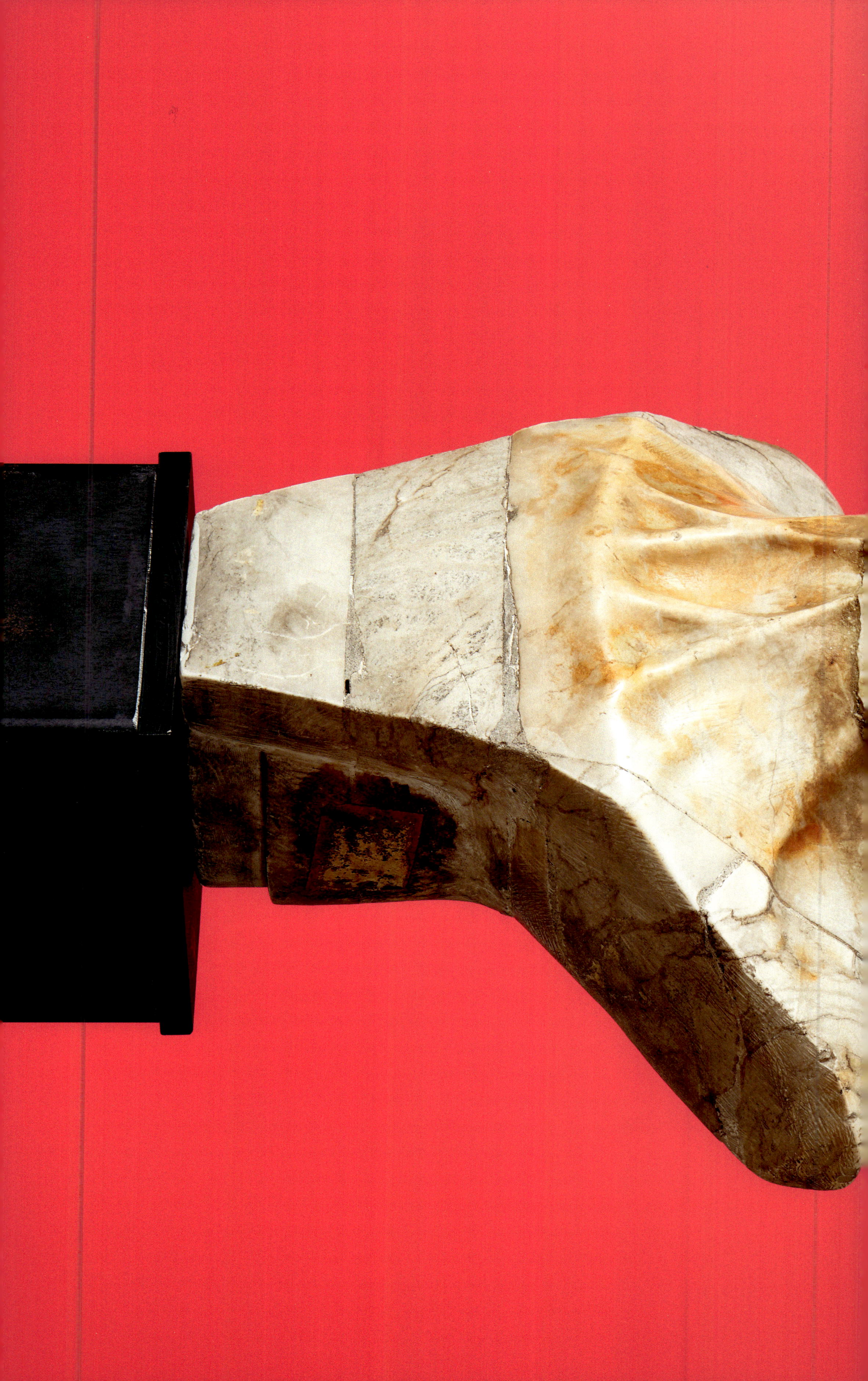

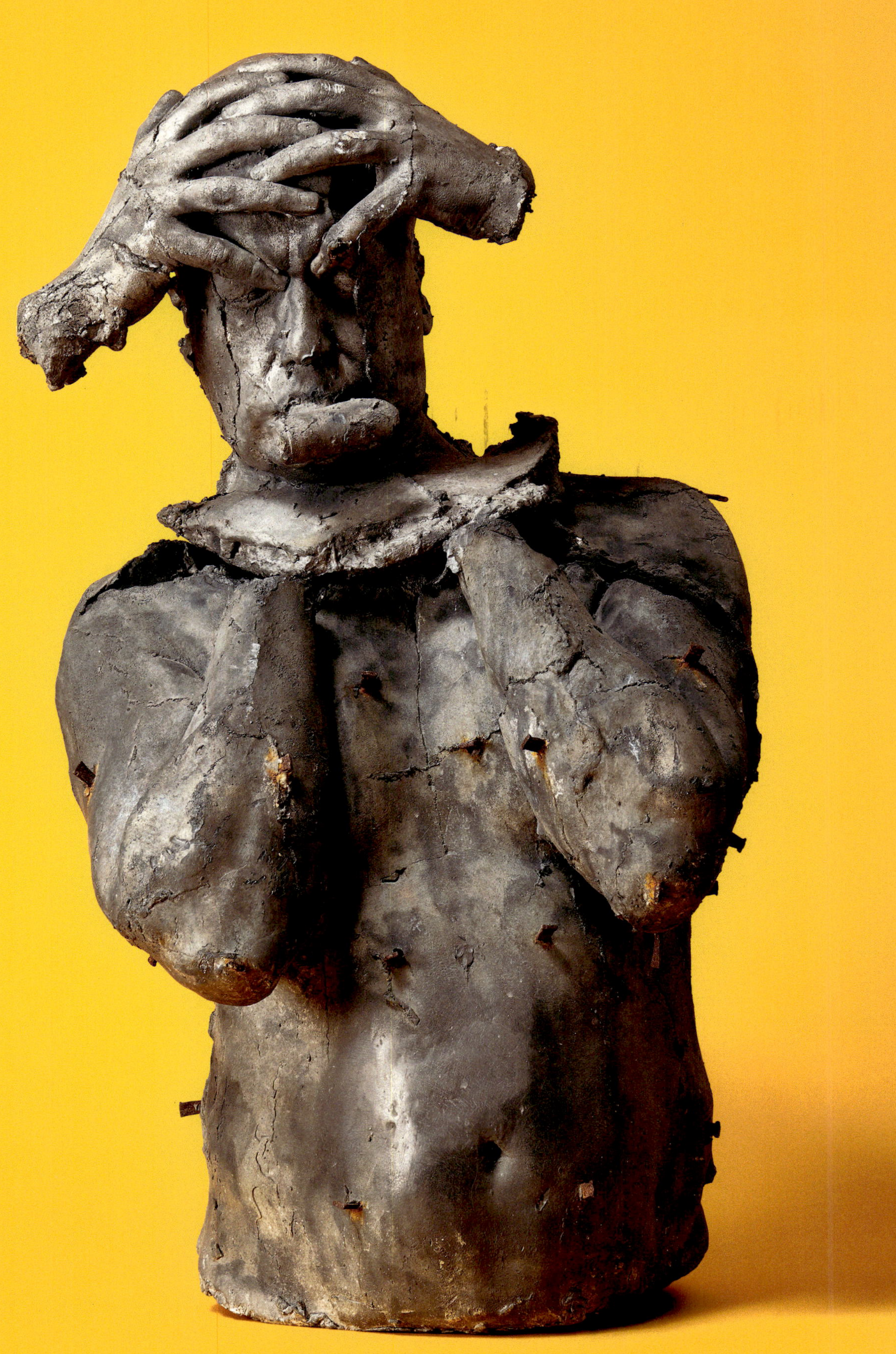

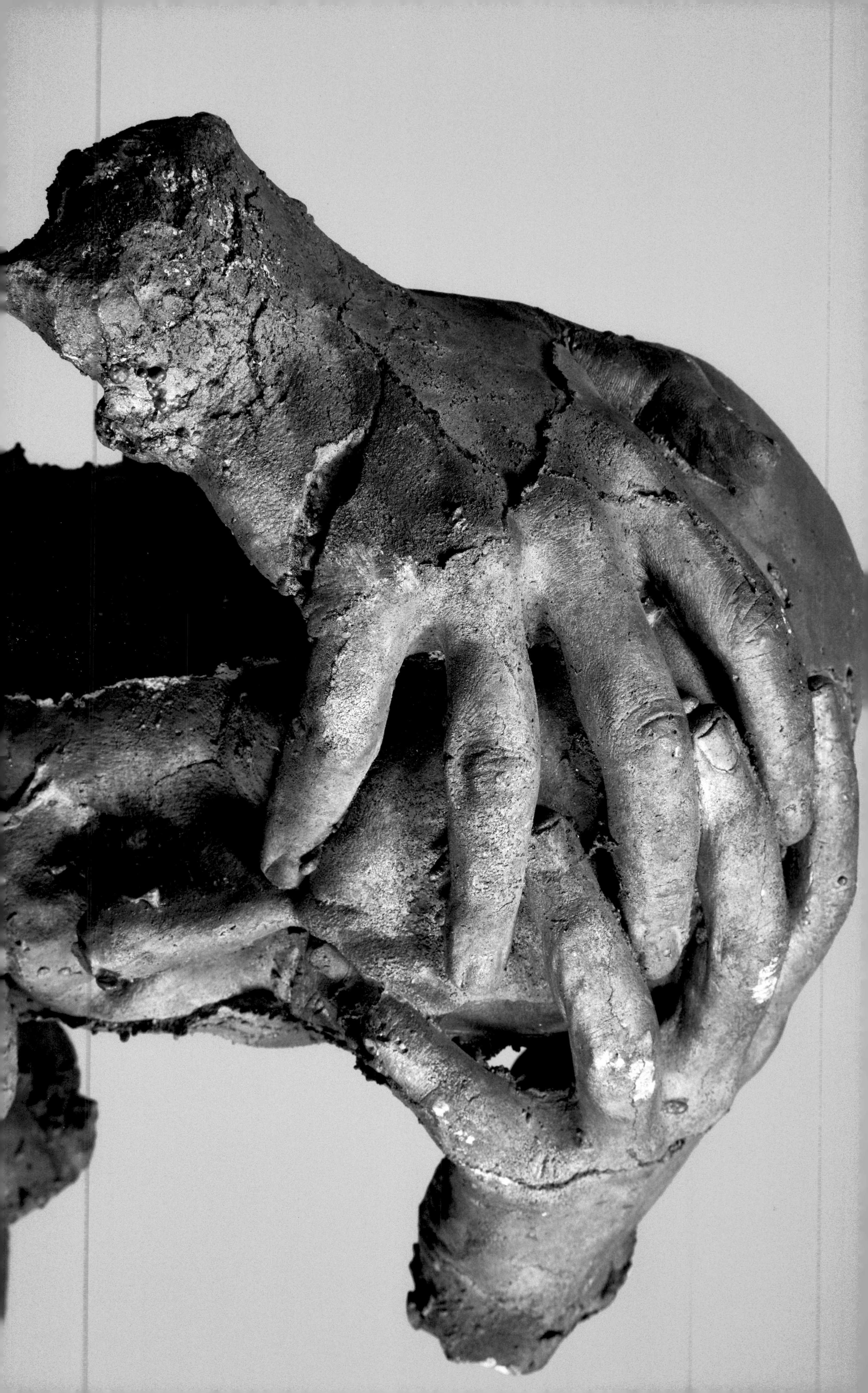

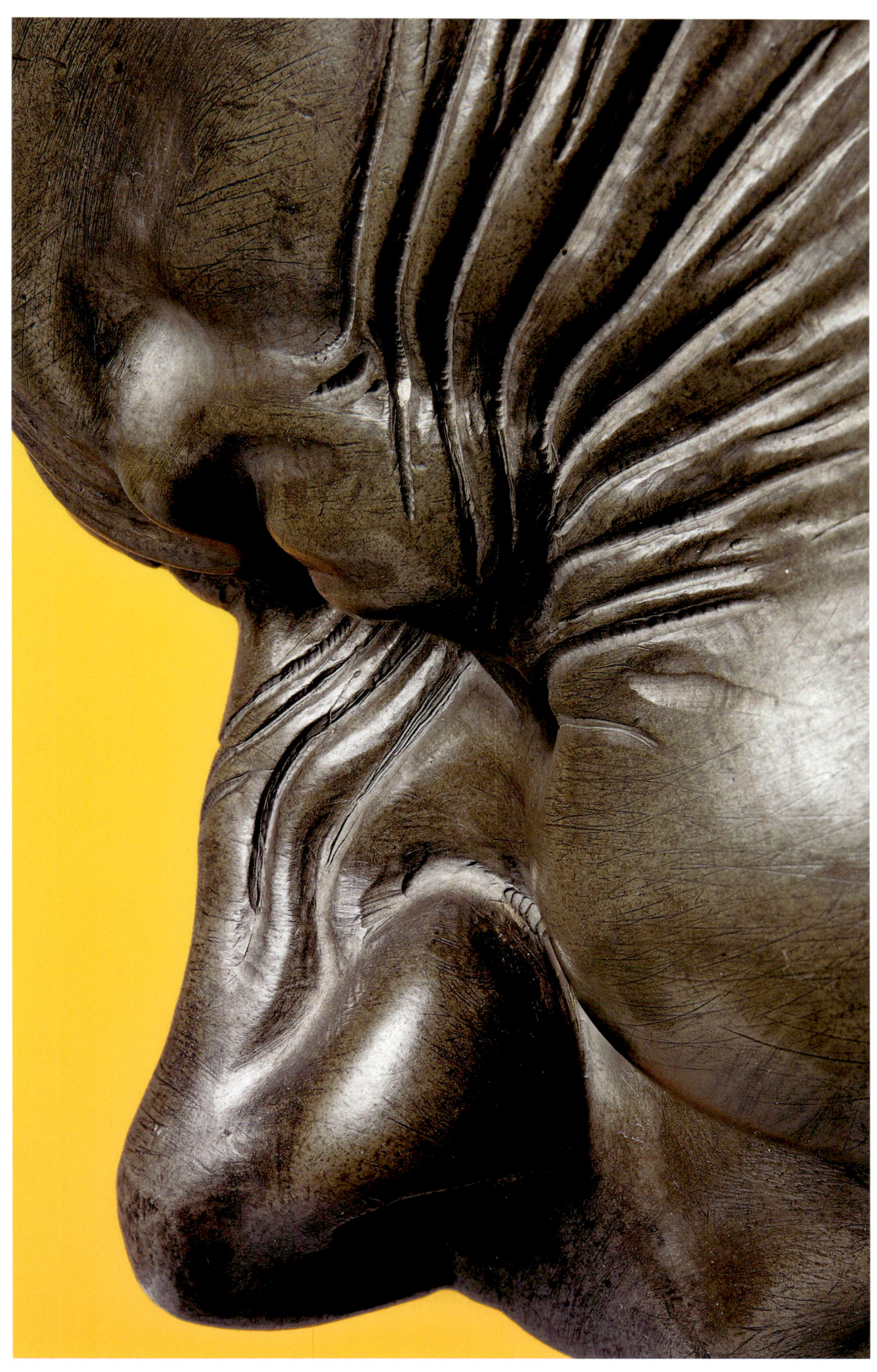

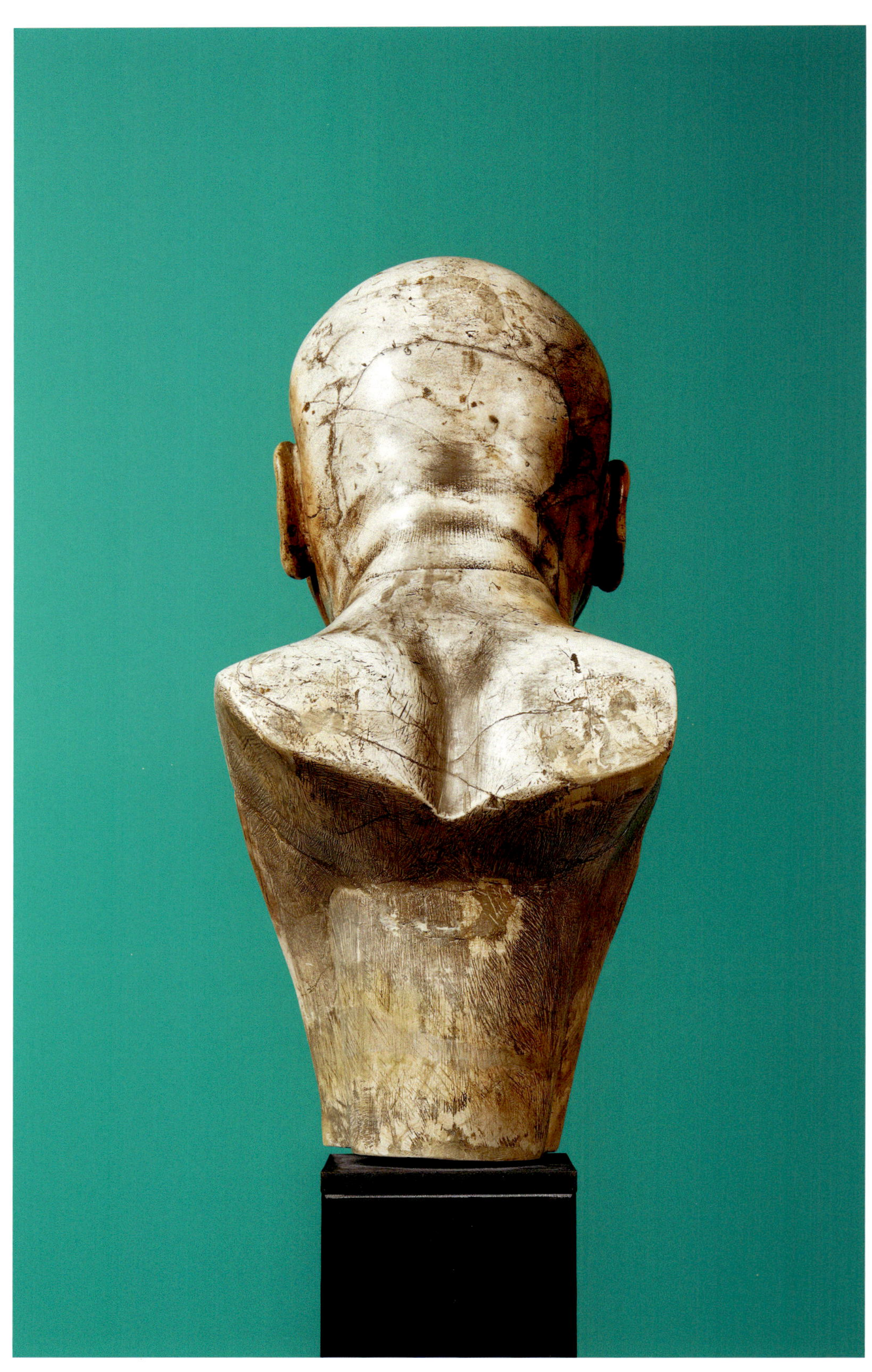

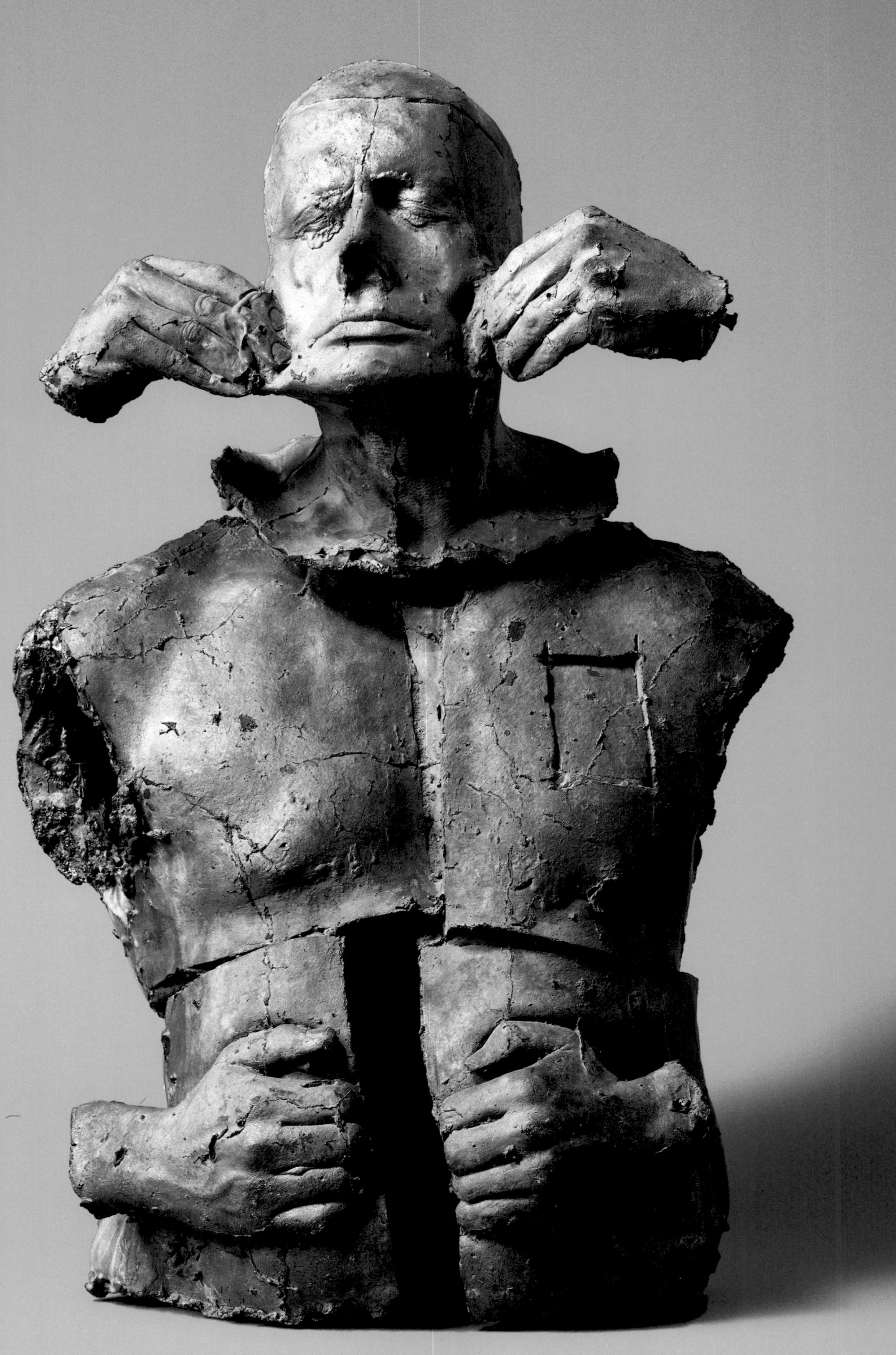

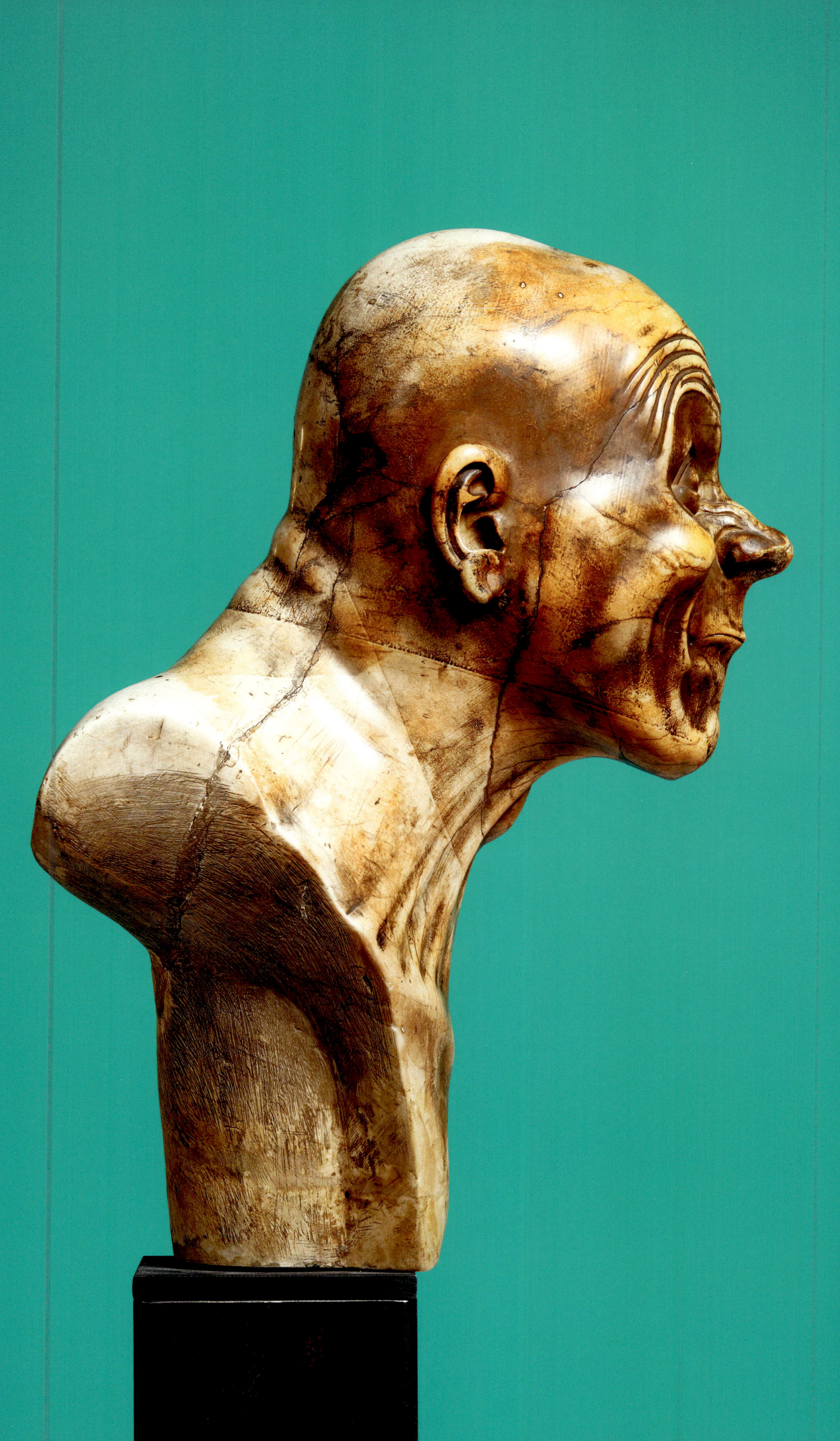

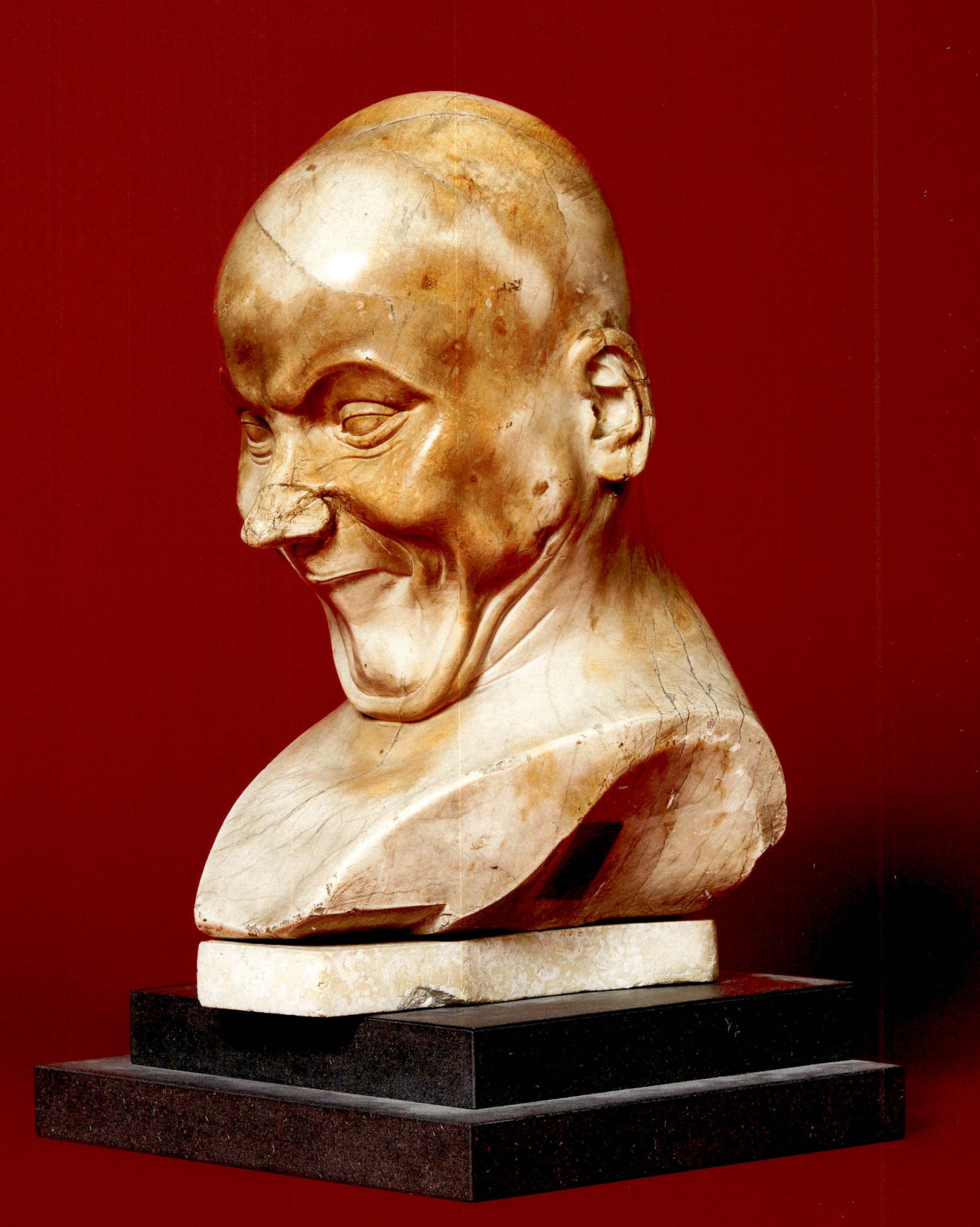

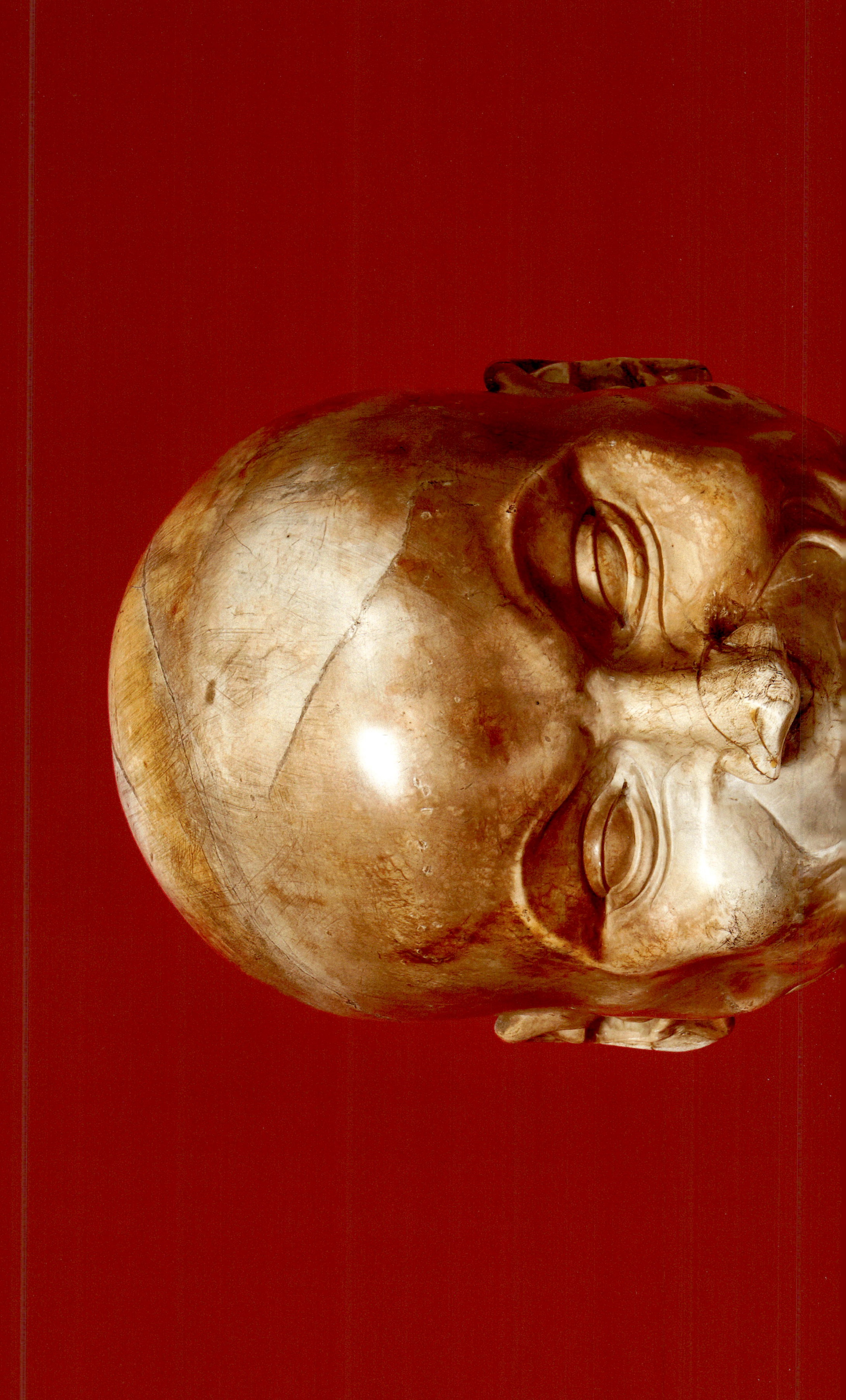

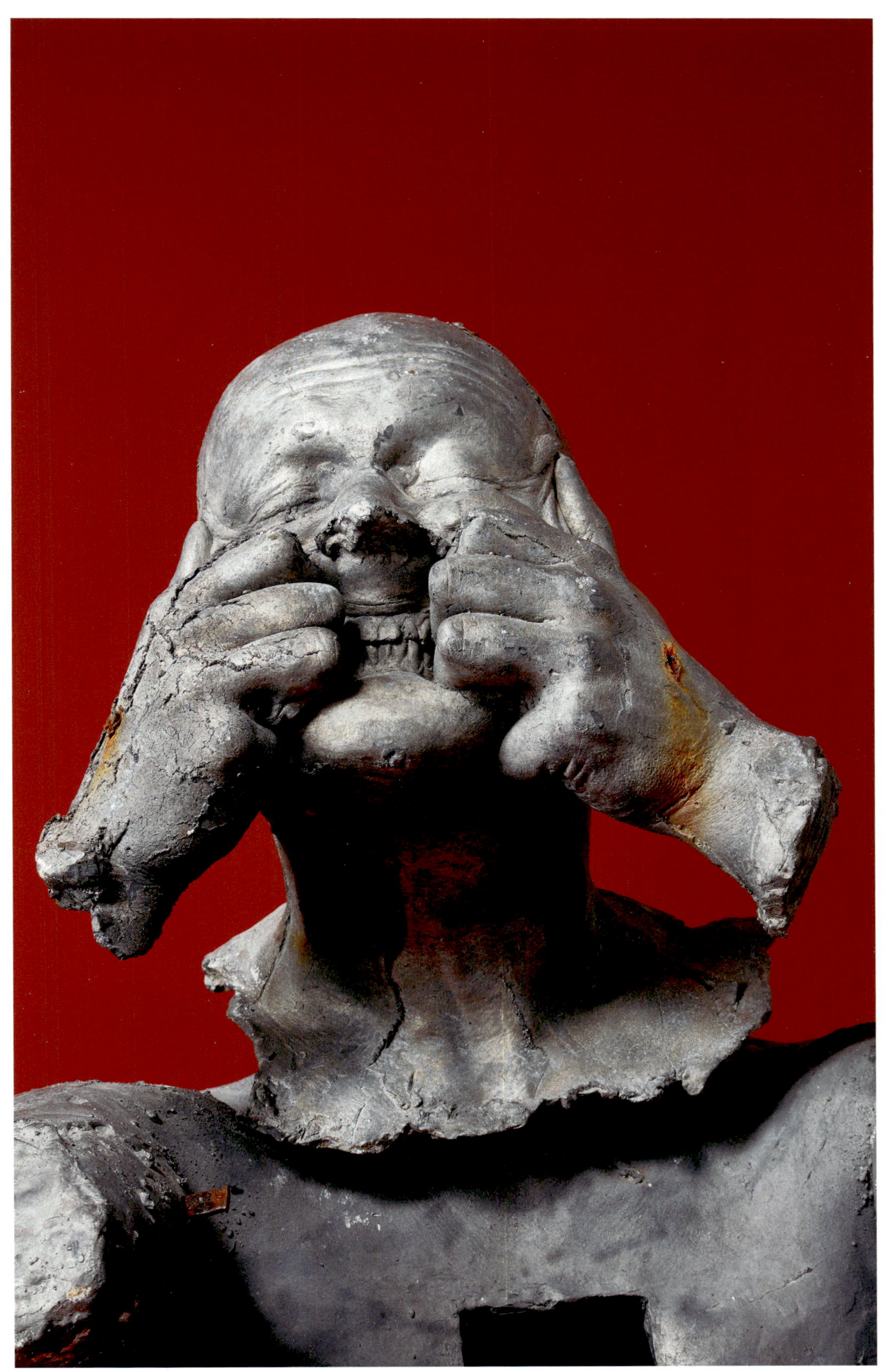

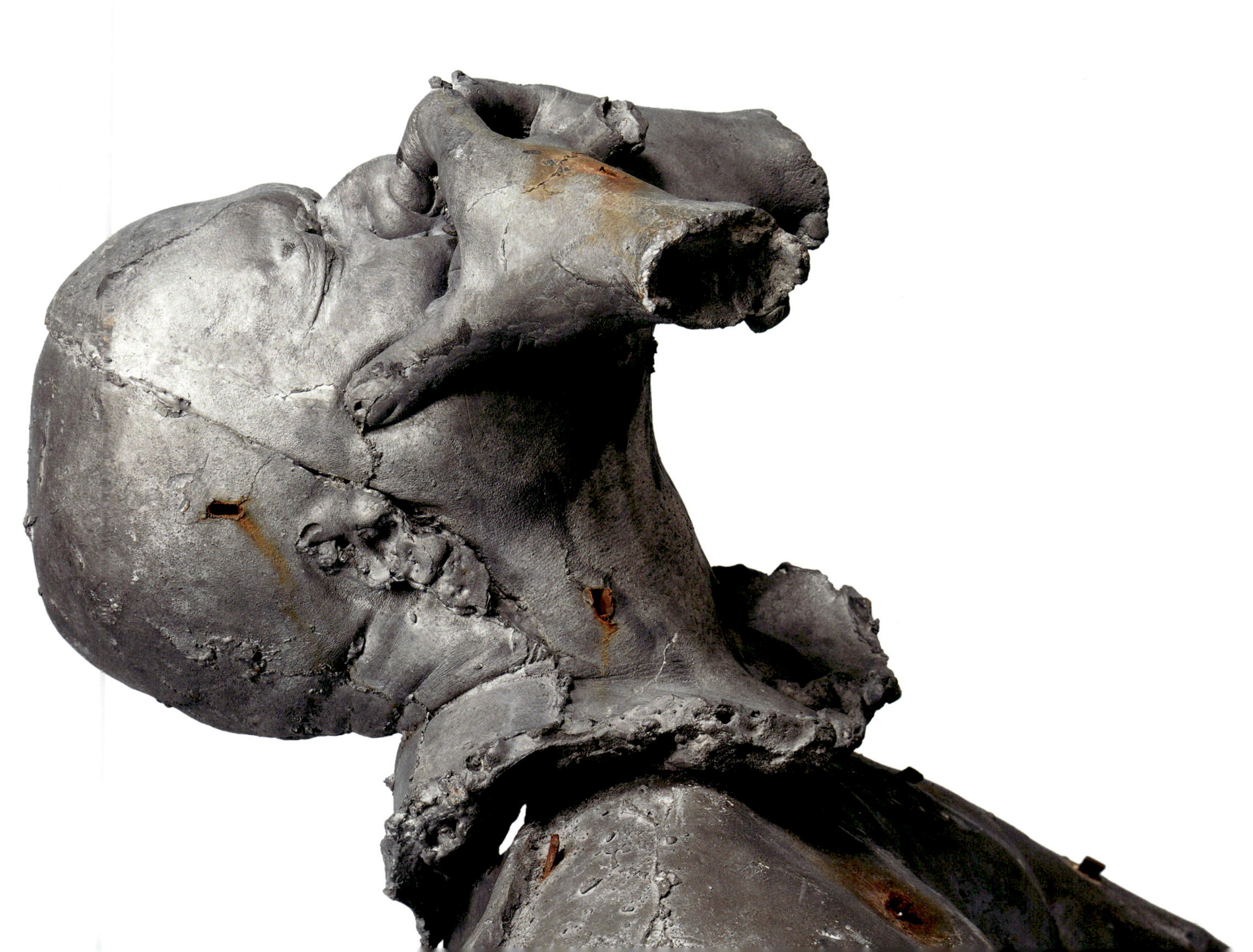

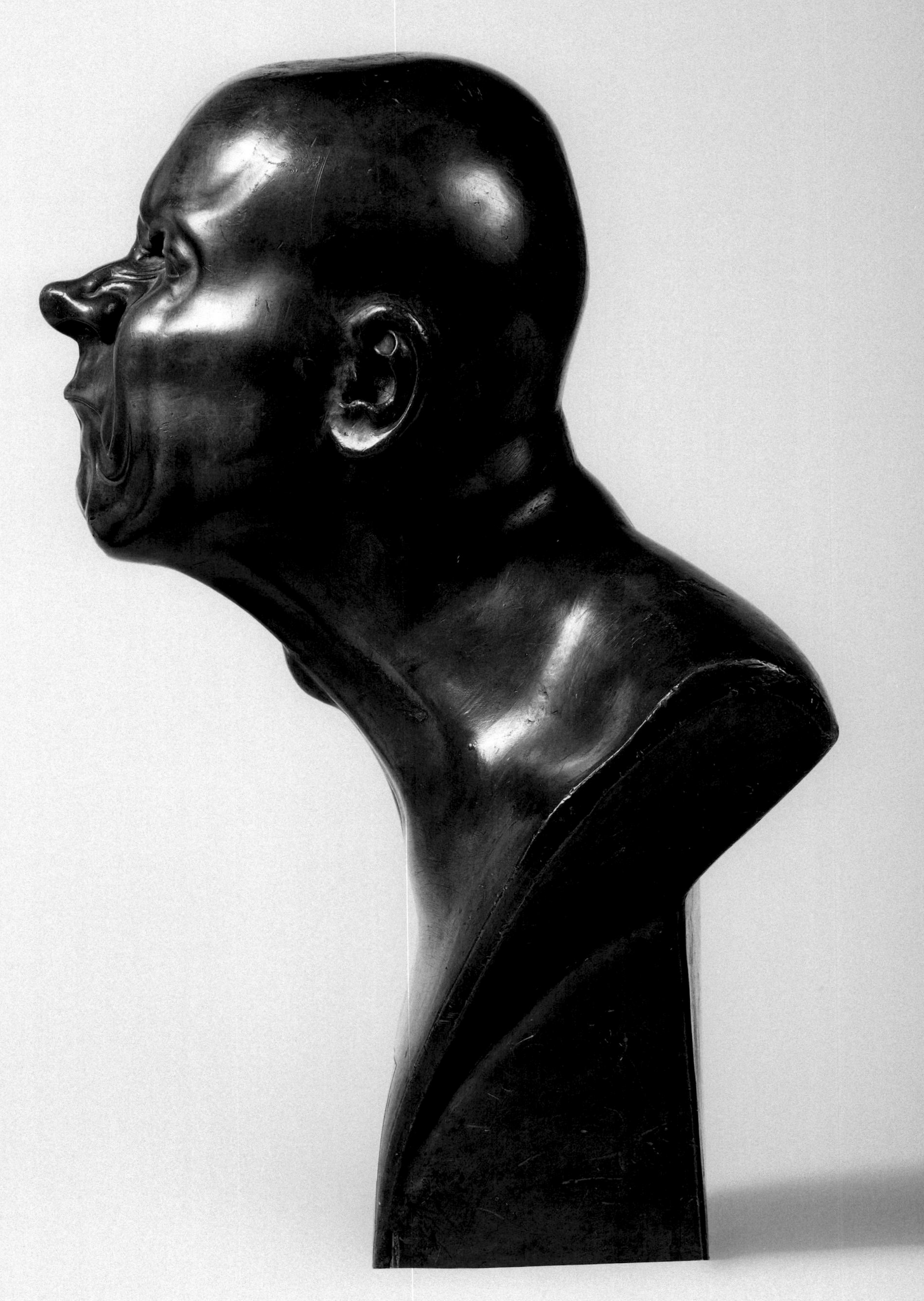

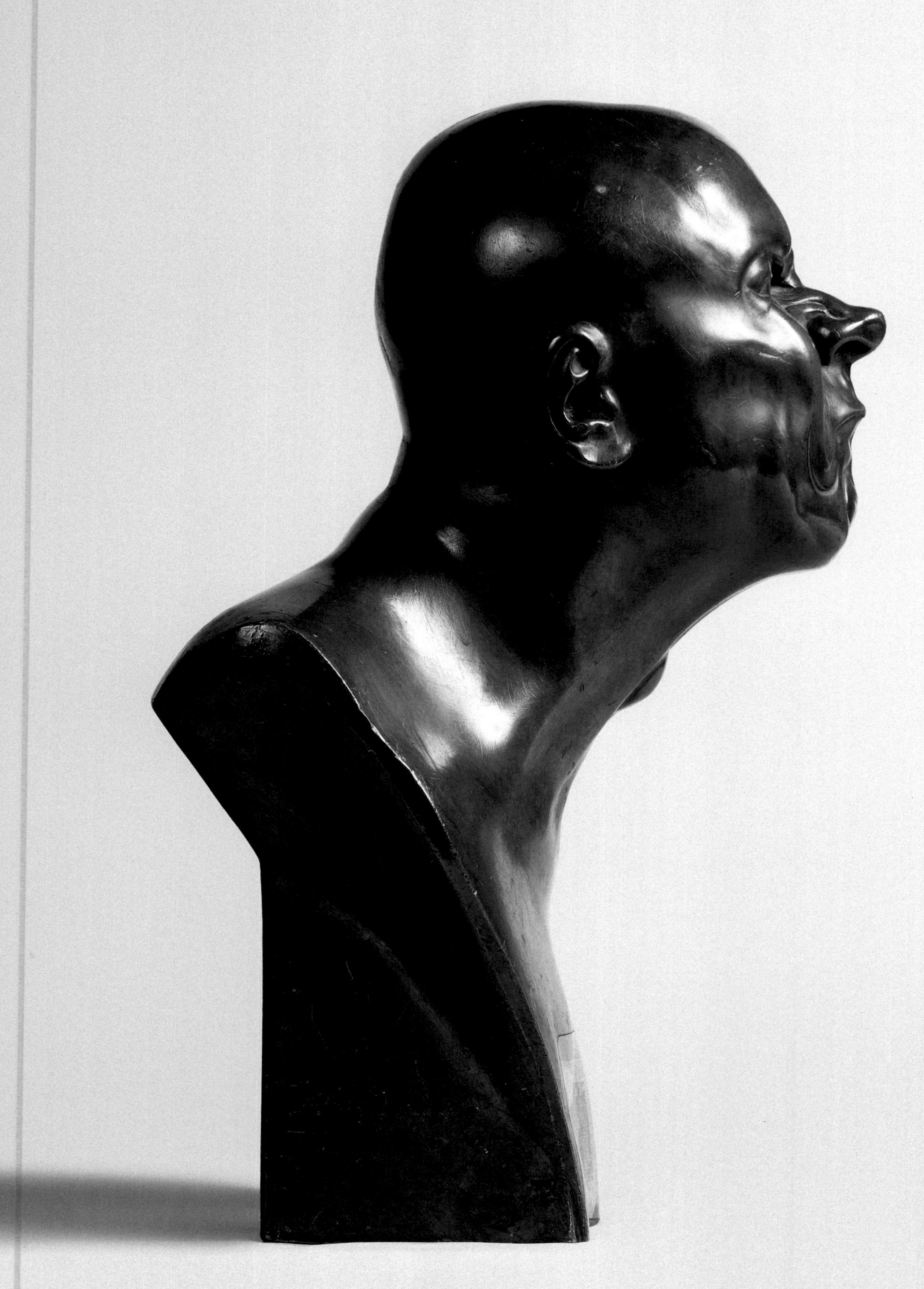

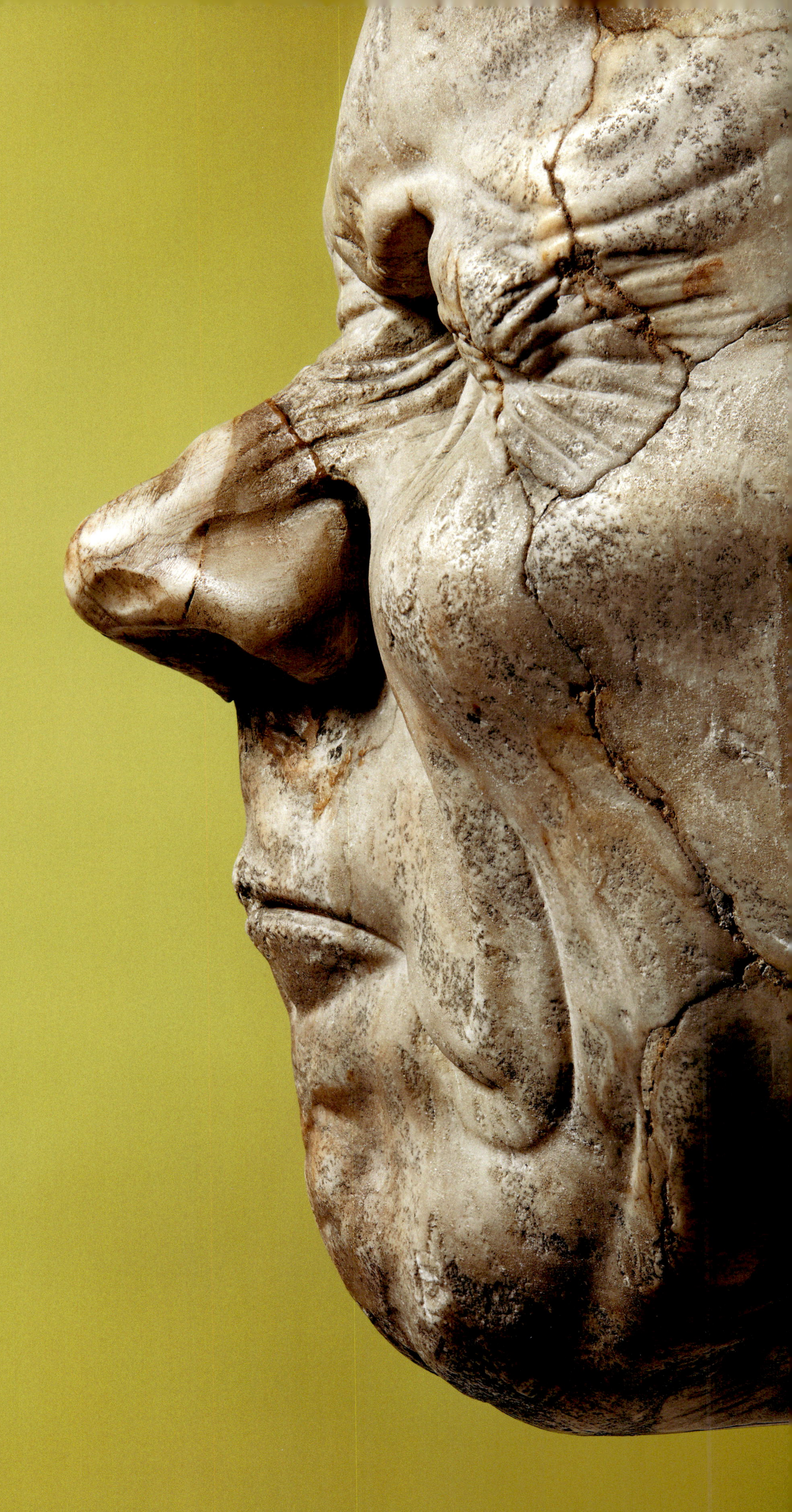

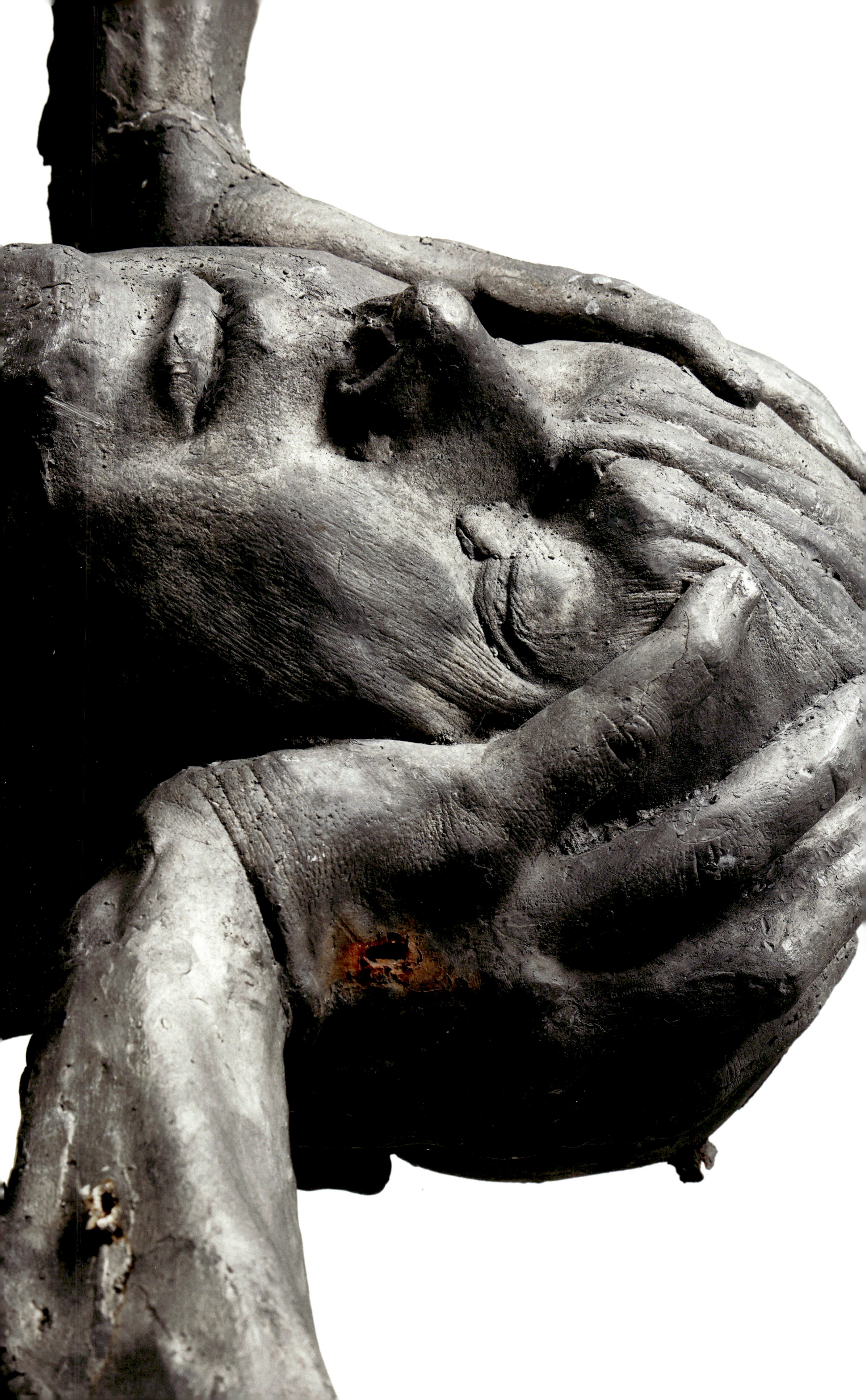

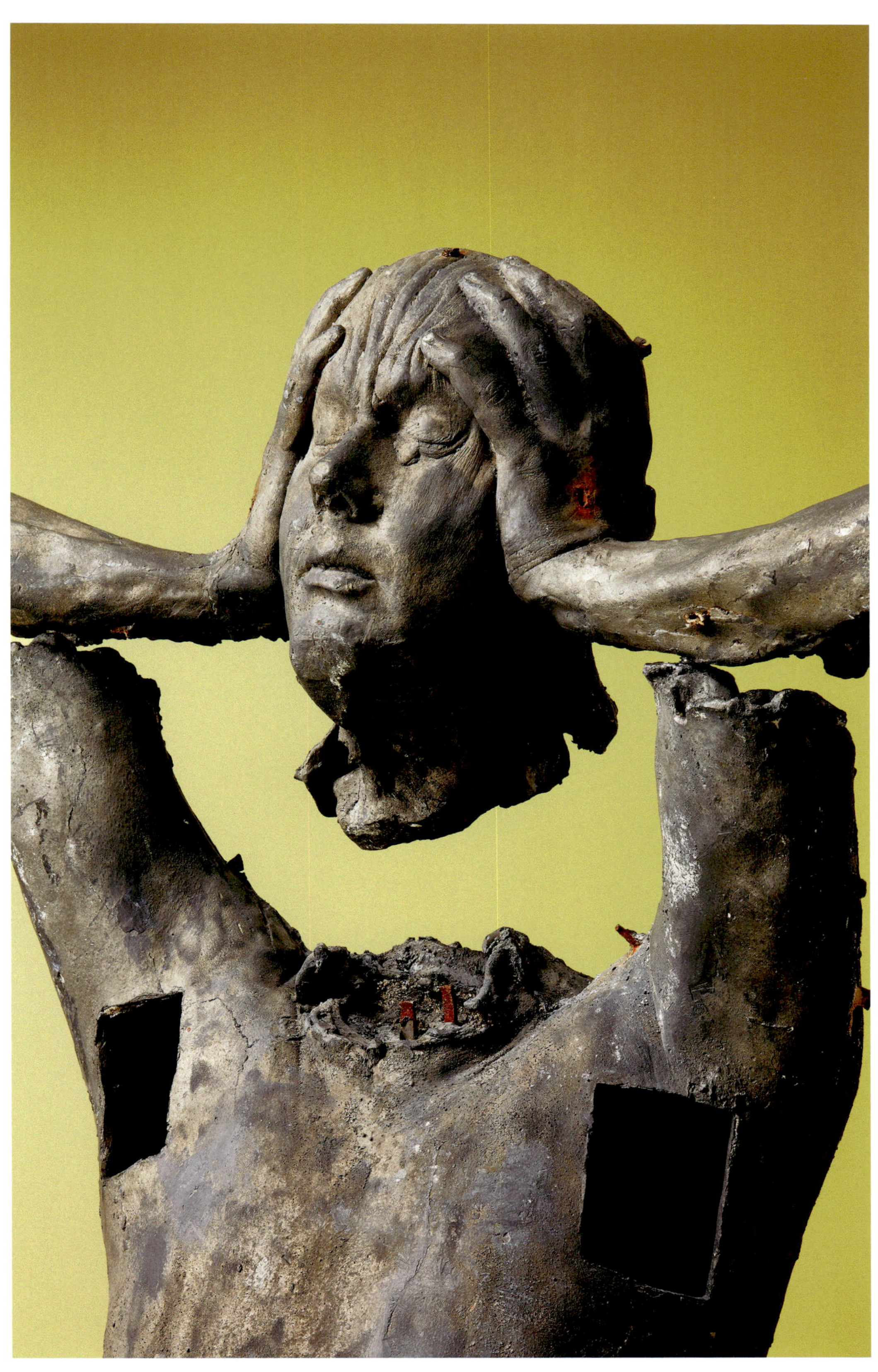

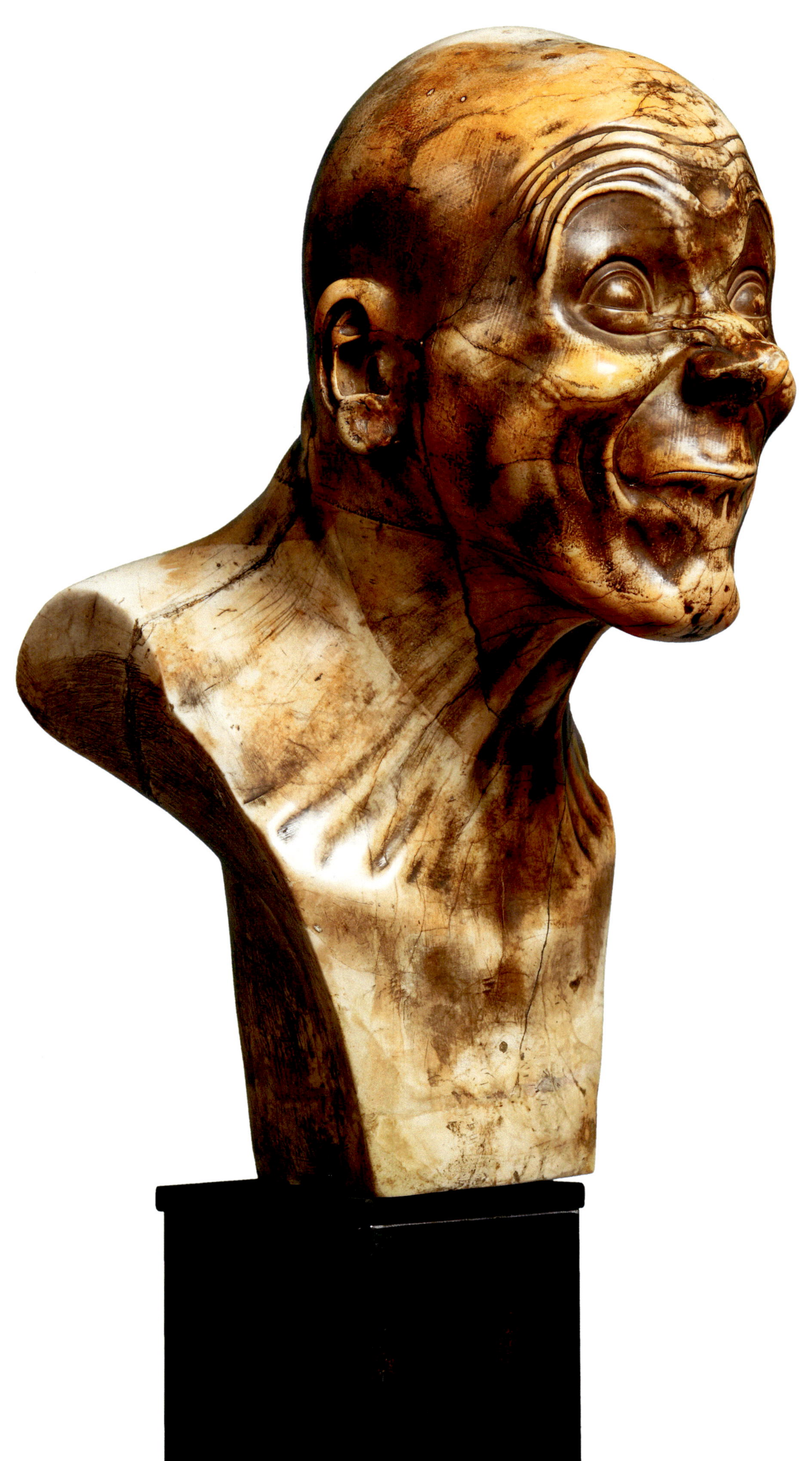

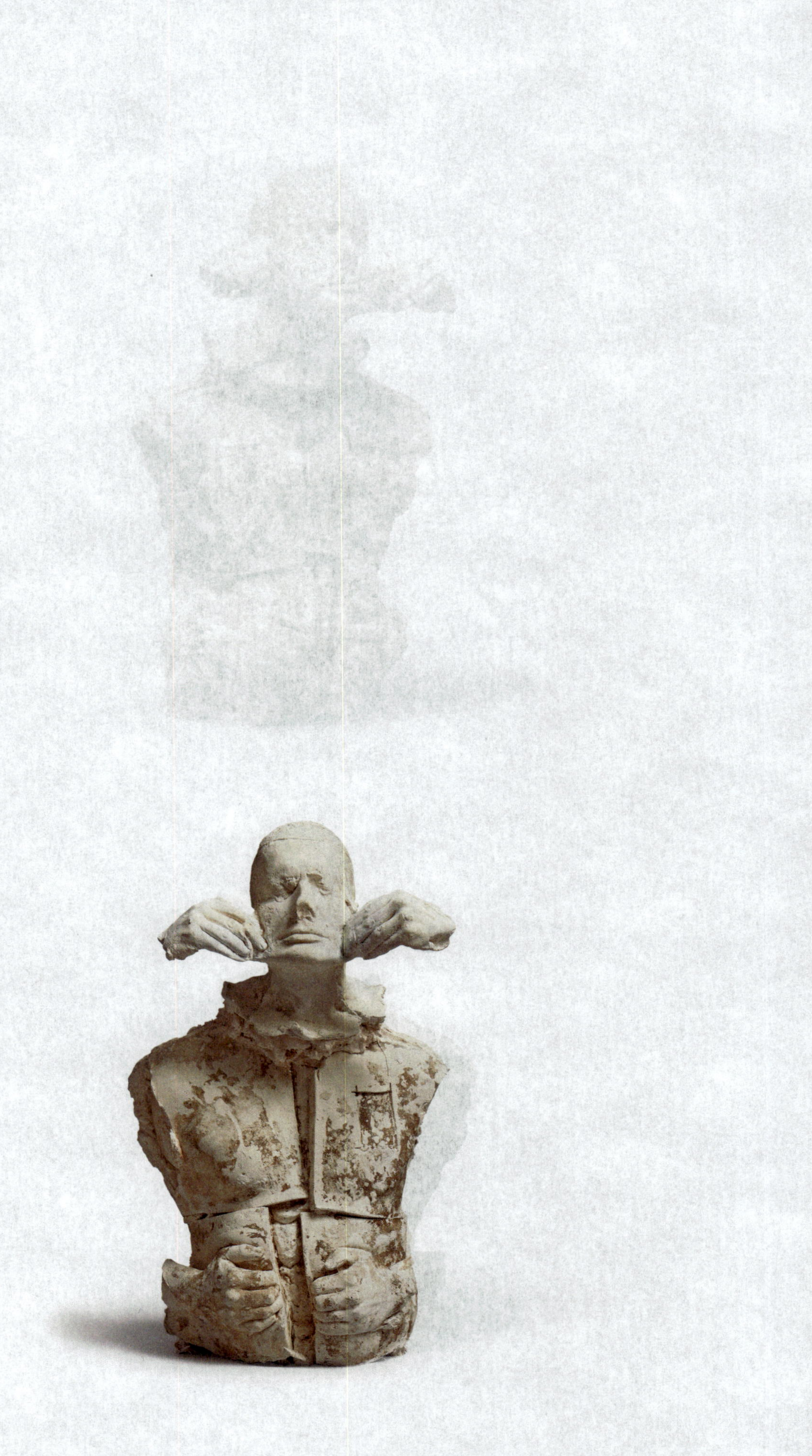

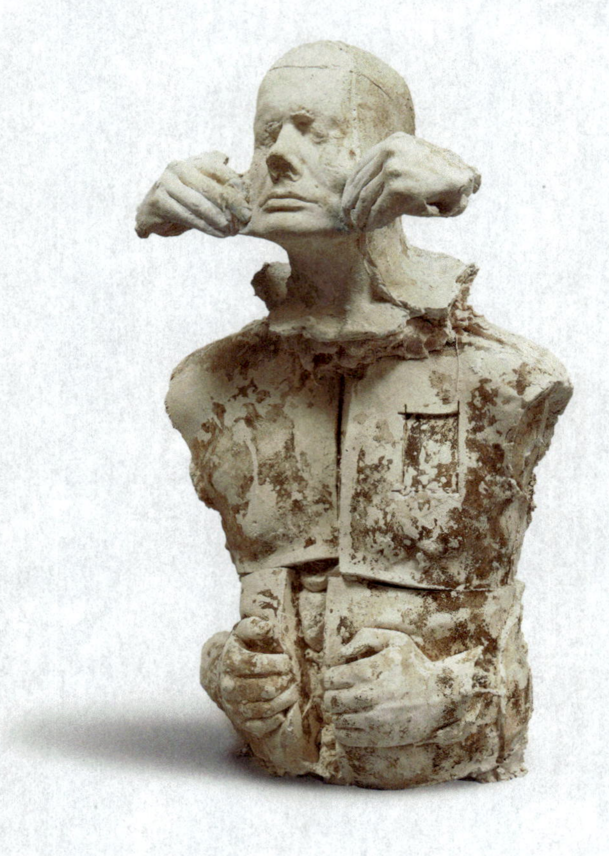

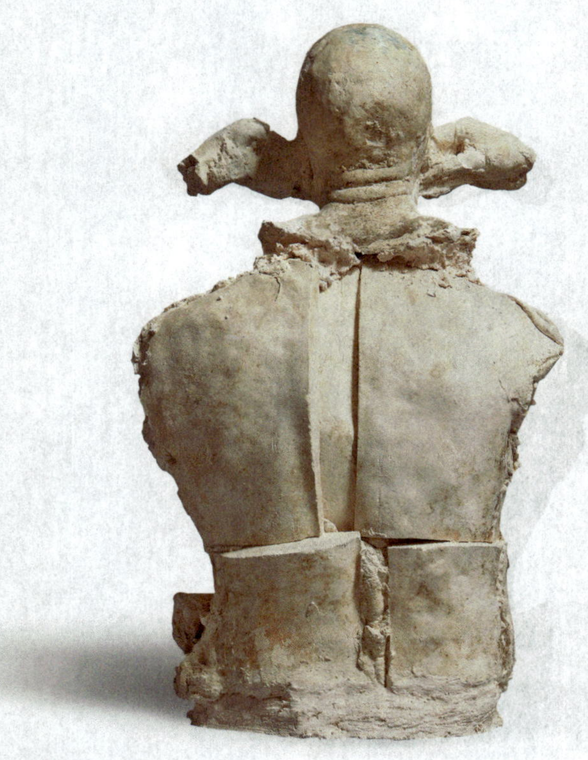

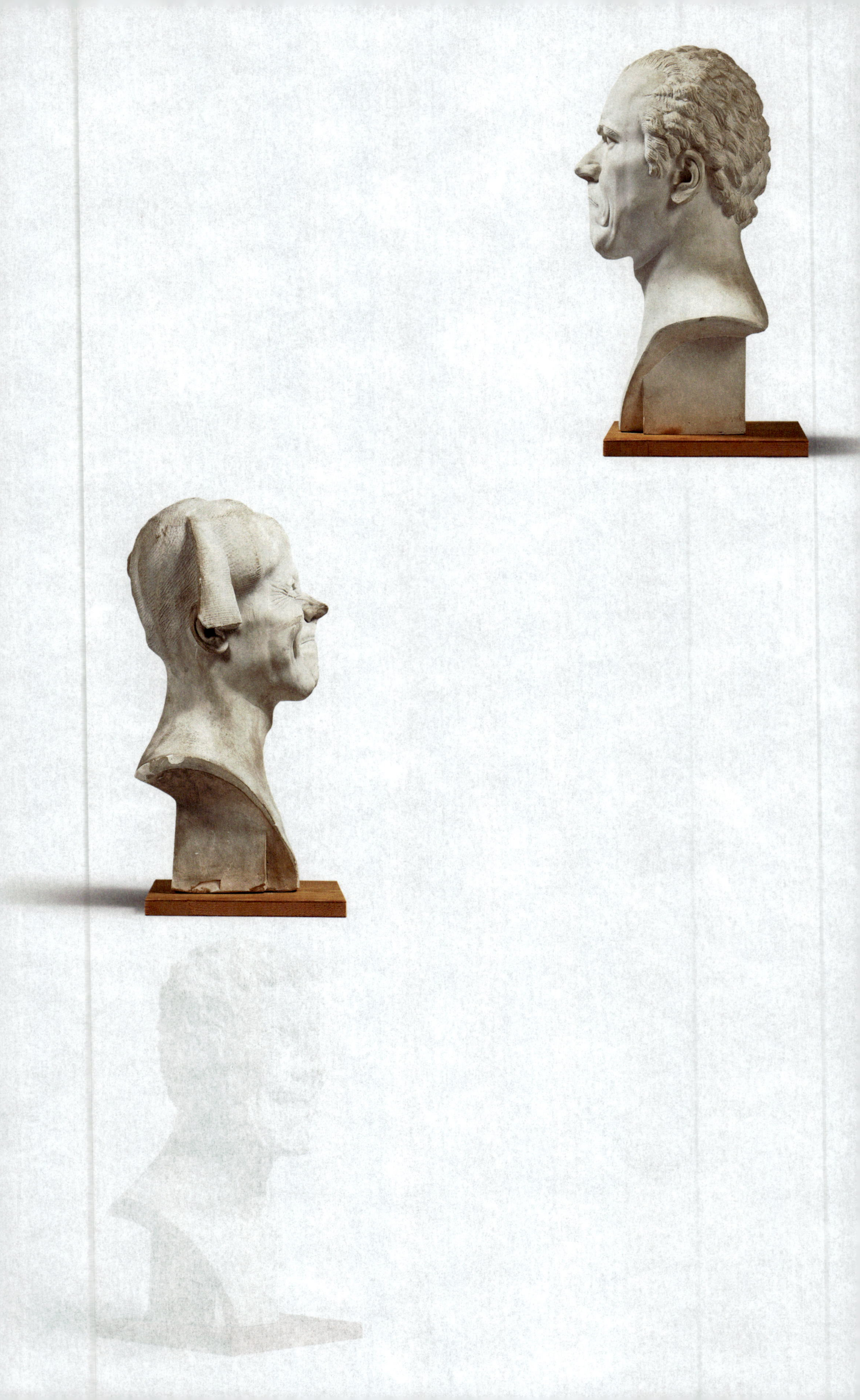

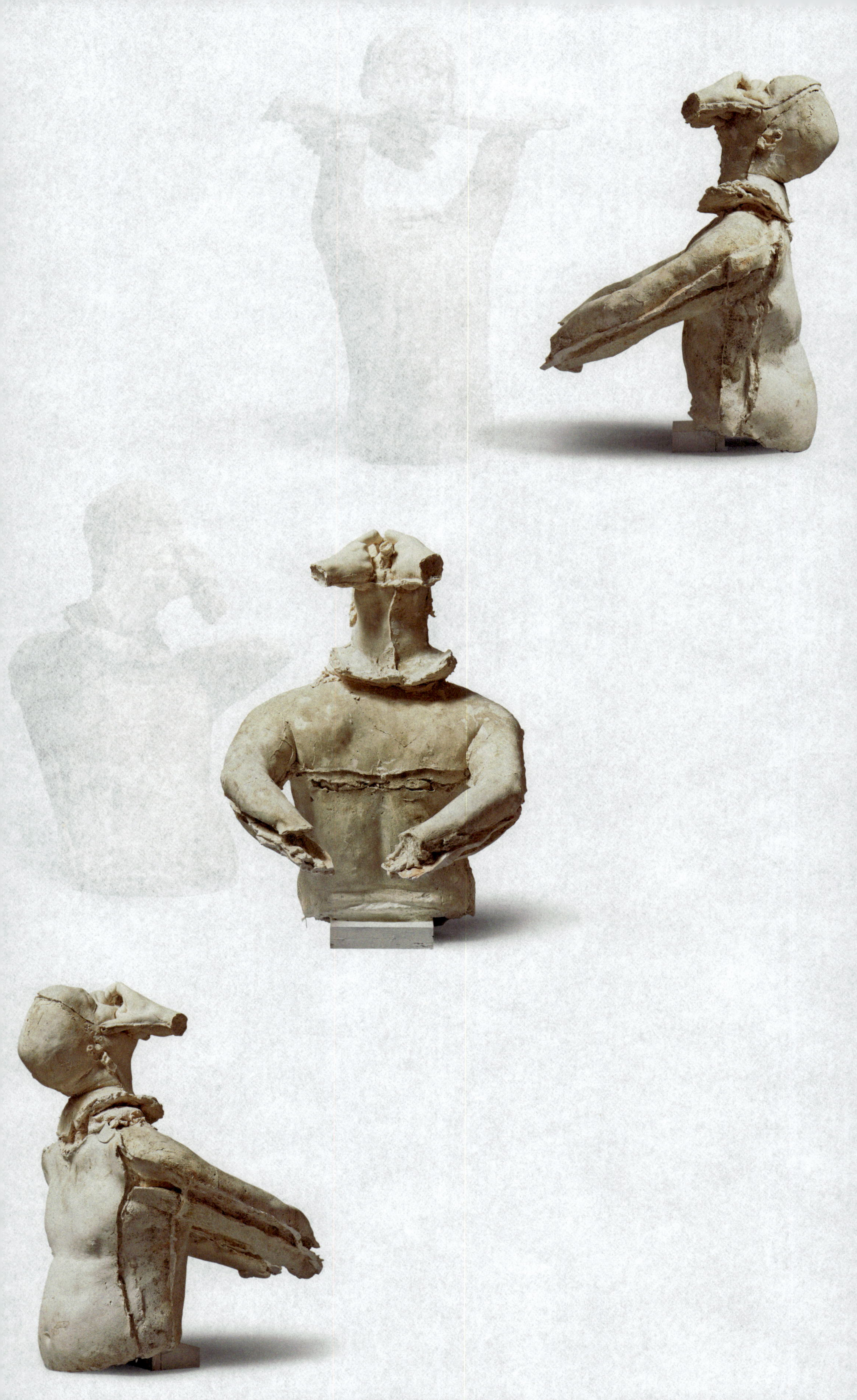

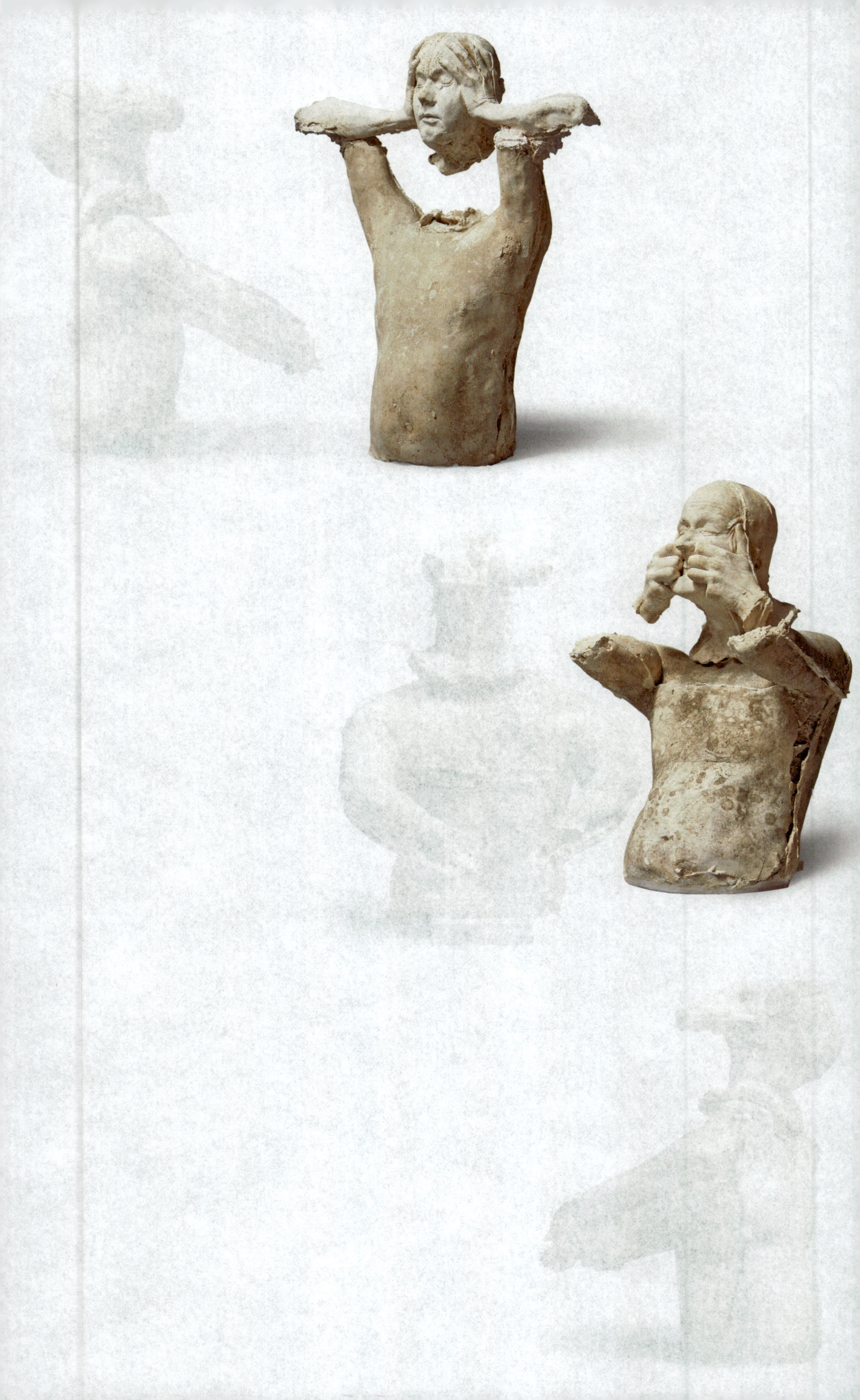

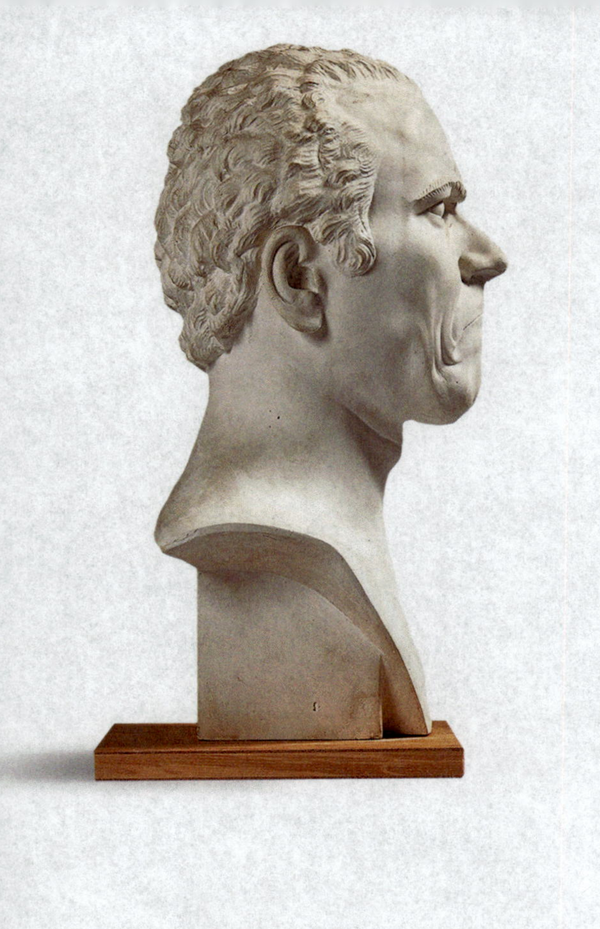

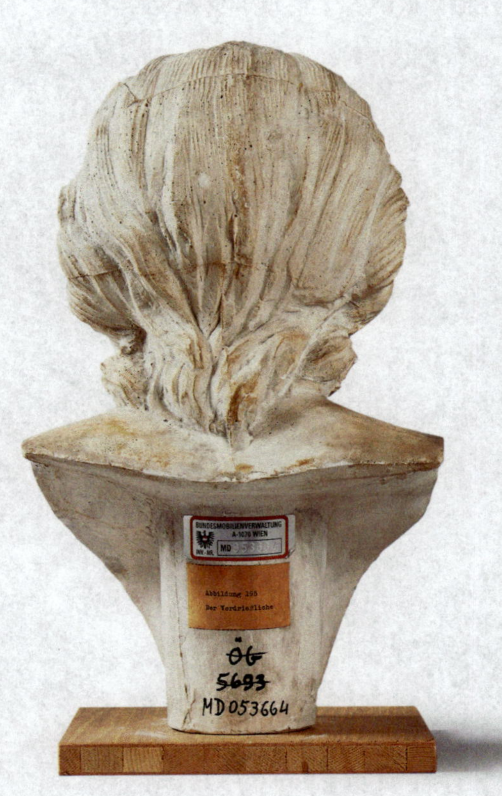
BUNDESMOBILIENVERWALTUNG
A-1070 WIEN
INV.-NR.
MD
Abbildung 195
Der Verdrießliche
ÖG
5693
MD053664

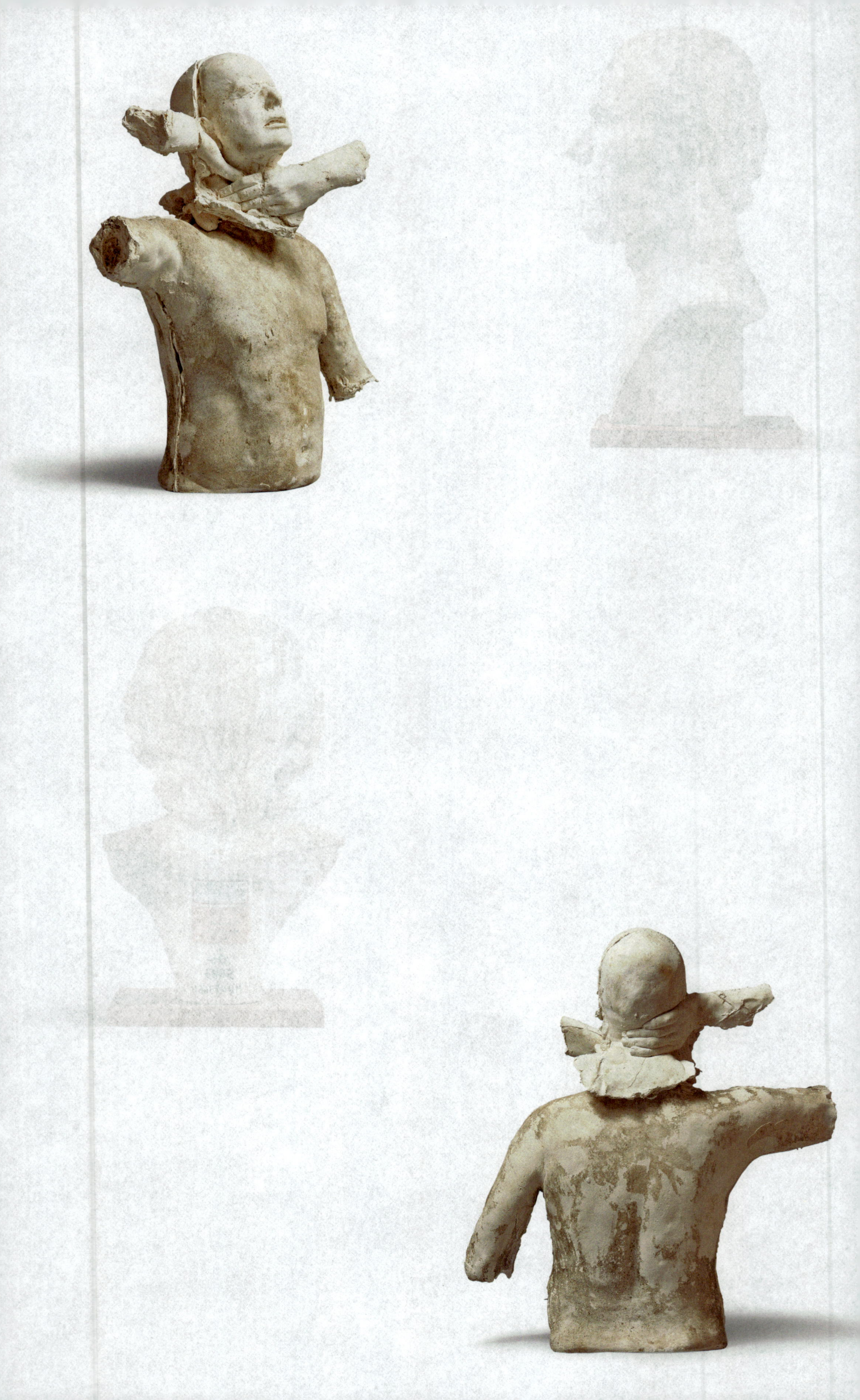

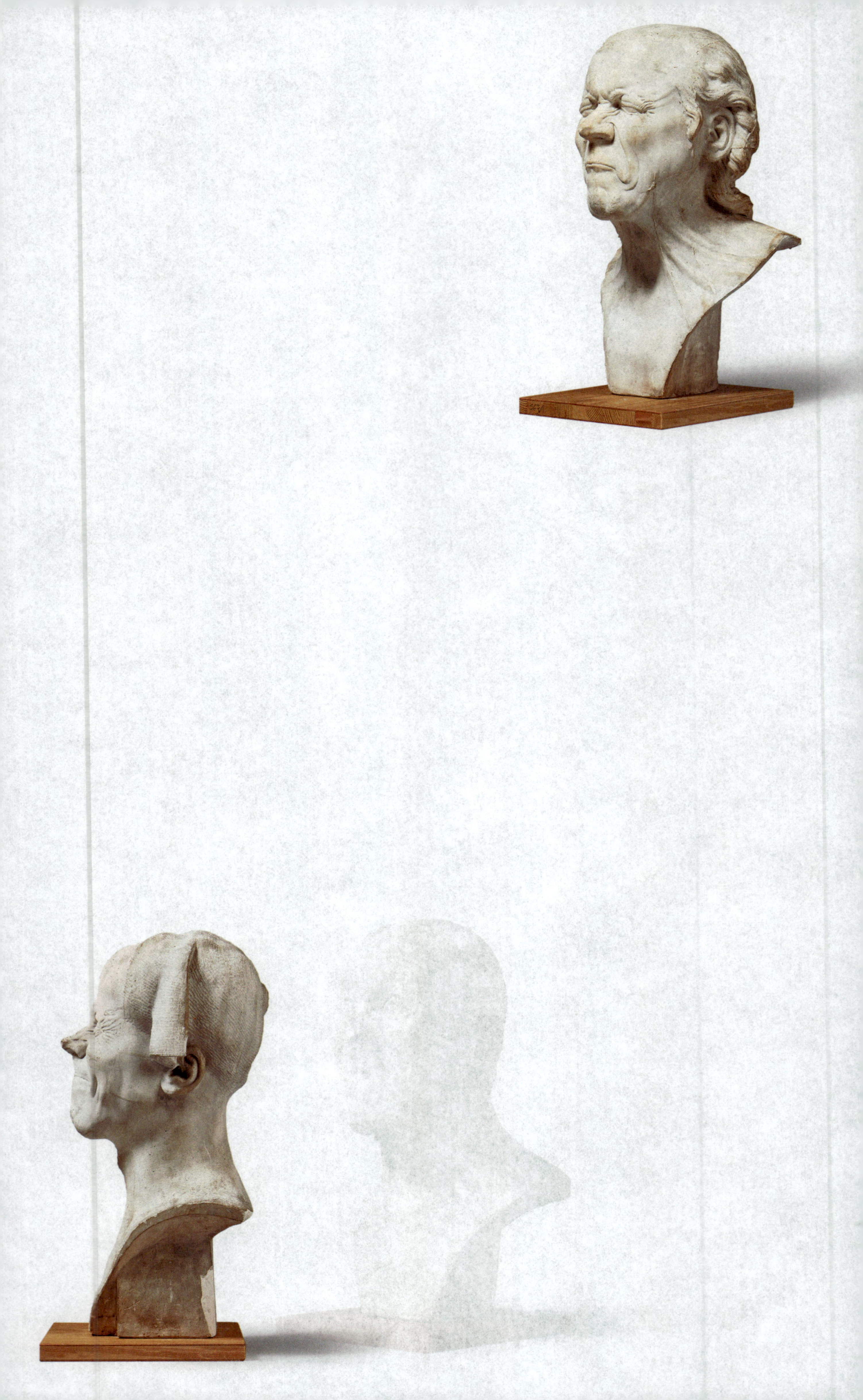

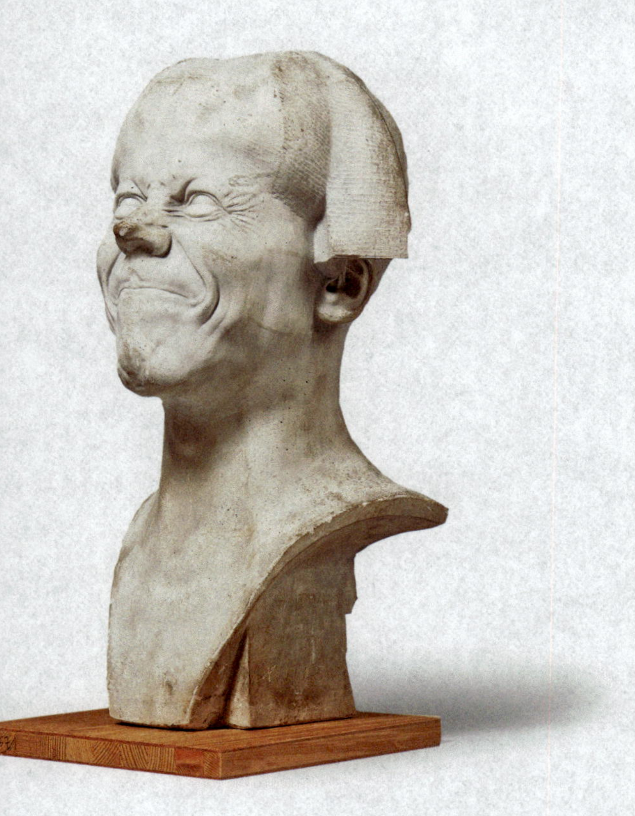

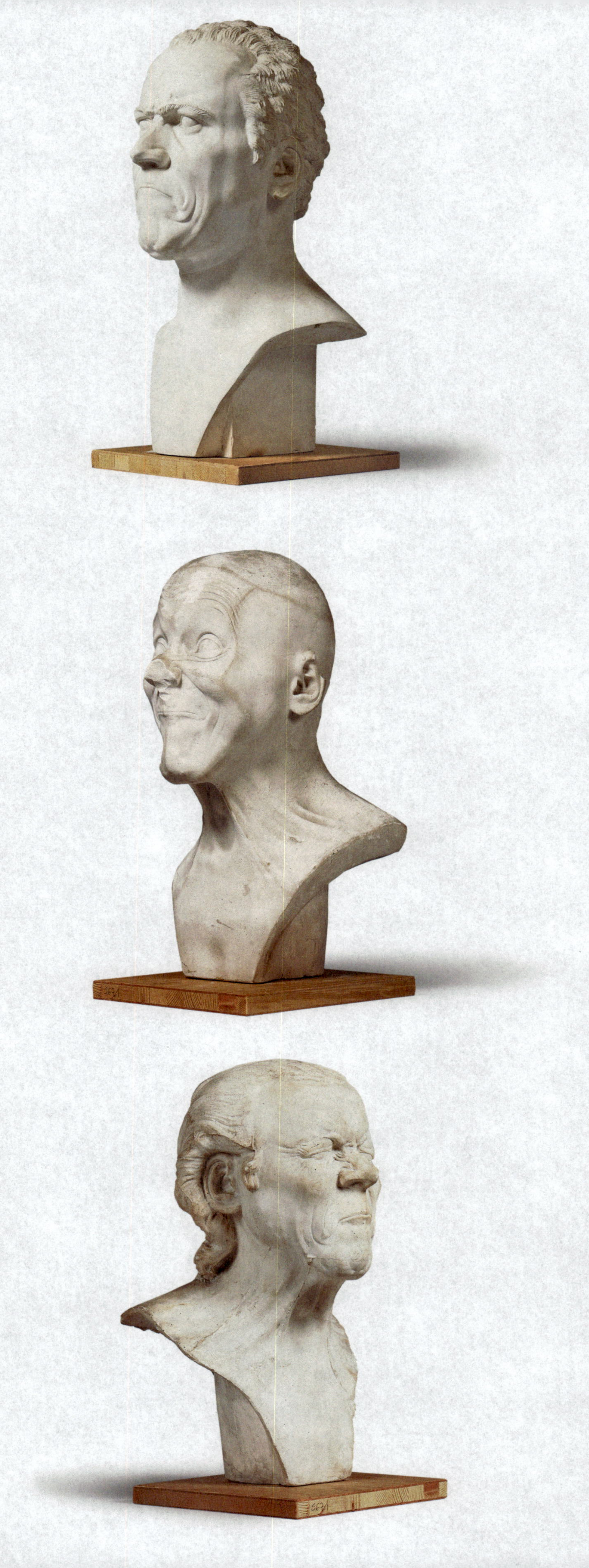

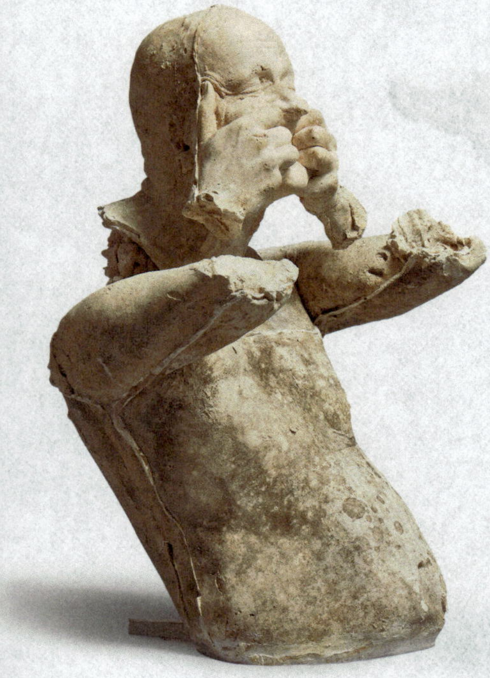

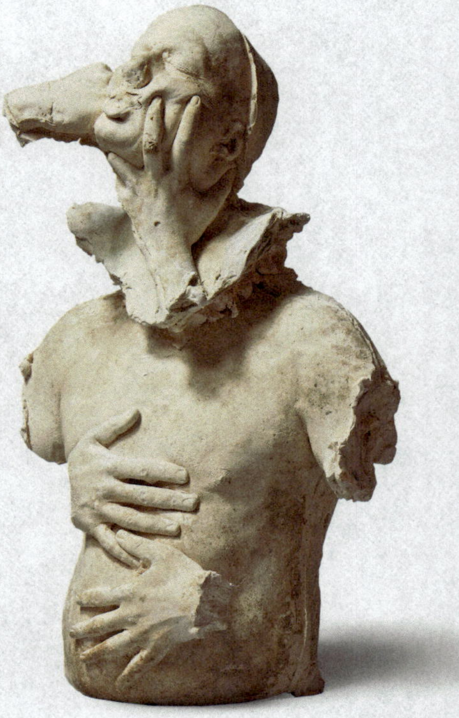

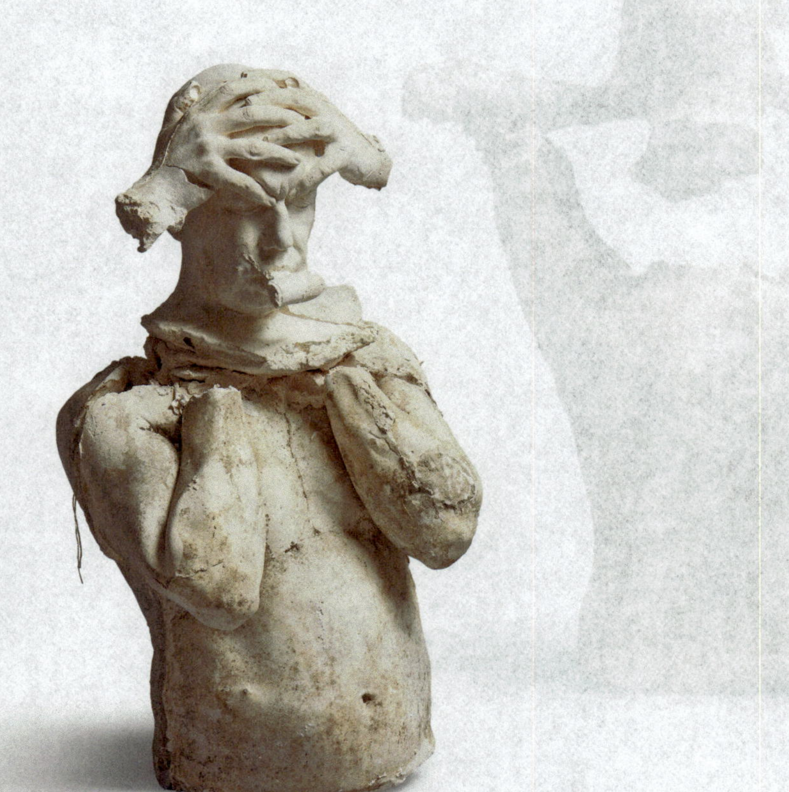
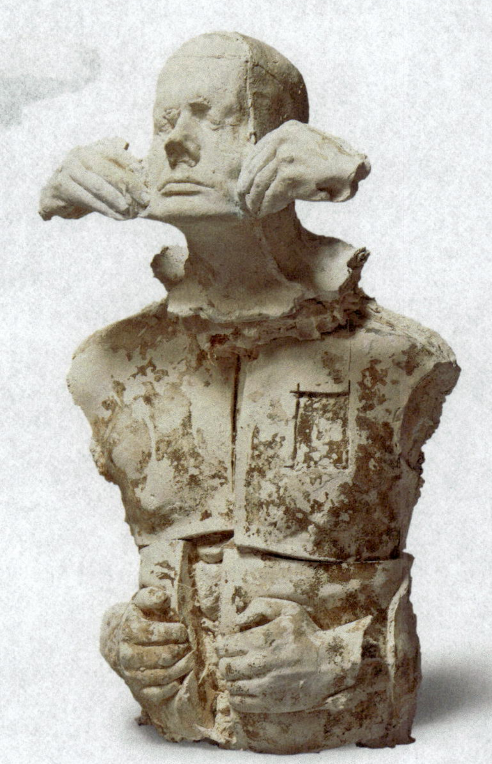

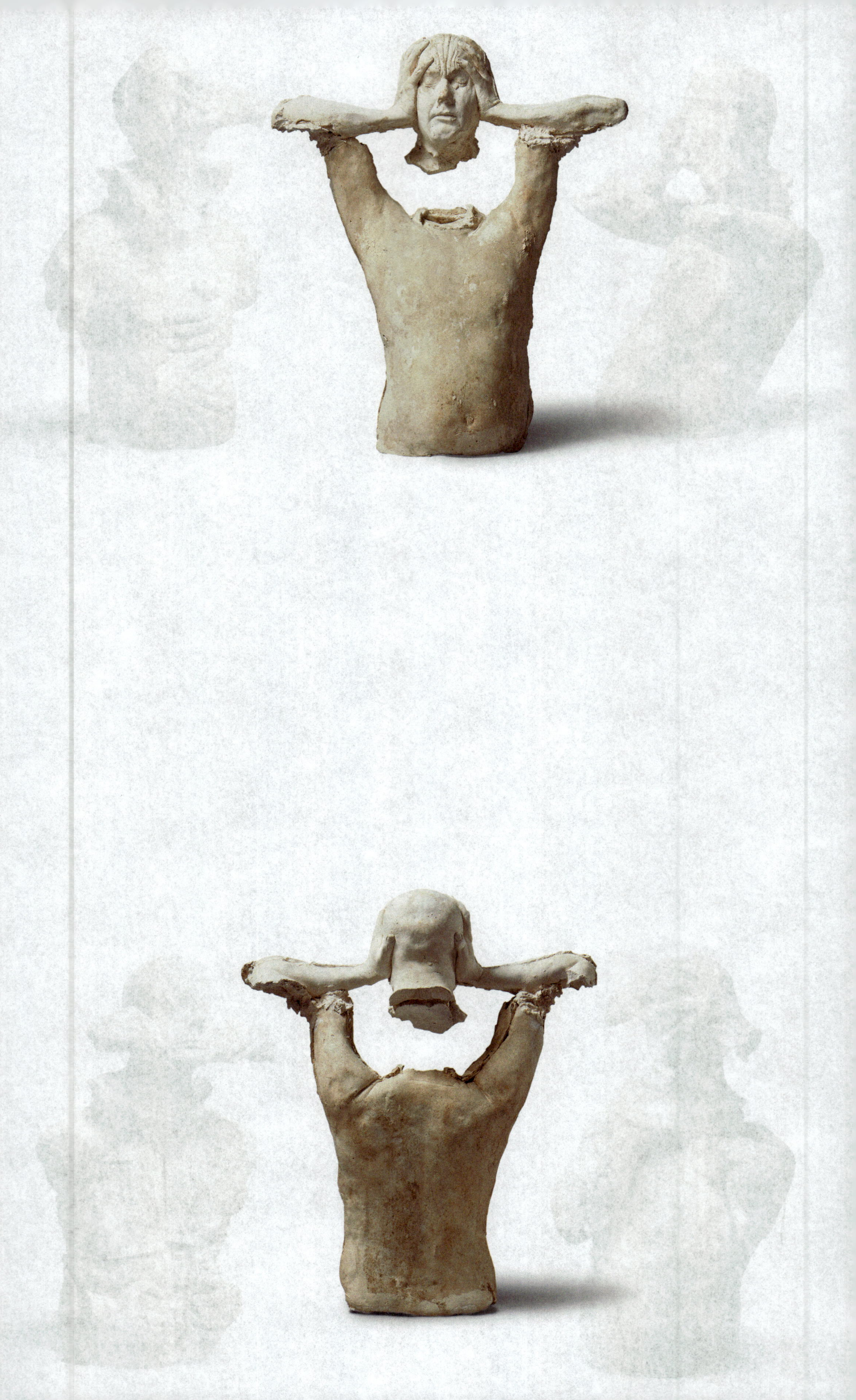

FACE TO FACE

Marc Quinn
meets
Franz Xaver Messerschmidt

Verlag der Buchhandlung Walther und Franz König

Die Hände des Bildhauers
Stella Rollig

Zwei Männer am Beginn des vierten Lebensjahrzehnts, nicht mehr blutjung, aber in Erwartung der „besten Jahre". Nur dass es sich für keinen der beiden so darstellt.

Marc Quinn ist dreißig, als er 1994 mit der Serie der Büsten beginnt, die unter dem Titel *Emotional Detox* heute eine der eindrucksvollsten Werkgruppen des Künstlers darstellt. Er macht einen Alkoholentzug durch. Wenn er davon spricht, klingt es nach einer Entscheidung zwischen Leben und Tod. *Emotional Detox* sind Selbstbildnisse dieser Erfahrung.

1770 ist Franz Xaver Messerschmidt 34 Jahre alt, er beginnt mit der Arbeit an den heute so genannten „Charakterköpfen". Es ist das Jahr, in dem sein bis dahin kontinuierlicher Aufstieg zum gut beschäftigten Bildhauer, Auftragnehmer des Kaiserhauses und Mitglied der Wiener Akademie einen Knick erleidet. Im folgenden Jahrzehnt wird ihm eine in Aussicht gestellte Professur verwehrt, geht die Auftragslage zurück, kehrt er der Hauptstadt Wien den Rücken und lässt sich schließlich im heutigen Bratislava nieder. Ihm wird eine psychische Erkrankung nachgesagt, die Quellenlage dazu ist spärlich. Wahrscheinlich ist er ein schwieriger Mensch, vielleicht paranoid oder schizophren, wie Forscher viel später nachzuweisen suchen. Er wird noch 13 Jahre leben. 13 Jahre, in denen er die Arbeit an den „Köpfen", wie er sie schlicht nennt, immer weitertreibt und schließlich ein paar Dutzend einer zunächst verständnislosen Nachwelt hinterlässt.

Gut zwei Jahrhunderte später: Die Gruppe der „Charakterköpfe" ist längst nicht mehr vereint, aber mittlerweile kunsthistorisch hoch geschätzt und in bedeutenden Museumssammlungen vertreten – die Österreichische Galerie Belvedere besitzt die größte Anzahl. Drei Jahre sind vergangen, seit Marc Quinn das radikalste und schockierendste Selbstporträt gemacht hat, das sich denken lässt. *Self* (1991) ist Quinns ikonische Arbeit, die das Potenzial hat, ihn unsterblich zu machen: der Kopf des Künstlers als Abguss aus seinem eigenen Blut, in gefrorenes Silikon getaucht. Wie, so frage ich mich, macht man weiter, nachdem man mit 27 ein solches Werk geschaffen, eine solche Tat gesetzt hat?

Es heißt, niemand könne je wissen, was ein*e Künstler*in gemacht hat, nur er*sie selbst. Aber ich weiß es doch selbst nicht, erwidert diese*r oftmals. Wohl selten vor historischen Kunstwerken ist der Wunsch so dringlich, mit dem Künstler über seine Arbeit zu sprechen, wie angesichts der „Charakterköpfe". Herr Messerschmidt, warum haben Sie das gemacht? Ach, ich habe dies und das probiert. Es gefiel mir, vor dem Spiegel Fratzen zu schneiden. Warum sollen nur Kinder Grimassen machen dürfen und sich damit belustigen? Ich wollte Köpfe formen, welche die hohe Kunst bis dato nicht kennt, nicht immer Majestäten oder Gelehrte. Ich weiß es doch selbst nicht.

Nun entdeckt Quinn im Victoria and Albert Museum diesen Kopf: *Der starke Geruch* (*The Strong Smell*) eines gewissen Franz Xaver Messerschmidt. Doch zeigt das Porträt einen Riechenden? (Wir wissen, dass die Titel der Köpfe nicht vom Künstler, sondern von anderen nach seinem Tod festgesetzt wurden.) Wenn man so will, entsprechen die gerümpfte Nase, die geschürzte Oberlippe dem Abscheu vor einem unangenehmen Odeur. Trifft man aber in einer Lebenskrise auf dieses Gegenüber, erscheint sein Ausdruck dann nicht als existenzieller Schmerz? Vielleicht sieht Quinn einen Mann, der die Augen so fest wie möglich zukneift, um die quälenden Bilder in seinem Kopf hinter Wälle von Schwarz und Sternenschauer zu sperren, der den Hals reckt und die Muskeln überdehnt, um den Körper zu spüren anstelle der Seele. Um die schrecklichen Gedanken für einen Moment im Korsett der physischen Anstrengung zu bannen.

Und vielleicht weiß er da plötzlich, wie es weitergehen kann nach der absoluten künstlerischen Entäußerung mit *Self* und nach den physischen und emotionalen Qualen des Entzugs. Er wird eine Serie von Werken schaffen, die ihn in seiner Hölle porträtieren. Er wird sich von der traditionellen Ikonografie der sieben Todsünden inspirieren lassen. Und er wird den Dämon zeigen, der ihm an die Gurgel geht: Er ist es selbst.

Die Hände des Bildhauers würgen und knuffen sein Abbild, boxen in sein Gesicht, pressen den Schädel. Die bis zur Taille reichende Büste ist stückhaft, roh, durchlöchert. Die Hände haben sich von den Armen gelöst und ein sadistisches Eigenleben begonnen. Und doch, wäre da nicht der gequälte Gesichtsausdruck, könnten diese Hände auch ein Spiel spielen, ein Spiel, wie es Kindern gefällt. Kleinen Kindern, die Erwachsenen ins Gesicht fassen, guck mal, wie lustig das aussieht, wenn ich deine Wangen auseinanderziehe.

Der Bildhauer legt Hand an (sich selbst). Das Großartige an *Emotional Detox* ist neben der packenden Darstellung und der meisterhaften Technik die bildhafte Vieldeutigkeit. Der Bildhauer zeigt das Grundprinzip seiner Arbeit, das Formen mit eigener Hand; das Leben geht durch den Körper und lässt Schrunden und Schrammen zurück. Unser schlimmster Foltermeister sind wir selbst, aber wie Münchhausen können wir uns am eigenen Schopf aus dem Sumpf ziehen.

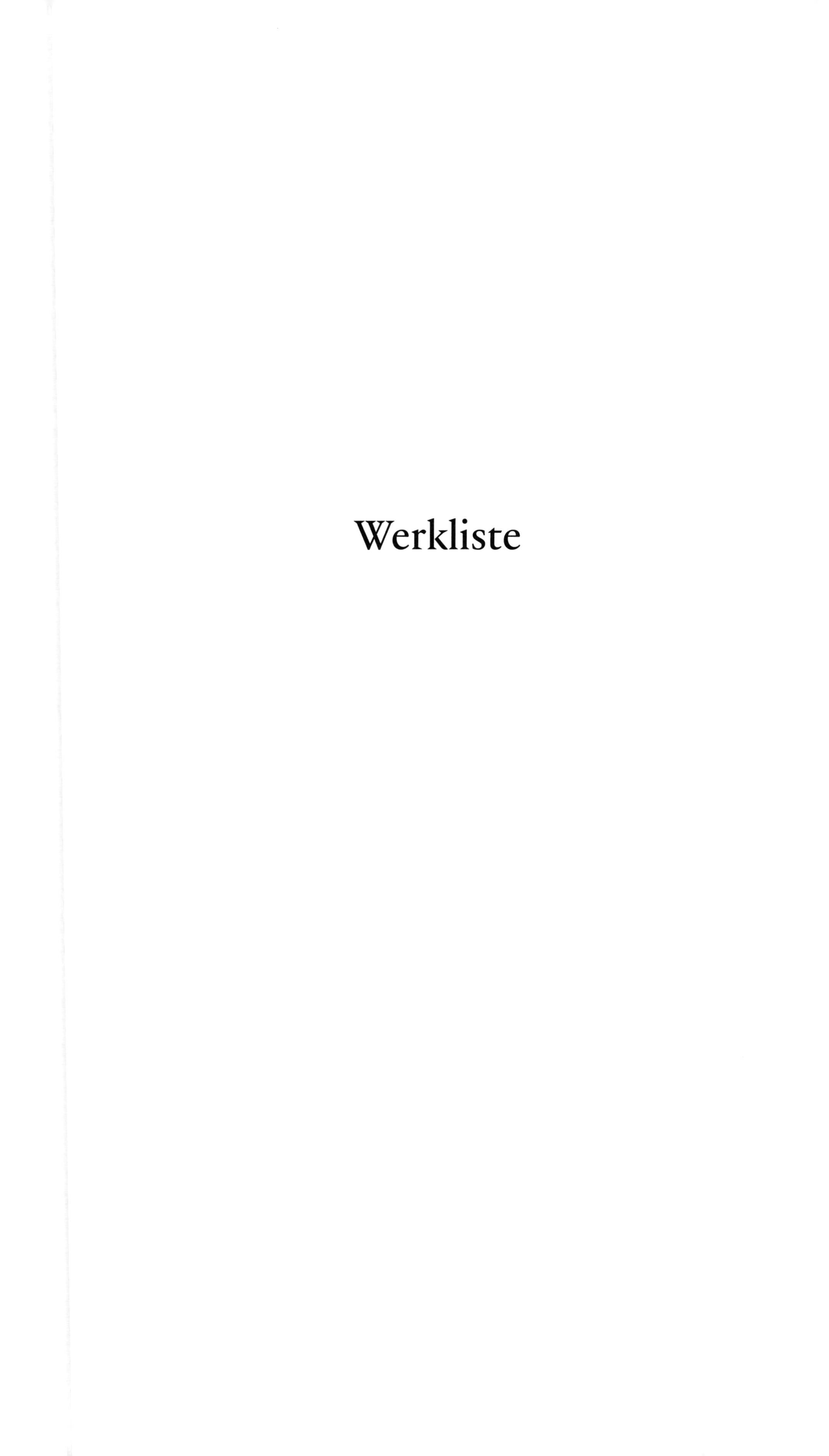

Werkliste

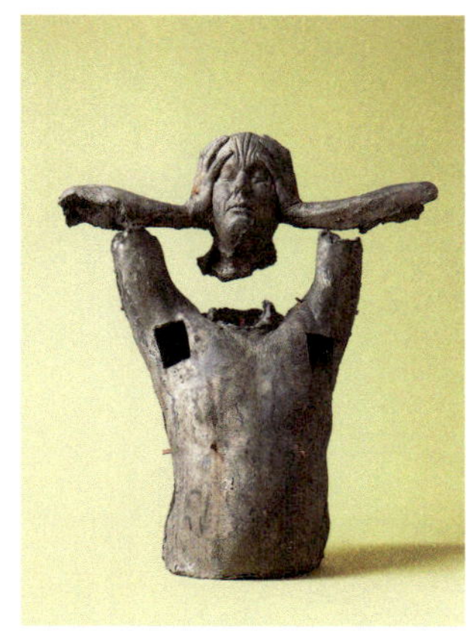

Marc Quinn
Emotional Detox IV, 1995
Edition von 3 mit 2 APs
Bleiguss und Wachs
90 × 80 × 30 cm

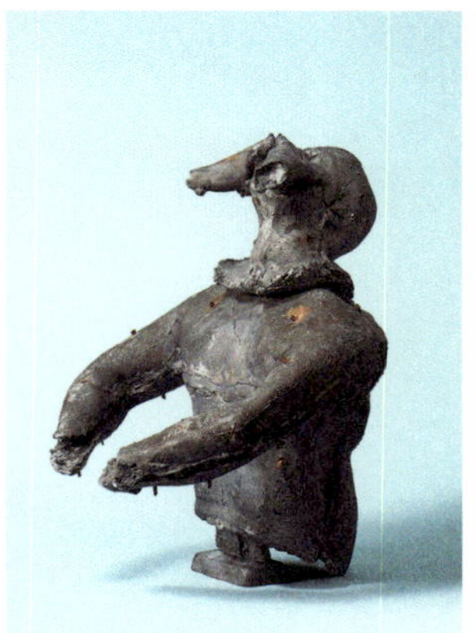

Marc Quinn
Emotional Detox III, 1995
Edition von 3 mit 2 APs
Bleiguss und Wachs
83 × 75 × 55 cm

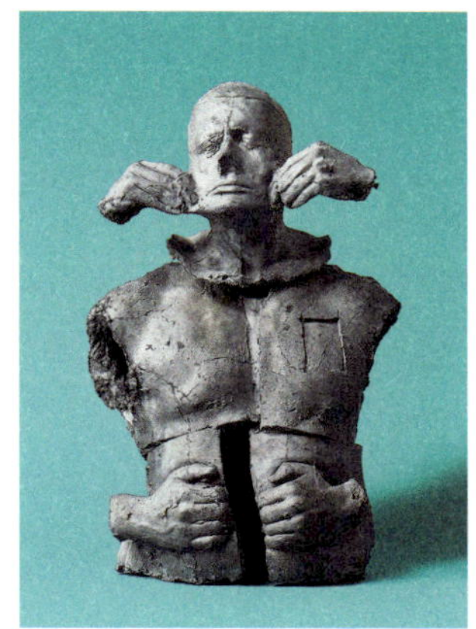

Marc Quinn
Emotional Detox V, 1995
Edition von 3 mit 2 APs
Bleiguss und Wachs
86 × 52 × 36 cm

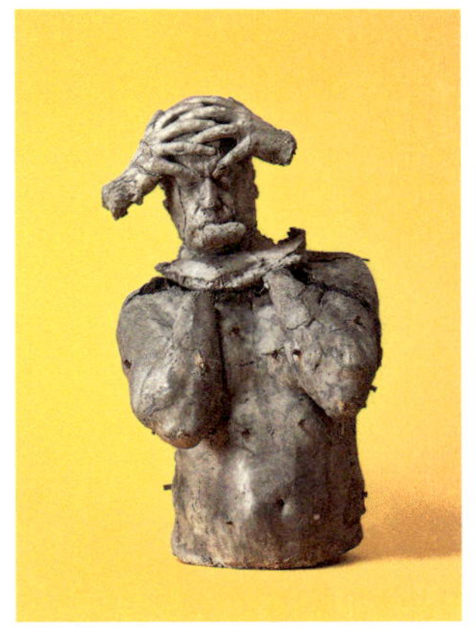

Marc Quinn
Emotional Detox II, 1995
Edition von 3 mit 2 APs
Bleiguss und Wachs
86 × 47 × 37 cm

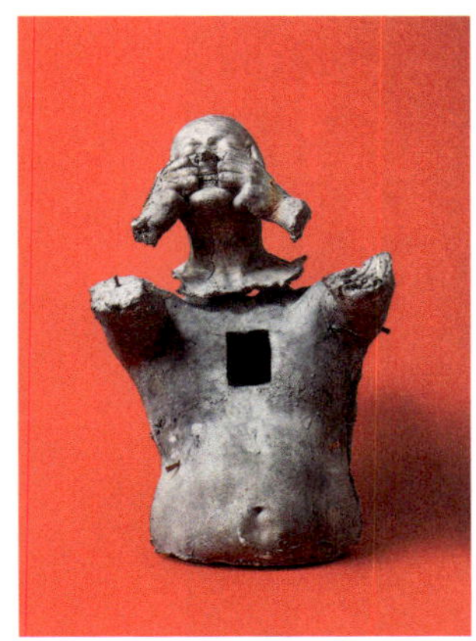

Marc Quinn
Emotional Detox VII, 1995
Edition von 3 mit 2 APs
Bleiguss und Wachs
90 × 80 × 30 cm

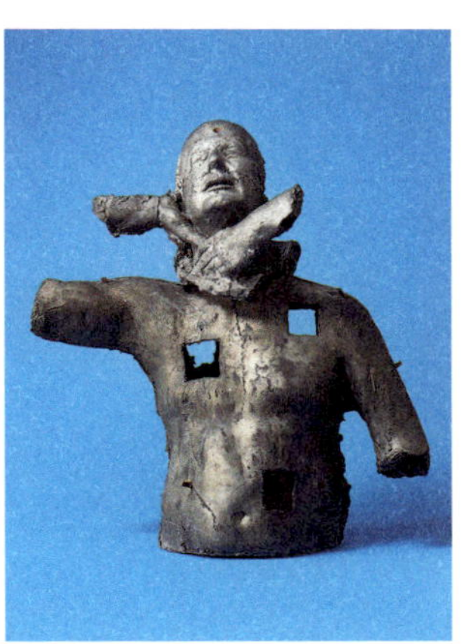

Marc Quinn
Emotional Detox I, 1994
Edition von 3 mit 2 APs
Bleiguss und Wachs
80 × 65 × 35 cm

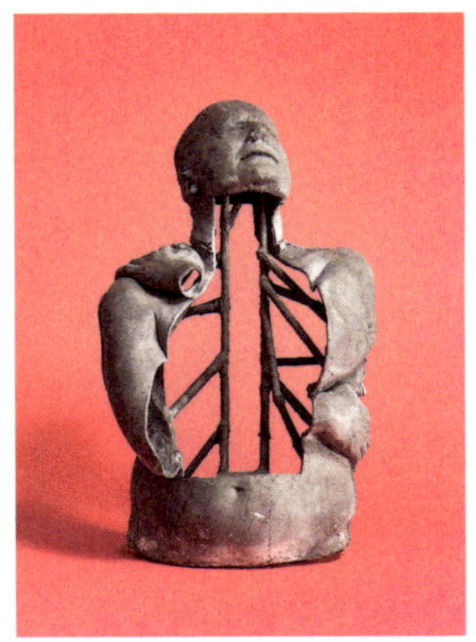

Marc Quinn
Fear of Fear, 1994
Edition von 5 mit 2 APs
Bleiguss
76 × 43 × 37 cm

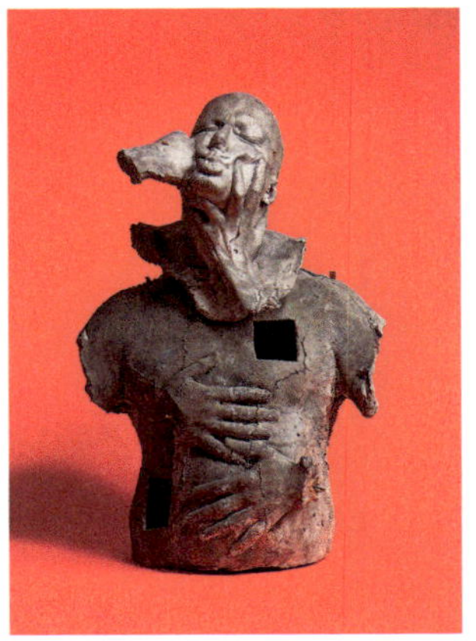

Marc Quinn
Emotional Detox VI, 1995
Edition von 3 mit 2 APs
Bleiguss und Wachs
86 × 55 × 40 cm

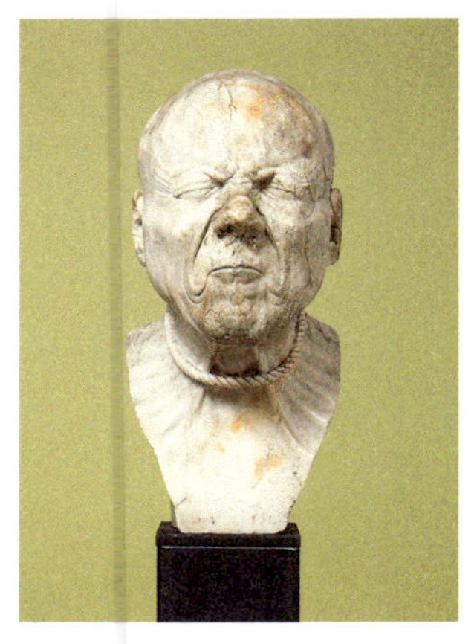

Franz Xaver Messerschmidt
Ein Erhängter, 1771/1783
Alabaster, grauweißer Stein mit bräunlichen Flecken
38 × 20 × 27 cm

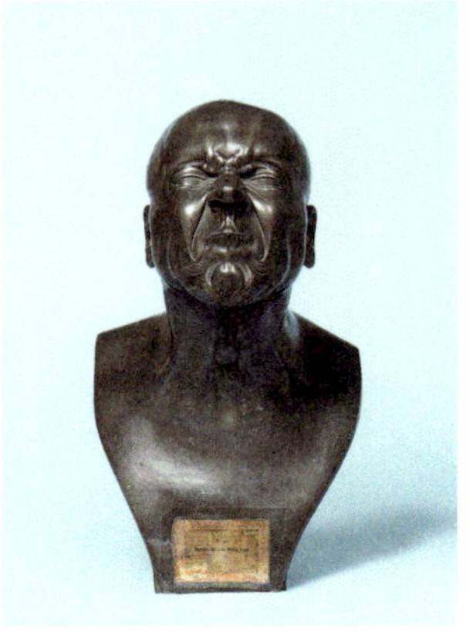

Franz Xaver Messerschmidt
Geruch der zum Niesen reizt, 1777/1783
Bleiguss
47 × 27 × 33 cm

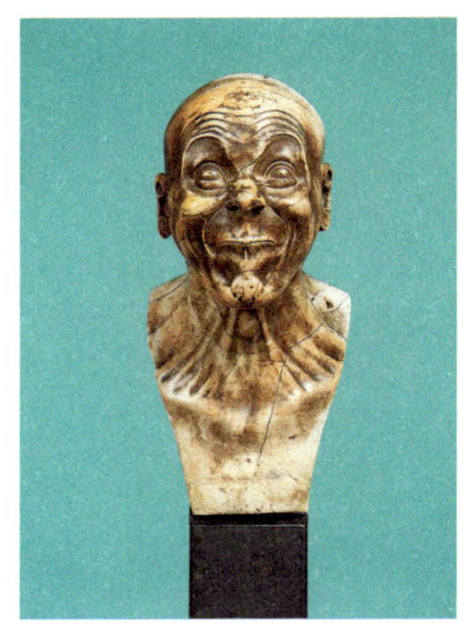

Franz Xaver Messerschmidt
Der Schaafkopf, 1777/1783
Braun gefleckter Alabaster
43,5 × 21 × 33 cm

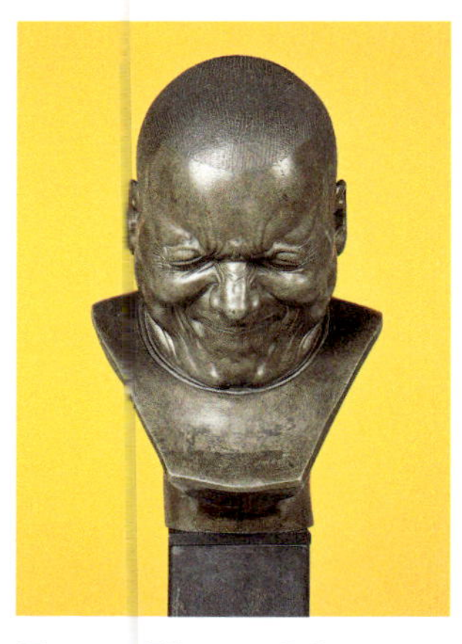

Franz Xaver Messerschmidt
Ein Erzbösewicht, 1777/1783
Zinnguss
39 × 26 × 25 cm

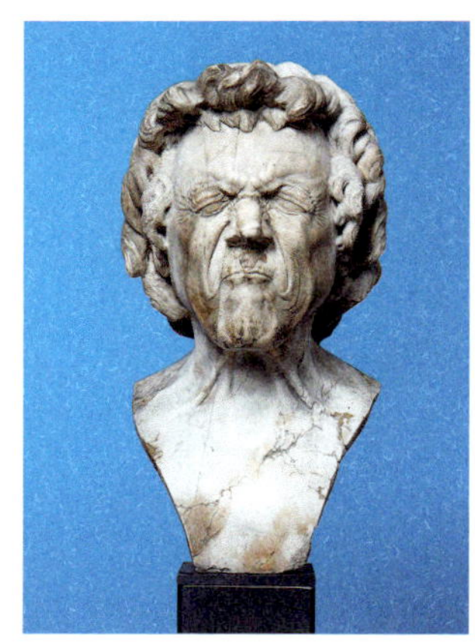

Franz Xaver Messerschmidt
Ein abgezehrter Alter mit Augenschmerzen, 1771/1783
Alabaster, fleckiger bräunlich-grauer Stein
44 × 23,5 × 26 cm

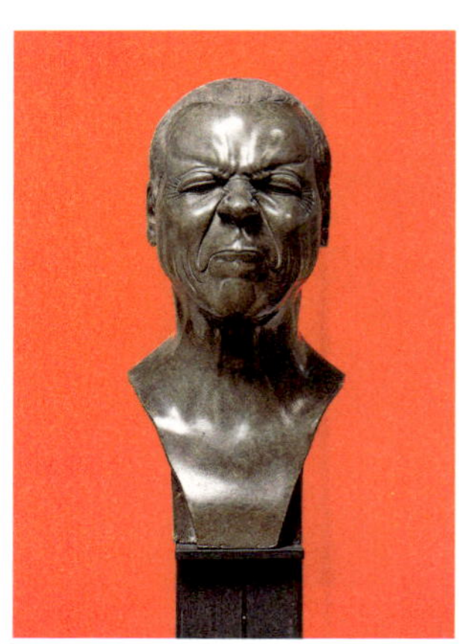

Franz Xaver Messerschmidt
Ein düstrer finsterer Mann, 1770/1783
Bleiguss
43 × 22 × 24 cm

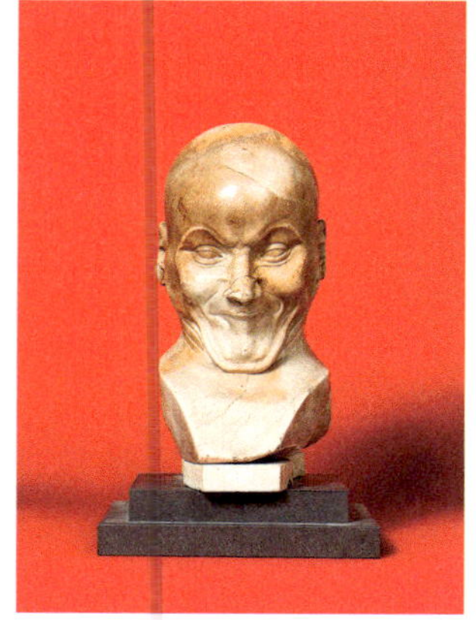

Franz Xaver Messerschmidt
Ein Schalksnarr, 1777/1783
Braun gefleckter Alabaster
37 × 18 × 23 cm

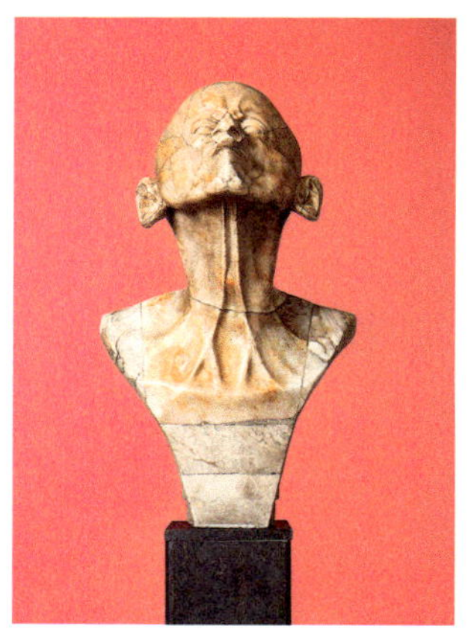

Franz Xaver Messerschmidt
Zweiter Schnabelkopf, 1777/1781
Braun gefleckter Alabaster
42,5 × 26 × 24,5 cm

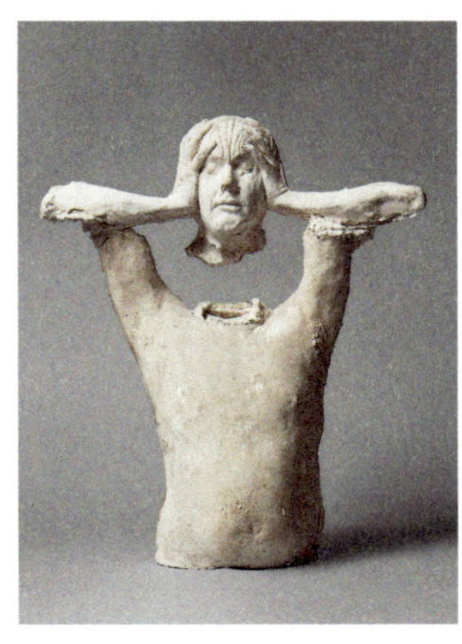

Marc Quinn
The Oneironaut IV (Emotional Detox), 1995
Gips
92 × 81 × 37 cm

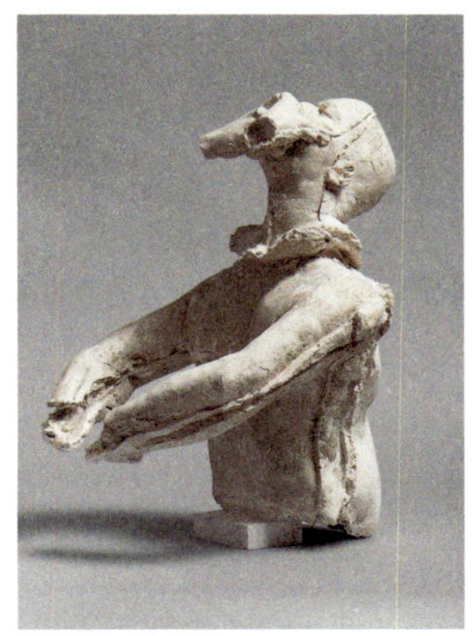

Marc Quinn
The Oneironaut III (Emotional Detox), 1995
Gips
80 × 56 × 64 cm

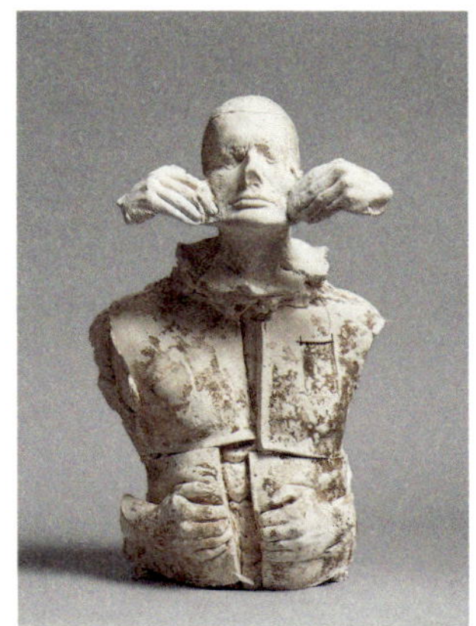

Marc Quinn
The Oneironaut V (Emotional Detox), 1995
Gips
81 × 52 × 39 cm

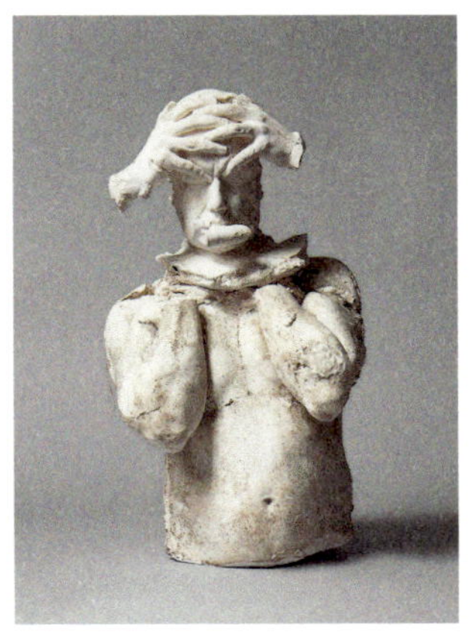

Marc Quinn
The Oneironaut II (Emotional Detox), 1995
Gips
81 × 46 × 35 cm

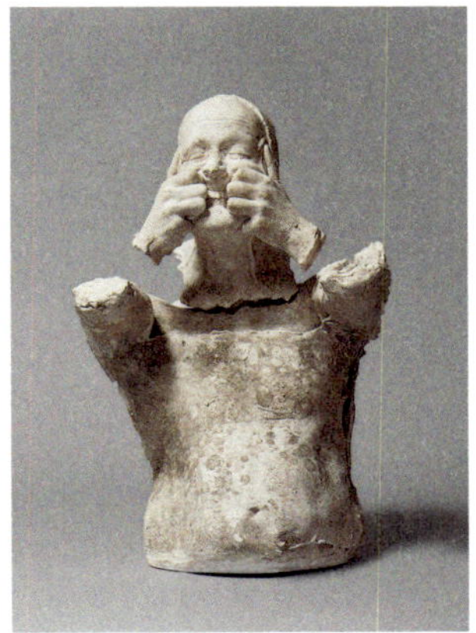

Marc Quinn
The Oneironaut VII (Emotional Detox), 1995
Gips
75 × 52 × 46 cm

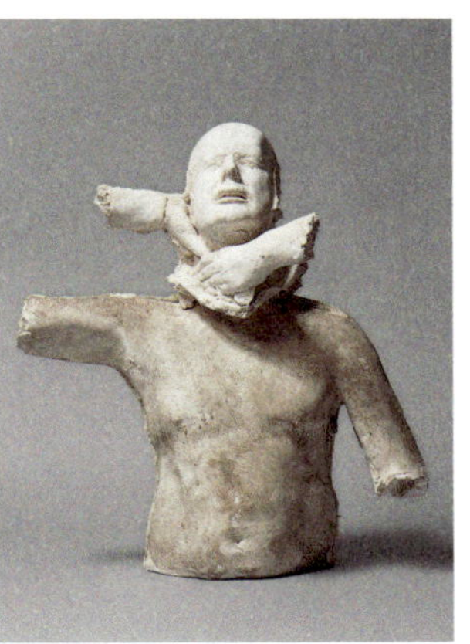

Marc Quinn
The Oneironaut I (Emotional Detox), 1995
Gips
80 × 70 × 34 cm

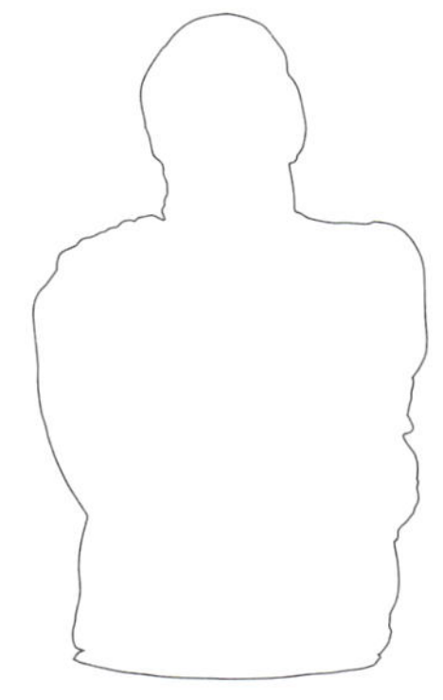

Marc Quinn
Fear of Fear, 1994

Der Originalabguss ist verschollen.

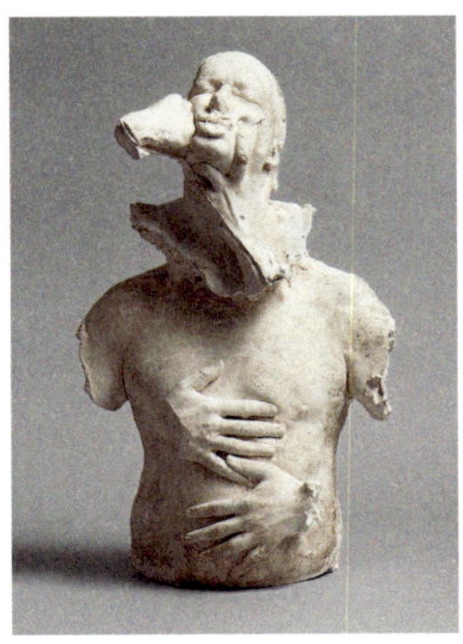

Marc Quinn
The Oneironaut VI (Emotional Detox), 1995
Gips
86 × 51 × 30 cm

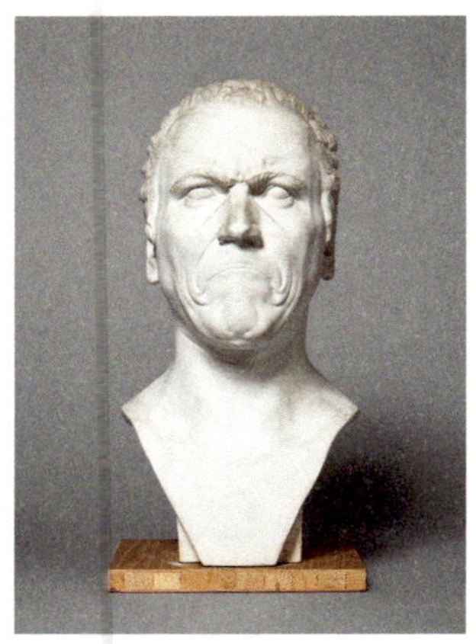

Nach Franz Xaver Messerschmidt
Ein mürrischer alter Soldat, 1964
Gipsabguss
Höhe: 42 cm

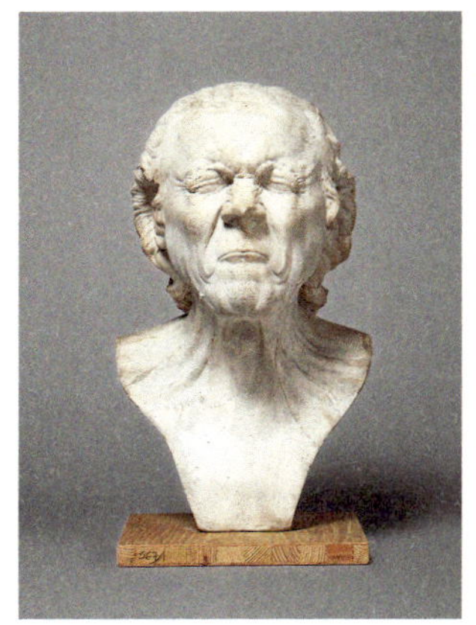

Nach Franz Xaver Messerschmidt
Der Verdrüßliche, vor 1923
Gipsabguss
Höhe: 42 cm

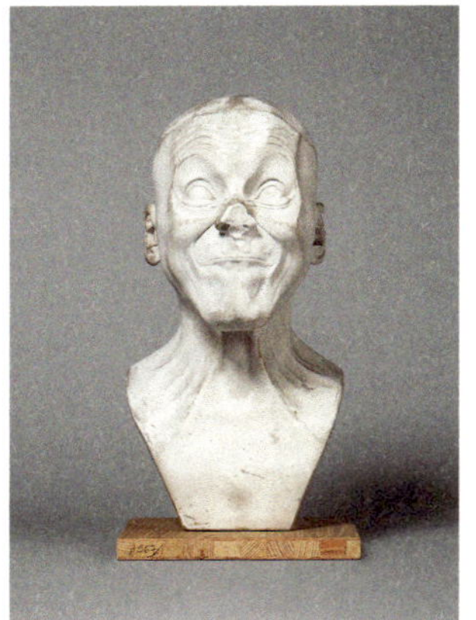

Nach Franz Xaver Messerschmidt
Ein wollüstig abgehärmter Geck, vor 1923
Gipsabguss
Höhe: 42 cm

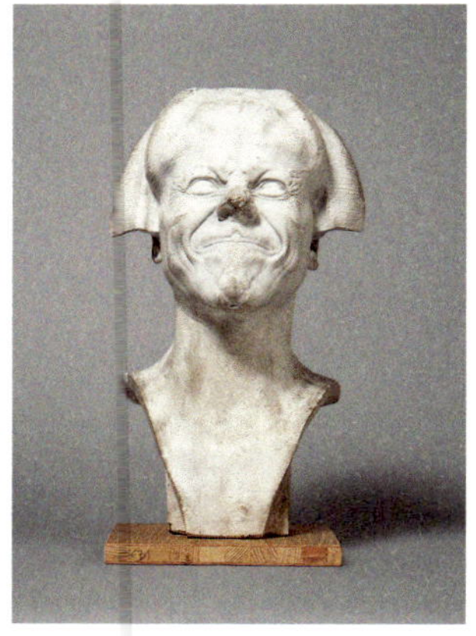

Nach Franz Xaver Messerschmidt
Ein schmerzhaft stark Verwundeter, vor 1923
Gipsabguss
Höhe: 45 cm

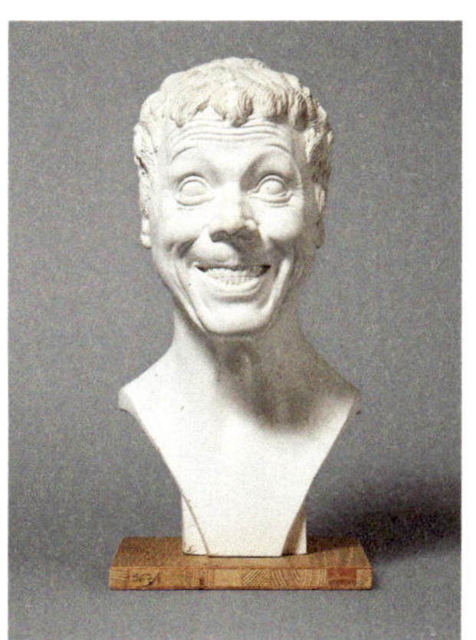

Nach Franz Xaver Messerschmidt
Der erboßte und rachgierige Zigeuner, vor 1923
Gipsabguss
Höhe: 45 cm

Die historischen Titel der „Charakterköpfe" stammen nicht von Franz Xaver Messerschmidt, sondern wurden nachträglich von Franz Friedrich Strunz in seinem Essay *Merkwürdige Lebensgeschichte des Franz Xaver Messerschmidt, k. k. öffentlichen Lehrer der Bildhauerkunst* (Wien 1793) anlässlich einer Ausstellung 1793 eingeführt. Bis heute dienen sie der behelfsmäßigen Betitelung und sind Teil der Provenienz der Werke. Aufgrund der subjektiven und abwertenden Benennung wird im aktuellen Forschungsdiskurs die reine Nummerierung der Arbeiten beabsichtigt.

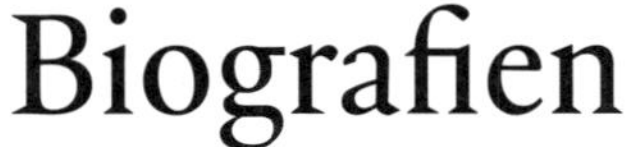

Biografien

Marc Quinn

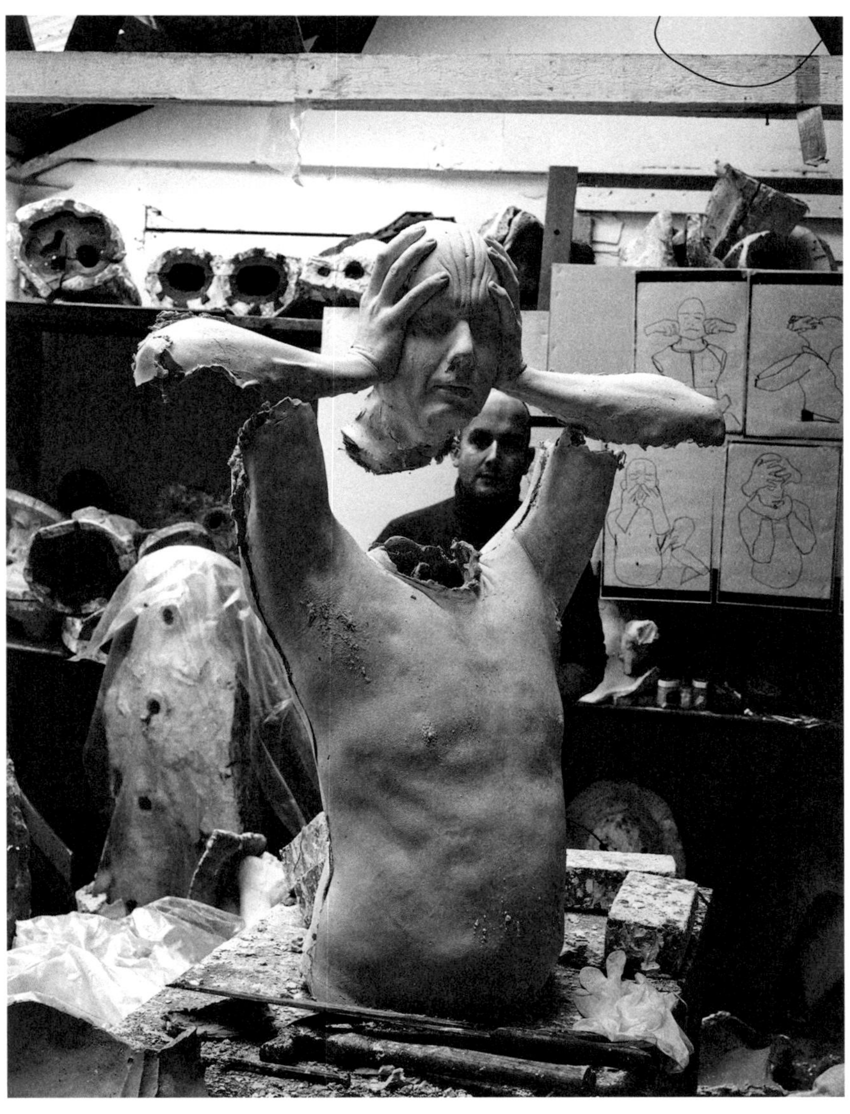

Abb. 1

Marc Quinn, geboren 1964, ist einer der wichtigsten Künstler*innen seiner Generation. Seine Skulpturen, Gemälde und Zeichnungen ergründen, was es heißt, im 21. Jahrhundert Mensch zu sein. Dabei schließt Quinn oft an die Kunstgeschichte von den modernen Meister*innen bis weit zurück in die Antike an. Bekannt wurde Quinn 1991 mit der Skulptur *Self*, einem Selbstporträt als Büste aus seinem gefrorenen Blut. Während sein Frühwerk vorwiegend der Erkundung des eigenen Ichs galt, begann der Künstler bald, sich mit der Darstellung der Erfahrungen anderer zu beschäftigen. Dabei stellte er stets Wertmaßstäbe, Wahrnehmung und gesellschaftliche Bruchlinien zur Diskussion. Von der Kritik mit Aufmerksamkeit bedacht wurden unter anderem *Alison Lapper Pregnant*, ausgestellt 2005 auf dem bekannten vierten Sockel am Londoner Trafalgar Square, *Siren*, eine Skulptur von Kate Moss aus massivem Gold, die im British Museum zeitgleich mit dem

Abb. 1
Marc Quinn im Studio mit *The Oneironaut IV (Emotional Detox)*, 1995

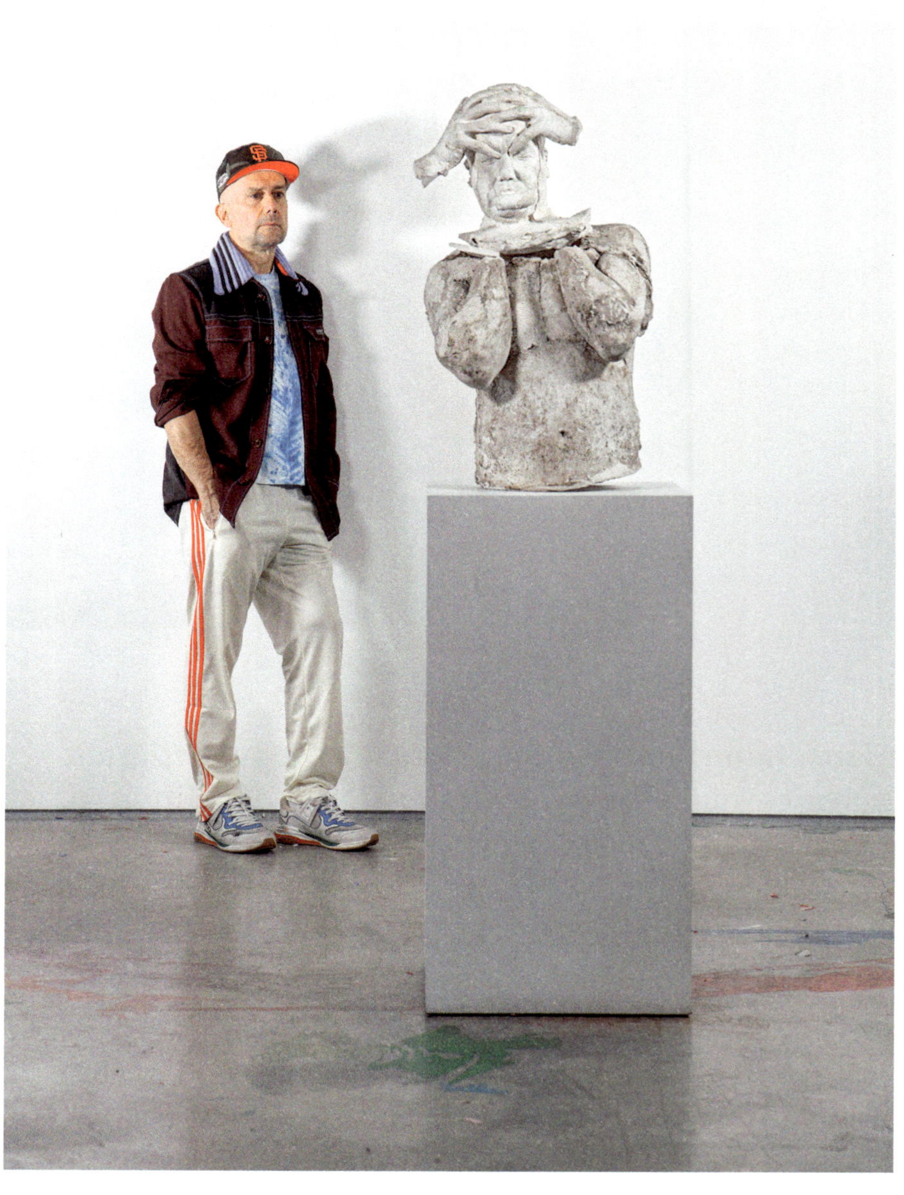

Abb. 2

Abb. 2
Marc Quinn mit *The Oreironaut II (Emotional Detox)*, fotografiert von Adiam Yemane Ende 2021.

Finanzkollaps 2008 gezeigt wurde und Fragen nach Werten und Glaubenssystemen in der Gesellschaft aufwarf, *Breath* (2012), eine monumentale Nachbildung von *Alison Lapper Pregnant*, die für die Eröffnungsfeier der Paralympischen Spiele in London 2012 in Auftrag gegeben wurde, und *Self-Conscious Gene* (2019), eine dreieinhalb Meter hohe Bronzeskulptur des „Zombie-Boy" Rick Genest, die nun permanent im Science Museum in London aufgestellt ist. In den vergangenen zehn Jahren beschäftigte sich Quinn in seiner Kunst mehr und mehr mit Medien, dem Tagesgeschehen und Weltpolitik. Die Serie *History Paintings* (2009–heute) besteht aus hyperrealistischen Ölbildern zu wichtigen Ereignissen der jüngsten Geschichte, deren Sujets Pressefotos entnommen sind. Als sich die Nachrichtenzirkulation im Zuge der COVID-19-Pandemie weiter beschleunigte, schuf Quinn *HISTORYNOW* (2020–heute), eine Gemäldeserie basierend auf iPhone-Bildschirmaufnahmen von News und Instagram-Posts.

Seit 2015 hat Quinn mehrere gemeinnützige Projekte entwickelt, die das Bewusstsein für die anhaltende globale Flüchtlingskrise schärfen und Geldmittel für das International Rescue Committee und andere Flüchtlingsorganisationen sammeln sollen. Dazu gehört auch *100 Heads* (2019–heute), eine Skulpturenserie bestehend aus einhundert Porträtbüsten aus Beton von Flüchtenden heute.

Quinns Werke befinden sich in Sammlungen weltweit, unter anderem in der Tate in London, im Metropolitan Museum of Art in New York, im Solomon R. Guggenheim Museum in New York, im SFMOMA in San Francisco, in der Fondazione Prada in Mailand, im Stedelijk Museum in Amsterdam sowie im Centre Pompidou in Paris.

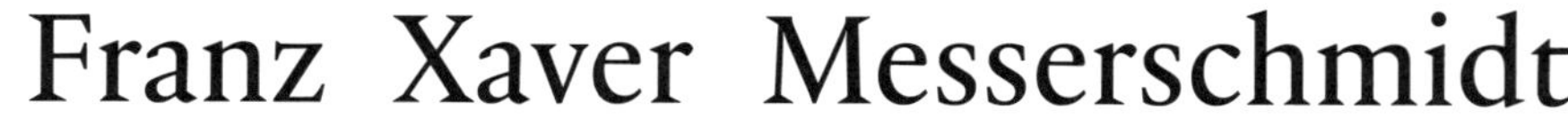
Franz Xaver Messerschmidt

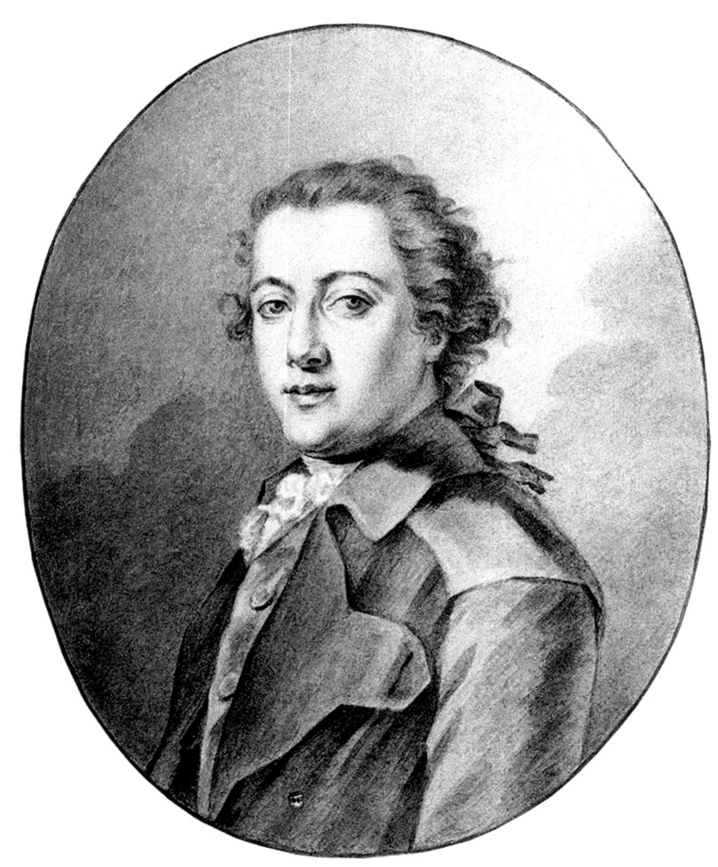

Franz Xaver Messerschmidt wird 1736 im schwäbischen Wiesensteig geboren. Nach dem Tod seines Vaters absolviert er ab 1746 eine Bildhauerlehre bei seinem Onkel Johann Baptist Straub in München. Im Jahr 1752 tritt der junge Messerschmidt als Geselle in die Werkstatt eines weiteren Onkels, Philipp Jakob Straub, in Graz ein. Ab 1755 studiert Franz Xaver Messerschmidt an der Akademie in Wien und wird dort von seinem Mentor, dem Maler Martin van Meytens dem Jüngeren, ab 1759 auch Direktor der Akademie, gefördert. Durch diese Beziehung erhält er seine erste Anstellung als Stuckverschneider im kaiserlichen Zeughaus, während der er Material- und Technikerfahrung sammelt. Ab 1760 wird Messerschmidt von Mitgliedern des Hochadels und vom Kaiserhaus selbst als Bildhauer beauftragt. Die Statuen von Maria Theresia und Franz I. Stephan sind heute in der Sala terrena im Oberen Belvedere ausgestellt. Ab 1770 sind die ersten „Charakterköpfe" nachweisbar. Aus Enttäuschung darüber, dass er als Mitglied der Akademie bei der Professorenwahl 1774 übergangen wird, verlässt Messerschmidt 1775 Wien. Nach Stationen in München und Wiesensteig lässt er sich in Bratislava nieder, wo er bis zu seinem Tod 1783 an den „Charakterköpfen" arbeitet.

Abb. 3
Unbekannter Künstler
Vermutliches Jugendbildnis Franz Xaver Messerschmidts, undatiert
Österreichische Nationalbibliothek, Wien

Marc Quinn
im Gespräch mit
Cat Marnell

CM Ich bin nicht gerade die konzentrierteste Gesprächspartnerin.

MQ Das passt ja vielleicht, wenn es um Kunst und Sucht geht.

CM Und um Messerschmidt?

MQ Seine Köpfe schauen jedenfalls recht intensiv aus.

CM War er das auch selber?

MQ Nun, für mich ist eine der eigentümlichsten Merkmale der Serie die technische Meisterschaft, die man jedem einzelnen der Köpfe ansieht. Deshalb sind sie ja so großartig. Sie sind wild und ausdrucksstark, aber trotzdem technisch perfekt – das geht normalerweise nicht zusammen. Ich denke, Messerschmidt muss, als er sie schuf, zumindest Phasen gehabt haben, in denen er klar im Kopf war, sonst hätte er das nicht geschafft – zum Beispiel wenn er im festen Griff einer Psychose gewesen wäre.

CM Ja. Ich fühle mich in die Zeiten versetzt, in denen ich selber drauf war. Da hab ich dann immer mit Lippenstift rumgeschmiert. [*Lacht.*] Von den Drogen bin ich total durchgeknallt. Plötzlich fand ich mich in einem 24-Stunden-Baumarkt wieder und schlief tagelang nicht. Das war mit das Verrückteste, das man sich vorstellen kann, und es erleichtert mich sehr, dass ich jetzt auf mich selbst aufpassen kann. Eines meiner Lieblingsbücher über die Sucht ist *Narcissus in Wonderland* von Richard B. Ulman und Harry Paul [New York 2006]. Im Wesentlichen werden darin Süchtige mit Fantasie-Junkies verglichen, die – wie Narziss im Spiegel – von sich selbst voll begeistert sind, weil die Sucht (so das Buch) den Narzissmus nachahmt.

MQ Auch Messerschmidt verbrachte viel Zeit vor dem Spiegel, um seine Mimik zu beobachten. Deswegen sind die Skulpturen so lebensecht modelliert. Einer der Aspekte, die mich an deinem Buch am meisten beeindruckt haben, ist, wie sachlich und lebensnah du schreibst. Dein Tonfall ist schonungslos gut gelaunt, aber gleichzeitig passieren viele verrückte Dinge. Das hat mich echt in den Bann gezogen. Wie ist das Buch denn zustande gekommen?

CM Na ja, ich war immer schon in der Publizistikbranche. Angefangen hab ich als Teenager, aber ich wollte immer Redakteurin bei einer Zeitschrift werden. So kam ich zu *Vanity Fair* und zu *Teen Vogue* und *Glamour* und landete schließlich bei *Lucky* – das war so ein Shopping-Magazin. Aber wegen meiner Medikamentensucht riss die Zeitschriftenkarriere ab, und ich begann, für das Internet zu schreiben, was damals – wir sprechen von 2010 – im Journalismus noch verpönt war. Das war mir *so* peinlich. Aber mit den Online-Beiträgen wurde ich viral und bekam dann diesen Buchvertrag. Damals war ich allerdings total krank. Ich war drogensüchtig. Und natürlich konnte ich, so tief in die Sucht abgesunken, nicht schreiben. Es war, als ob ich mit einem Holzbein Marathon laufen wollte. Schließlich begann ich das Buch dann auf Therapie in einem Behandlungszentrum in Thailand zu schreiben – an einem Schreibtisch im Dunkeln mit all diesen Affen rundherum … die brüllten.

MQ [*Lacht.*] Das klingt ja surreal. Ich weiß noch, dass ich glaubte, nicht mehr kreativ sein zu können, wenn ich mit dem Alkohol aufhören würde. Mir schwant, dass viele deswegen weitertrinken. Sie haben Angst, dass das, was sie als den verrückten, kreativen Teil von sich ansehen, abstirbt, sobald sie aufhören. Wie bei dir in Thailand ist aber das Gegenteil richtig! Dann gewinnt man erst die Fähigkeit, auf kontrollierte Weise kreativ zu sein, ohne sich selbst zu zerstören.

CM Wäre ich Malerin oder Bildhauerin – alles *außer* Schriftstellerin –, dann hätte ich mich vielleicht auch mit diesem Argument selbst widerlegt. Aber das Schreiben ist für mich schlicht zu technisch, als dass die Sucht jemals etwas anderes als ein Handicap sein könnte. Schreiben ist so höllisch wirr. Was die Kreativität angeht, so *kann* die dunkle Trance, in die man sich manchmal durch die Sucht versetzt, schon Gold wert sein, aber die Gesundheit – die ist Diamanten wert! Sie macht dich zu einer Athletin! Ich meine, all diese fantastischen Ideen habe ich immer noch – und du natürlich auch –, aber erst jetzt bringen wir sie rüber. Ich jedenfalls würde meinen klaren Kopf gegen nichts mehr eintauschen wollen.

MQ Ja, ohne klaren Kopf ist es ein Albtraum. Da bist du nie in Bestform.

CM Ich versuche gerade, meine Arbeit Trainingsprinzipien unterzuordnen. Hast du schon mal von hochintensivem Intervalltraining gehört? Dabei geht es darum, maximale Wirkung in minimaler Zeit zu erzielen. Man strafft den Zeitplan, macht keine Pausen, und – schwupp – ist es *erledigt*. So schreibe ich jetzt am liebsten: streng, geordnet, so früh am Morgen wie möglich.

MQ Also bist du jetzt süchtig nach Arbeit und Training?

CM Weißt du, dass es noch besser geht? Ich komm jetzt zur *Reinigung*.

MQ [*Lacht.*] Es ist schon erstaunlich, dass wir so kreativ damit umgehen können, oder? Wir haben beide wirklich Glück, dass wir das hinkriegen.

CM Das ist das große Privileg meines Lebens. Man muss seine ganze Suchtenergie irgendwo umsetzen, denn verschwinden wird sie ja nie. Weißt du, dass Trainer*innen sehr gerne mit Ex-Süchtigen arbeiten? Da gibt es so einen berühmten Trainer in Hollywood, der sagt immer: „Engagiert ehemalige Alkis, weil die sind immer pünktlich." Ja, es ist ein Traum, so weit gekommen zu sein. Ich meine, ist es nicht großartig für dich, dass deine Ausstellung in einem Schloss stattfindet? Ich weiß schon, dass das in Europa normal ist, aber es ist ja trotzdem fabelhaft.

MQ Es ist schon ein bisschen surreal. Ich konnte die Skulpturen von *Emotional Detox* sehr lange nicht einmal anschauen. Sie haben mich zu stark an diese Phase in meinem Leben erinnert. Ich hab sie damals gemacht und mich dann weiterentwickelt.

CM Noch einmal: Es ist schon erstaunlich, wie reinigend kreative Arbeit wirken kann. Für mich persönlich ist alles, was ich schreibe, erledigt, sobald es geschrieben ist.

MQ Das ist für Kunstschaffende ein ganz wesentlicher Aspekt der Anziehungskraft von Kunst. Eine Theorie besagt übrigens, dass Messerschmidt mit den Köpfen böse Geister verscheuchen wollte, die ihn in der Nacht verfolgten.

CM Das ist ja witzig, wenn ich an meine nächtlichen Erinnerungen an Österreich denke. Warst du schon einmal im Vergnügungspark im Wiener Prater? Ich schwöre dir, das ist, als würdest du in einem menschlichen Gehirn herumspazieren. Da gibt es riesige Clownmünder, ein Spukhaus, Drachen, Schlangen. Als ich dort herumlief, hab ich mich gefragt: „Was zum Teufel ist denn das?“ Ich steh ja eigentlich total auf Karneval. Ich hatte immer den Eindruck, dass mein Gehirn tagsüber so flach und uninteressant war, wie untertags die Attraktionen im Vergnügungspark sind. Da sehen sie nach gar nichts aus. Aber sobald es dunkel wird, gehen alle Lichter an. Mein ganzes Leben lang war ich von solchen Orten angezogen. Erst jetzt merke ich, dass die guten Sachen ganz in der Früh passieren. Den jungen Menschen, die unser Gespräch lesen, sage ich so wasnur ungern.

MQ Du zerstörst alle ihre Illusionen. Ich stehe jetzt früh auf und mache Sport, was ich nie für möglich gehalten hätte. Aber ich fühle mich nicht mehr gut, wenn ich's nicht mache.

CM So wie Gwen Stefani einmal gesagt hat: „Ich denke gar nicht daran, es nicht zu tun.“ Die besten Ideen hab ich jetzt immer beim Laufen.

MQ Ja, jede Art von Bewegung löst auch bei mir Gedankenblockaden. Ich finde, dass beim Sport etwas in meinem Kopf passiert. Erst da merke ich, wie ich das, was ich denke, auch ausdrücken kann.

CM Hast du vom Dichter John Berryman gehört? Er gewann den Pulitzer-Preis für *The Dream Songs* und sprang dann irgendwann von einer Brücke – er war ein krasser Alkoholiker. Als ich deine Skulpturen sah, fiel mir jedenfalls als Erstes sein Buch ein. Bei deinen Arbeiten wird mir ziemlich ungut zumute. Auch Berrymans Gedichte sind so verworren und düster. Immer wenn ich betrunken nach Hause kam, nahm ich sie aus dem Regal und verstand alles. Aber als ich sie dann nüchtern las, fragte ich mich: „Was ist denn das?" Die sind so surreal – und hässlich zugleich. Der Autor ist einfach sehr, sehr krank, und die Texte kommen aus seinem Unbewussten. Hast du dich letztlich dann wegen der Sucht behandeln lassen?

MQ Ja. Eines Tages, nachdem ich mit meiner Freundin aus einem Frankreichurlaub zurückgekommen war, der nicht so gut gelaufen war, wachte ich auf und fand mich inmitten von Flaschen in so einer Art besetztem Haus wieder, in dem ich damals wohnte. Da schnappte ich eine Zeitschrift und blätterte darin herum, bis ich eine Liste mit dem Titel „Londons Top Doctors" fand. Und da stand auch der Arzt drin, bei dem ich schon zur Blutabnahme für meine Blutskulptur *Self* gewesen war. Ich las, dass er auf Suchtkrankheiten spezialisiert war. Da machte es plötzlich klick, ich nahm den Hörer in die Hand und fragte ihn: „Kann ich zu Ihnen kommen?" Und er antwortete: „Oh, ich habe mich schon gefragt, wann Sie endlich auftauchen, um mit mir darüber zu reden." Er besorgte mir einen Platz in einer Reha-Klinik, und ich ging noch am selben Tag hin. Ich beschloss ziemlich schnell, dass ich mich therapieren lassen wollte. Warum, weiß ich nicht – nachdem ich doch vorher so unfähig gewesen war aufzuhören.

CM Wie alt warst du da?

MQ Dreißig. Danach konnte ich etwa anderthalb Jahre lang nicht arbeiten, und dann begann ich mit diesen Skulpturen, die ich mir erst jetzt wieder ansehen kann.

CM Ich verstehe gut, warum du sie nicht ansehen wolltest. Weißt du, ich reiße gerne Seiten aus Zeitungen, und sogar die Fotos und Porträts, die ich um mich herum aufhänge, sind heute andere als früher. Je älter ich werde, desto mehr will ich nur noch gesunde Menschen um mich sehen – und keine Marilyn Monroe mehr. Das läuft nicht bewusst ab, aber man weicht dem kranken Zeug aus.

MQ Andererseits ist es meiner Meinung nach definitiv auch hilfreich, dass man während der Behandlung andere Kranke kennenlernt. Das Leben als Süchtiger ist ja recht einsam. Man redet sich ein, einzigartig zu sein und dass noch nie jemand so etwas erlebt hat, und dort muss man dann einsehen: „Oh Gott, das ist ja ganz normal, gar keine große Sache!" Und es entspannt schon, dass es andere gibt, die dasselbe durchmachen. Was an den Gruppentherapiesitzungen wirkte, war, wie schnell sie das Fantasieren stoppten. Du gehst da hin und redest dir ein, dass die Sauferei eigentlich gar nicht so schlimm war – da war doch dieser eine tolle Abend da und so weiter. Und dann erzählt jemand, wie es *wirklich* war gestern – und schon verflüchtigt sich deine Fantasie. Menschen fantasieren ja so gern. Sie scheuen schon zurück, eine Konfrontation mit der Realität überhaupt nur zu *riskieren*. Denk an die Titel der „Charakterköpfe". Nach Messerschmidts Tod kaufte sie ein Schausteller und gab ihnen so lachhafte Titel wie *Ein naseweiser spitzfindiger Spötter* oder *Die Einfalt im höchsten Grade*. Und diese Titel gelten heute *immer noch*. Das ist witzig, denn ohne Titel sind sie ja gerade deswegen so wirkungsvoll und verstörend, weil sie namenlose Gefühle darstellen. Man muss sie nachfühlen, was eben schwierig ist. Fast scheint es so, als würden sie die Leute erst wegen dieser doofen Titel akzeptieren können. Die Titel zähmen sie. Dieser Kontrast hat auch etwas mit deinem Buch *How to Murder Your Life* [New York 2017] zu tun, in dem Inhalt und Tonfall gegeneinander arbeiten. Es ist *schrecklich*, aber auch *wirklich witzig*.

CM Genau. Ich wollte tatsächlich, dass meine Ich-Erzählerin irgendwie … „frech" klingt.

MQ Frech in der Hölle, ja. Dieses Unheimliche macht den Reiz deines Buches aus, finde ich. Es ist wie eine ganz extreme Form der Neigung, alles, was einem wirklich zustößt, hinter einer seltsamen Schicht von ... Frechheit zu verbergen.

CM Danke, das freut mich, denn das war ja definitiv eine bewusste Entscheidung. Ich wollte, dass sich das Buch leicht wie Popmusik liest, nicht so wie *Heroin* von The Velvet Underground zum Beispiel, das ja typisch für dieses Thema ist. Wenn man als Frau über sich selbst schreibt, dann, habe ich festgestellt, werten die Leute manchmal die Schreibtechnik wie alle Entscheidungen, die man bewusst trifft, ein wenig ab. Sie sagen dann, das Buch sei einfach „bekenntnishaft". Und ja, ich verwende autobiografisches Material. Aber ich habe jeden einzelnen Taktschlag auf jeder einzelnen Seite konstruiert! So hat jedes Kapitel im Buch zum Beispiel die gleiche Wortanzahl, nämlich 4.400 Wörter.

MQ Ich glaube, dein Buch wird bleiben. Ich glaube, in der Kunst ist es die Authentizität, die überdauert. Vielleicht ist das auch der Grund, warum wir immer noch über Messerschmidt sprechen. Es spielt keine Rolle, was die Zeitgenoss*innen denken, denn wenn sich etwas aus der Realität speist, dann hat es noch Jahrhunderte vor sich. Die Menschen werden auch in tausend Jahren noch dieselben Probleme haben wie wir – das Gehirn des Menschen wird sich nicht verändern. Daher bleiben all diese Kunstwerke über menschliche Stärken und Schwächen – im Guten wie im Schlechten – für immer relevant.

Gesichter machen
Tim Smith-Laing

„Wenn die Seele unruhig ist, wird das menschliche Gesicht zum Tableau vivant, auf dem sich die Leidenschaften mit ebenso viel Feinheit wie Energie abzeichnen, wo jede Bewegtheit der Seele durch ein Merkmal, jede Handlung durch einen hervorstechenden Zug ausgedrückt wird, dessen lebhafter, flüchtiger Eindruck dem Willen zuvorkommt, uns verrät und in unserem Äußeren, durch Anzeichen der Empfindung, die Bilder unserer geheimsten Regungen wiedergibt.“

– Comte de Buffon, *Histoire naturelle, générale et particulière*[1]

„Kein Wissen gibts / Der Seele Bildung im Gesicht zu lesen.“

– Duncan in Shakespeares *Macbeth*[2]

Emotional Detox zeigt uns, wie Marc Quinns Körper wieder und wieder unter dem Zugriff seiner eigenen Hände leidet. Diese können frei agieren, um sich ihm zu widersetzen, sie können ihn stoßen, schlagen, würgen, und sie können sich sogar vervielfachen, um mehrere Aufgaben gleichzeitig zu erledigen. In Nummer VI hält eine Hand den Kopf fest, während die andere ihn schlägt; in Nummer V ziehen zwei Hände an den Wangen, als ob sie das Gesicht öffnen wollten, und weiter unten reißen zwei andere säuberlich den Bauch auf. Es wird schreckliche Gewalt angetan. Doch das Gesicht, das bei all dem im Mittelpunkt steht, bleibt seltsam ruhig. Quinns Kopf, der buchstäblich losgelöst auf dem Körper balanciert, erträgt seine Strafen mit merkwürdiger Fassung. Die Augen sind in der gesamten Serie geschlossen, aber nicht in Angst oder Agonie zusammengepresst. Skulptur Nummer I kommt der Sichtbarkeit von Schmerz am nächsten: mit einem Stirnrunzeln, einem lautlosen Keuchen unter dem fester werdenden Würgegriff. Ansonsten könnte man die Gesichtsausdrücke – soweit man sie unter den Behandlungen, die sie erfahren, erkennt – als duldsam bezeichnen. Vielleicht hat man sich darauf geeinigt, dass die bei dieser Handarbeit verübte Gewalt kein Selbstzweck ist. Hier, in Nummer VI, streichelt ein Paar Hände den Torso wie zur Besänftigung. In Nummer IV scheint es sogar, als sei durch ihre Fürsorge eine gewisse Linderung

1
„Lorsque l'ame [sic] est agitée, la face humaine devient un tableau vivant où les passions sont rendues avec autant de délicatesse que d'énergie, où chaque mouvement de l'âme est exprimé par un trait, chaque action par un charactère dont l'impression vive & prompte devance la volonté, nous décèle & rend au dehors, par des signes pathétiques, les images de nos plus secrettes [sic] agitations." Georges-Louis Leclerc, Comte de Buffon, *Histoire naturelle, générale et particulière, Tome second*, Paris 1749, S. 519.

2
William Shakespeare, *Macbeth*, 1. Akt, 4. Szene, Verse 11–12. Übersetzung von Dorothea Tieck.

eingetreten. Schließlich ruht der nun ganz vom Körper losgelöste Kopf zwischen den Händen, die ihn hochhalten und wiegen. Oder so ähnlich.

Oder so ähnlich, weil es beim Gesichtsausdruck und seiner Deutung auf so vieles ankommt. *Emotional Detox* bietet eine Reihe von Interpretationswegen, die man beschreiten und auf denen man Bedeutungen sammeln kann, doch diese Wege sind so zahlreich, dass sie zu einem Labyrinth werden. Da ist der angebotene Schlüssel des Titels: *Detox*, ein anderes Wort für Katharsis; doch die Reihe endet nicht mit dem Gleichgewicht von Nummer IV, sondern mit den gewaltsam auseinandergezogenen Lippen und den entblößten Zähnen von Nummer VII. Sieht so Läuterung aus oder geht dieser Vorgang endlos weiter? Da ist die biografische Information: Quinns früherer Alkoholismus; aber das allein ist zu dürftig, um zu beschreiben, was vor sich geht. Da sind die Kunstgeschichte und die Inspiration: Franz Xaver Messerschmidts „Charakterköpfe"; doch Quinns Reaktion auf sie ist mindestens ebenso nebensächlich wie unmittelbar. Da ist das bedeutsame Material: Blei, mit seiner Giftigkeit, seiner alchemistischen Symbolik, seiner Formbarkeit, seinem geringen Wert und seinem Potenzial ... Da sind die Anliegen, die sich durch Quinns gesamte Laufbahn hindurchziehen: die Identität und das Selbst, das Körper-Geist-Problem, die Veränderung ... Wir wissen, dass all dies im Spiel ist; alles beeinflusst unsere Deutung und unsere Reaktion. Nichts davon hilft uns, innezuhalten. Wenn es einen Punkt gibt, an dem die Zuschreibung von Bedeutungen zum Stillstand kommen könnte, muss es das Gesicht sein.

Die Frage, wie man ein Gesicht deuten soll, ist allerdings strittig, und das gilt nicht nur für *Emotional Detox*. Diese Frage verbindet Quinn sogar enger mit Messerschmidt als die unmittelbare Inspiration. Bei *Emotional Detox* stoßen unsere Versuche, zu verstehen, was mit der Figur – also gewissermaßen mit der Person *im* Körper – geschieht, auf etwas, das man als Ausdrucksarmut bezeichnen könnte. Wir verspüren einen gewissen Abstand zum schwebenden Lächeln von *Self* (1991) und eine noch größere Distanz zur ekstatischen Verrenkung von *Blind Leading the Blind* (1995). In den Gesichtern von *Emotional Detox* findet sich eine Art Minimierung des Ausdrucks: Es entsteht kein prägnanter *Gesichtsausdruck*, dem wir eine Bedeutung zuschreiben könnten. Bei Messerschmidts Werk steht man vor dem gleichen Problem, wenn auch unter umgekehrten Vorzeichen: einem Übermaß an Ausdruck. Die sogenannten „Charakterköpfe" bieten nichts als *Gesichtsausdrücke*. Aber was für welche! In der Serie der Köpfe verzerrt sich das menschliche Gesicht in einer Unzahl abstruser Gestaltungen: Von den zusammengepressten Lidern gehen tiefe Falten aus; hochgezogene Brauen zerfurchen die Stirn; Wangen und Kinne bilden Grübchen, dehnen und wellen sich zu straff gespannten Symmetrien. Die Skulpturen selbst bieten nur einen einzigen Anhaltspunkt, das Gesicht, das aller anderen Teile des Körpers beraubt ist; doch die Bedeutung des einzelnen Gesichts und der gesamten Serie entzieht sich uns.

Dieses Sichentziehen ist entscheidend, denn ebenso wie bei *Emotional Detox* haben wir das Gefühl, uns in der Anwesenheit einer oder mehrerer Personen zu befinden. Auf den ersten Blick sind die „Charakterköpfe" realistische, ja sogar hyperrealistische Skulpturen; wenn man von dem speziellen Anblick der „Schnabelköpfe" einmal absieht, versuchen wir ganz selbstverständlich, intuitiv die Geisteszustände zu erahnen, in denen sie sich scheinbar befinden. Dieser Versuch ist jedoch zum Scheitern verurteilt. Daher die bemühten Titel, mit denen die Köpfe von ihrem ersten Katalogisierer und Aussteller überfrachtet wurden.[3] Die Oberflächlichkeit von narrativen Bezeichnungen wie *Ein aus dem Wasser Geretteter* oder *Der unfähige Fagottist* oder von moralisierenden Beschreibungen wie *Ein absichtlicher Schalksnarr* oder *Ein Heuchler und Verleumder* deutet vor allem auf die Weigerung der Köpfe hin, sich interpretieren zu lassen.[4] Selbst ein vermeintlich einfacher Fall wie *Der Gähner* stellt uns vor Probleme. Könnte dieses Gähnen, in Anbetracht der Stummheit der Skulptur, nicht auch ein Schrei sein?[5]

Das Interesse an Messerschmidts eigenem Leben, das seine Köpfe weckten, hat in den zweieinhalb Jahrhunderten seit ihrer Entstehung stetig zugenommen. Die berühmte zeitgenössische Schilderung von Friedrich Nicolai, der Messerschmidt als einen buchstäblich von Geistern verfolgten Einsiedler darstellt, der an seinen Köpfen arbeitet, um mit ihnen den „Geist der Proportion" abzuwehren, liest sich noch heute faszinierend.[6] Mehr oder

3 Siehe *Merkwürdige Lebensgeschichte des Franz Xaver Messerschmidt, k. k. öffentlichen Lehrer der Bildhauerkunst*, Wien 1794. Als Verfasser wurde vor einigen Jahren Franz Friedrich Strunz identifiziert. Siehe Anna Schirlbauer, „Die Charakterköpfe F. X. Messerschmidts und ihr erster Aussteller Franz Strunz", in: *Ars*, 46. Jg., Nr. 2, 2013, S. 292–308.

4 In dieser Reihenfolge: Privatsammlung, Belgien; Sammlung Gerolamo und Roberta Etro; Belvedere, Wien, Inv.-Nr. 2284; Metropolitan Museum of Art, New York, Inv.-Nr. 2010.24.

5 Szépművészeti Múzeum, Budapest, Inv.-Nr. 53.655.

6 Friedrich Nicolai, *Beschreibung einer Reise durch Deutschland und die Schweiz, im Jahre 1781*, Bd. 6, Berlin/Stettin 1785, S. 401–420, hier S. 412.

weniger übergriffige Retrodiagnosen haben Messerschmidt wahlweise als schizophren, analfixiert oder an Dystonie leidend beschrieben.[7] Eine wachsende Zahl moderner Forschungsarbeiten verortet ihn zurückhaltender in seiner Zeit, etwa im Kontext der Intrigen und der Politik des Wiener Hofs und der Kunstakademien oder in den proto- und pseudowissenschaftlichen Strömungen, die das Europa der Aufklärung und Wien prägten.[8] Neben kunsthistorischen Parallelen bieten die Physiognomik, der Spiritismus und der Hermetismus des 18. Jahrhunderts mögliche Deutungsansätze. Die Zahlenmystik drängt sich auf. Die Beziehung des Bildhauers zu Franz Anton Mesmer, dem charismatischen Heiler und Erfinder des „animalischen Magnetismus", übt eine besondere Anziehungskraft aus.[9] Doch weder Spekulationen noch die Archäologie führen letztlich zu Erklärungen. Wie Michael Yonan bemerkt, bleiben Messerschmidts Köpfe trotz aller Anstrengungen, ihre Bedeutung zu erfassen, „semantisch schwer greifbar".[10] Sie entziehen sich uns, selbst wenn wir vor ihnen stehen.

Wenn man jedoch vor *Emotional Detox* steht, kann man dieses Sichentziehen als konkretes Beispiel für ein generelles Problem betrachten, das man als „Wissensproblem" des Gesichts bezeichnen könnte. Einerseits stellen Gesichter in zwischenmenschlichen Beziehungen einen besonderen Punkt der Gewissheit dar: Sie sind entscheidend für unsere Identität in der Welt der Sehenden, der Fixpunkt unseres sozialen Selbst. Zwar gibt es andere Optionen – wir können einen geliebten Menschen an der Stimme, am Gang oder am Geruch erkennen –, doch diese Möglichkeiten sind vager und intimer. Das Gesicht bietet Gewissheit und ist für alle Welt erkennbar. Aus diesem Grund dominiert in Ausweisen – zwölf Jahrzehnte seit der Verwendung von Fingerabdrücken und vier Jahrzehnte seit dem Einsatz von DNA-Analysen und Retina-Scans – immer noch das Passfoto. Quinn hat all diese anderen Formen des Selbstporträts verwendet, doch nur *Self* besaß in allen fortlaufenden Wiederholungen die Fähigkeit, mit der veränderlichen Kontinuität seiner Identität in der Welt Schritt zu halten. Wir sehen und wissen, und wir vertrauen diesem Instrument des Wissens so sehr, dass wir in den letzten Jahren – wenn auch unvollkommen und mit enormem technischem Aufwand – sogar unsere Smartphones und Computer trainiert haben, dasselbe zu tun.

7 Begründer dieser bis heute bestehenden Tendenz war der Psychoanalytiker und Kunsthistoriker Ernst Kris. Siehe Ernst Kris, „Die Charakterköpfe des Franz Xaver Messerschmidt: Versuch einer historischen und psychologischen Deutung", in: *Jahrbuch der kunsthistorischen Sammlungen in Wien*, N. F., Bd. 6, 1932, S. 169–228; wiederveröffentlicht als „A Psychotic Sculptor of the Eighteenth Century", in: ders., *Psychanalytic Explorations in Art*, New York 1952, S. 128–150. Zur Dystonie siehe Michal Maršálek, „Dystonia in Art: The Impact of Psychiatric and Neurological Disease on the Work of the Sculptor F. X. Messerschmidt", in: Petr Kanovsky / Kallash P. Bhatia / Raymond Rosales (Hg.), *Dystonia and Dystonic Syndromes*, Wien 2015, S. 227–244.

8 Siehe etwa Maria Pötzl-Malikova, *Franz Xaver Messerschmidt*, Wien 1982.– Miriam Szőcs, „Intrigue or Insanity? The Case of Franz Xaver Messerschmidt", in: *Sculpture Journal*, Bd. 20, Nr. 1, 2011, S. 55–70.

9 Siehe Michael Yonan, *Messerschmidt's Character Heads: Maddening Sculpture and the Writing of Art History*, London 2017, Kap. 3, S. 196–262.

10 Yonan 2017 (wie Anm. 9), S. 26.

Darüber hinaus gibt es die Offenheit von Gesichtern als Verbindungswegen. Das Gesicht ist der Punkt, an dem sich das innere und das äußere Selbst am nächsten kommen; im Gesicht tritt das, was im Kopf vor sich geht, dank der Zeichenträger unserer Gesichtsmuskeln nach außen. Die tote Metapher *expression* (Ausdruck) bringt diese These auf den Punkt. Sie hatte im Englischen zuerst die Doppelbedeutung von „auspressen" und „sprachlich formulieren". Ab der Mitte des 18. Jahrhunderts stand *expression* auch für den Gesichtsausdruck; dies beruhte auf der Erkenntnis, dass er Bedeutungen von innen nach außen transportiert.[11] An den entgegengesetzten Enden der Skala, wenn Gesichtsausdrücke aufhören, Bedeutungen zu vermitteln, sind sie keine *Ausdrücke* mehr: Dann deuten sie auf ein gewisses Defizit des inneren Erlebens hin. Ausdruckslosigkeit heißt in der Sprache der modernen Medizin, an *Affektschwäche* zu leiden: Man wird von der Welt nicht mehr bewegt. Über den Ausdruck hinauszugehen bedeutet, *ein Gesicht zu machen* oder *Grimassen zu schneiden*: eine Entsprechung zum sinnlosen Stammeln. Zwischen diesen beiden Extremen erzeugen unsere Gesichter Bedeutungen.

Bedeutungen sind nützlich, wenn man sie – etwa mit einem Lächeln oder einem stechenden Blick – gezielt einzusetzen vermag. Doch als Wissensform sind Gesichtszüge noch interessanter, wenn sie außer Kontrolle geraten. Unkontrollierte Gesichtsausdrücke zeigen, wie der Comte de Buffon, ein Gelehrter des 18. Jahrhunderts, formulierte, „unsere geheimsten Regungen" – jene tiefsten Gefühle, die man eigentlich vor den Blicken anderer schützen will. Ein Wissen, das ansonsten unzugänglich ist. Gesichtsausdrücke eröffnen auch eine Möglichkeit für das, was Buffon und Messerschmidts Zeitgenosse Johann Caspar Lavater als *Physiognomik*[12] bezeichneten: der Versuch, an den Gesichtszügen die Leidenschaften der Seele abzulesen.[13] Die Physiognomik verspricht ungehinderte Blicke auf Wahrheiten, die andere vielleicht lieber verbergen möchten.

Doch genau hier liegt das Problem. Gerade weil Gesichter ein bestimmtes Wissen enthalten können, sind sie nicht vertrauenswürdig. Unser Verständnis für sie könnte getrübt sein, oder es könnte, was noch bedeutsamer ist, manipuliert werden. Der Gesichtsausdruck entzieht sich nicht *vollständig* der Kontrolle.

11
Siehe *Oxford English Dictionary* (OED), *expression*, I.1.a: „The action of pressing or squeezing out" (earliest citation 1594); II.4.a: „Manner or means of representation in language" (earliest citation 1628); and II.5.a: „Of the countenance, voice, or (occasionally) attitude, etc.: Capacity or fact of expressing feeling or character; expressive quality" (earliest citation 1774); (*expression*, I.1.a: „Die Handlung, etwas auszupressen oder auszuquetschen" [frühester Textbeleg 1594]; II.4.a: „Art oder Mittel der sprachlichen Darstellung" [frühester Textbeleg 1628]; und II.5.a: „Über die Mimik, Stimme oder [gelegentlich] Haltung usw.: Fähigkeit oder Tatsache des Ausdrucks von Gefühl oder Charakter; Ausdrucksqualität" [frühester Textbeleg 1774]).

12
Siehe dazu Maria Pötzl-Malikova, *Franz Xaver Messerschmidt 1736–1783. Monografie und Werkverzeichnis*, Wien 2015, S. 119f.: „Die Köpfe sind nicht so beschaffen, dass sich [Franz Friedrich] Strunz bei der Erfindung ihrer Namen leicht getan hätte. Seine Abhängigkeit von Johann Caspar Lavater ist zwar offenkundig, dessen Lehre der Physiognomie konnte er jedoch nicht konkret anwenden, da bei der Interpretation der Werke nicht die individuellen Merkmale des Schädelbaues wesentlich waren, sondern die veränderliche Mimik. Sie entsprächen damit eher der Pathognomik Georg Christoph Lichtenbergs, die für Strunz allerdings kein Leitfaden gewesen sein dürfte."

13
Johann Caspar Lavater, *Physiognomische Fragmente zur Beförderung der Menschenkenntnis und Menschenliebe*, 4 Bde., Leipzig/Winterthur 1775–78.

14 William Shakespeare, *Hamlet*, 1. Akt, 5. Szene. Übersetzung von August Wilhelm Schlegel.

Und wer seine Gesichtszüge bewusst kontrollieren kann, verfügt über einen unlauteren Vorteil. König Duncan in *Macbeth*, der gerade von einem Menschen verraten wurde und bald von einem anderen ermordet werden wird, ist bei Weitem nicht die einzige Shakespeare'sche Figur, die beklagt, dass es kein verlässliches „Wissen [gibt], der Seele Bildung im Gesicht zu lesen". Als guter Schüler, der er ist, nimmt Hamlet sogar seine „Schreibtafel", um aufzuschreiben, dass „einer lächeln kann und immer lächeln / Und doch ein Schurke sein".[14] Alle Formen von Kommunikation bieten die Möglichkeit zur Täuschung; das Gesicht ist insofern einzigartig, als es zugleich das Versprechen enthält, eine Täuschung durchschauen zu können.

In der Kunst besteht keine dringende Notwendigkeit, die Unwahrheit in gleicher Weise zu durchschauen. Selbst wenn man sagen könnte, dass man getäuscht wird, so wird man doch nicht gleich verraten. Und trotzdem treibt uns die Frage nach dem Gesicht um: In den stummen Welten der Malerei und der Skulptur gibt es nur wenige andere Anhaltspunkte. Wo ein expressives Gesicht auftaucht, fesselt es unsere Aufmerksamkeit wie kaum etwas anderes, und zwar umso mehr, wenn das, was *wie ein Ausdruck* aussieht, sich weigert, seine Geheimnisse preiszugeben. Wenn man *Emotional Detox* und die „Charakterköpfe" einander gegenüberstellt, wirken sie nicht zuletzt wie gegensätzliche Experimente mit dieser gefesselten Aufmerksamkeit. In der Serie *Emotional Detox* scheint Quinns Gesicht knapp oberhalb der Schwelle zur Ausdruckslosigkeit zu verharren: Es drückt etwas aus, flüstert jedoch so leise, dass man die Worte nicht versteht. In der Serie der „Charakterköpfe" verharrt das menschliche Gesicht knapp unterhalb der Schwelle, *Grimassen zu schneiden*: Wie eine Vielzahl erhobener Stimmen drücken sich die „Charakterköpfe" so laut und eindringlich aus, dass man ihre Botschaften nicht versteht. Beide lassen uns immer wieder nähertreten, in der Hoffnung, es vielleicht doch zu können.

Der Ausdruck des Wahnsinns
Lou Stoppard

„Äußerlich lebte er wie der gemeine Mensch, und war auch so gekleidet", schrieb der deutsche Schriftsteller der Aufklärung und Buchhändler Friedrich Nicolai über den österreichischen Bildhauer Franz Xaver Messerschmidt, den er im Juni 1781 besucht hatte.[1] In dem Bericht über den Künstler schimmern Idealvorstellungen und Erwartungen durch. Wer oder was ist denn der gemeine, gewöhnliche Mensch? Wie lebt – oder verrichtet – man denn ein normales Leben? Kommt es darauf an, was man isst, anzieht, kauft und konsumiert? Kann man gewöhnlich sein und zugleich Kunst machen? Normal sein und zugleich wahnsinnig? Normal sein und trotzdem hin und wieder aus dem Alltag in eine frenetische Innenwelt voll Chaos und Verwirrung absinken? Normal sein und dauernd trinken, tagein, tagaus, bis man endlich der normalen Wirklichkeit entflieht und sich an einen ruhigeren, langsameren, aber dennoch helleren Ort zurückzieht? Kann man gewöhnlich sein und zugleich süchtig (wegen dieser Erfahrung ersann Marc Quinn dieses Projekt)?

1
Friedrich Nicolai, *Beschreibung einer Reise durch Deutschland und die Schweiz im Jahre 1781*, Bd. 4, Berlin/Stettin 1785.

Interessanterweise steht das eingangs erwähnte Zitat Nicolais im Gegensatz zu dem meisten, was er sonst über Messerschmidt berichtet. Obwohl, anders als einige seiner pompöseren Kollegen, bescheiden in Sachen Kleidung, erschien er Nicolai „merkwürdig". Er litt unter Anfällen und Ekstasen – und hatte ein Mitglied der Akademie der bildenden Künste in Wien mit dem Tod bedroht (übrigens war er dort als Professor abgelehnt worden, aber nicht wegen seiner Kunst, sondern weil er mancher*manchem mit seinem Temperament und seinen Anfällen Angst eingejagt hatte). Andere Male war er offenbar dermaßen in Wut geraten, dass er ganze Werkgruppen zerstört hatte, weil sie ihm nicht ausdrucksstark genug erschienen waren oder weil er sich über Kaufinteressent*innen echauffiert hatte. Und wenn er nachts, um vor der Alltagsqual in den Schlaf zu entfliehen, seine Arbeit unterbrach, bedrängten ihn Geister, die ihn gellend verhöhnten, bedrohten, peinigten und verspotteten.

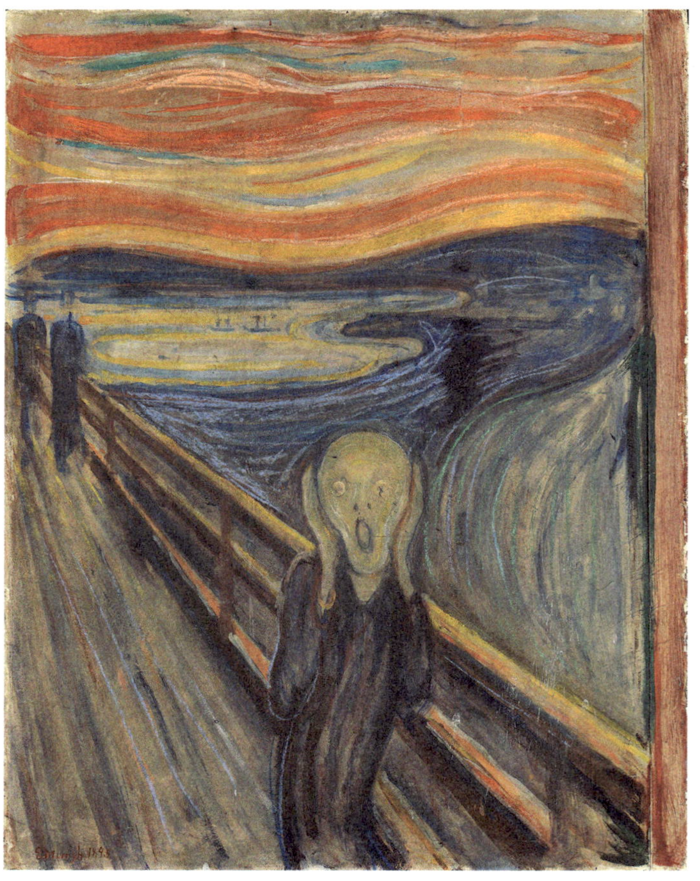

Abb. 1

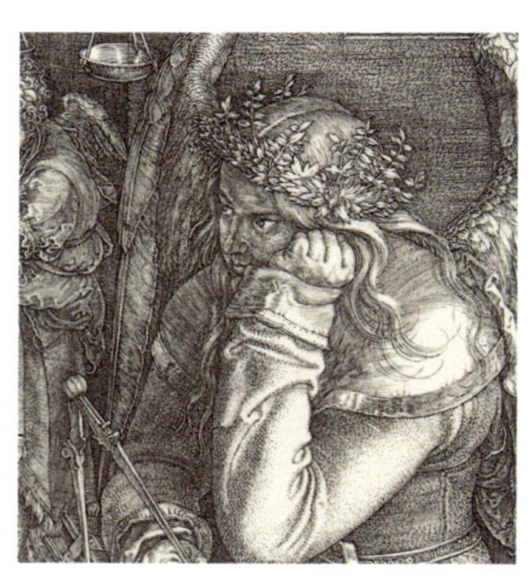

Abb. 2

Als Messerschmidt mit der Arbeit an den später so genannten „Charakterköpfen" begann, verlor er nach übereinstimmender Auffassung, die unter anderem durch Berichte wie jenen von Nicolai geprägt wurde, jeden Bezug zur Realität. Diese Theorie erhärtete sich 1932, als der Wiener Kunsthistoriker Ernst Kris eine Studie über die „Charakterköpfe" veröffentlichte, in der er darlegte, dass der Künstler ab ca. 1770 an Schizophreniesymptomen litt und dass die Köpfe ergo im Zusammenhang mit dieser Störung gesehen werden müssen. Auch andere hatten rasch Diagnosen parat: narzisstische Persönlichkeitsstörung, verdrängte Sexualität, Bleivergiftung. Selbst Biograf*innen und Kritiker*innen, die der spekulativen Medizin und der Pseudowissenschaft weniger zuneigen, sind sich zumeist einig, dass die „Charakterköpfe" Ergebnisse des Ausbruchs einer Psychose oder eines Wahns sind.

Messerschmidt selbst sah die „Charakterköpfe" als Hilfe, als Lösung, als Schutzschild gegen die Geister, die ihn verfolgten. Er glaubte, wenn er nur ihre Ausdrücke richtig festhalten könnte, würden diese von ihm ablassen. (Bei der Beurteilung von Messerschmidt ist natürlich zu beachten,

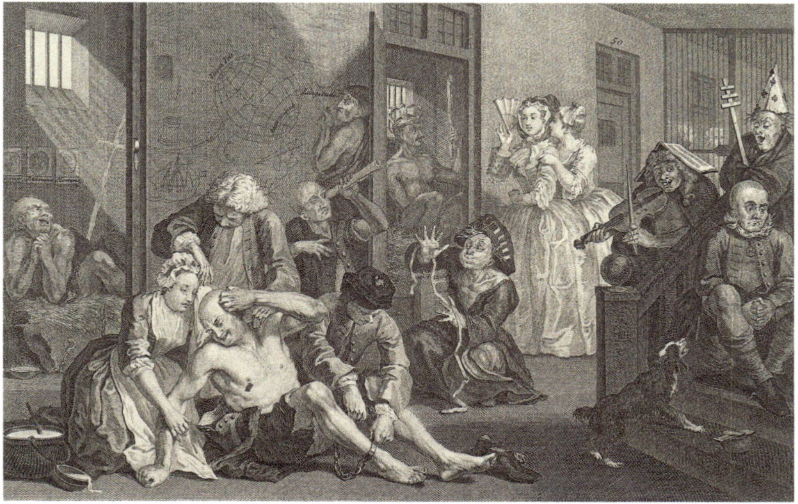

Abb. 3

dass der Geisterglaube zu seiner Zeit weitverbreitet war.) Er machte sich an dieses Projekt, das in seinem ehrgeizigen Umfang von mehr als sechzig Skulpturen bizarr und großartig wirkt und sämtliche Mienen des Menschen, die ganze Pracht seiner 43 Gesichtsmuskeln zeigen sollte, ohne jeden Auftrag und ohne jede Garantie auf Vergütung. Angespornt war er einzig von einem größeren und persönlicheren Bedürfnis. Wir dürfen interpretieren, dass das Gesicht für ihn ein Einfallstor war – zum Verständnis, zur Selbstkontrolle, zum Wissen, zur Seele. So betrachtet könnte man sagen, dass Messerschmidt, wenn man die Diagnose der Psychose akzeptiert, jene besondere Eigenschaft des Wahnsinnigen hatte, die Michel Foucault in *Wahnsinn und Gesellschaft* (1961) beschreibt, nämlich die Fähigkeit, den Unterschied zwischen dem, was der Mensch ist, und dem, was er vorgibt zu sein, aufdecken zu können.[2]

2
Michel Foucault, *Wahnsinn und Gesellschaft*, Frankfurt am Main 1969 (*Histoire de la folie*, Paris 1961).

Natürlich tragen Kleidung und Besitz, um auf Nicolais einleitendes Zitat zurückzukommen, viel dazu bei, wer wir sind oder als wen wir uns darstellen wollen. Aber sie zeigen auch, wenn man sich verirrt hat, überfordert ist oder die Normen von Schicklichkeit und Anstand unterschreitet – Flecken, Gestank, die zu großen, zerschlissenen Mäntel der Obdachlosen, der Verlassenen, der Unglücklichen, der Kranken. Sie alle stehen überall für Leid und Ungleichheit. Und doch ist es das Gesicht und nicht die Garderobe, das die Eigenarten, die Tiefen und die persönliche Geschichte des Leids vermittelt. Man sagt, dass der Körper die Partitur aufbewahrt, es aber das Gesicht ist, das diese in ihrer ganzen gleißenden Individualität anderen offenbart.

Abb. 1
Edvard Munch
Der Schrei, 1893
National Museum of Art, Architecture and Design, Oslo

Abb. 2
Albrecht Dürer
Melancholie I, 1514
Metropolitan Museum of Art, New York

Abb. 3
William Hogarth
Der Werdegang eines Wüstlings, 1735
Metropolitan Museum of Art, New York

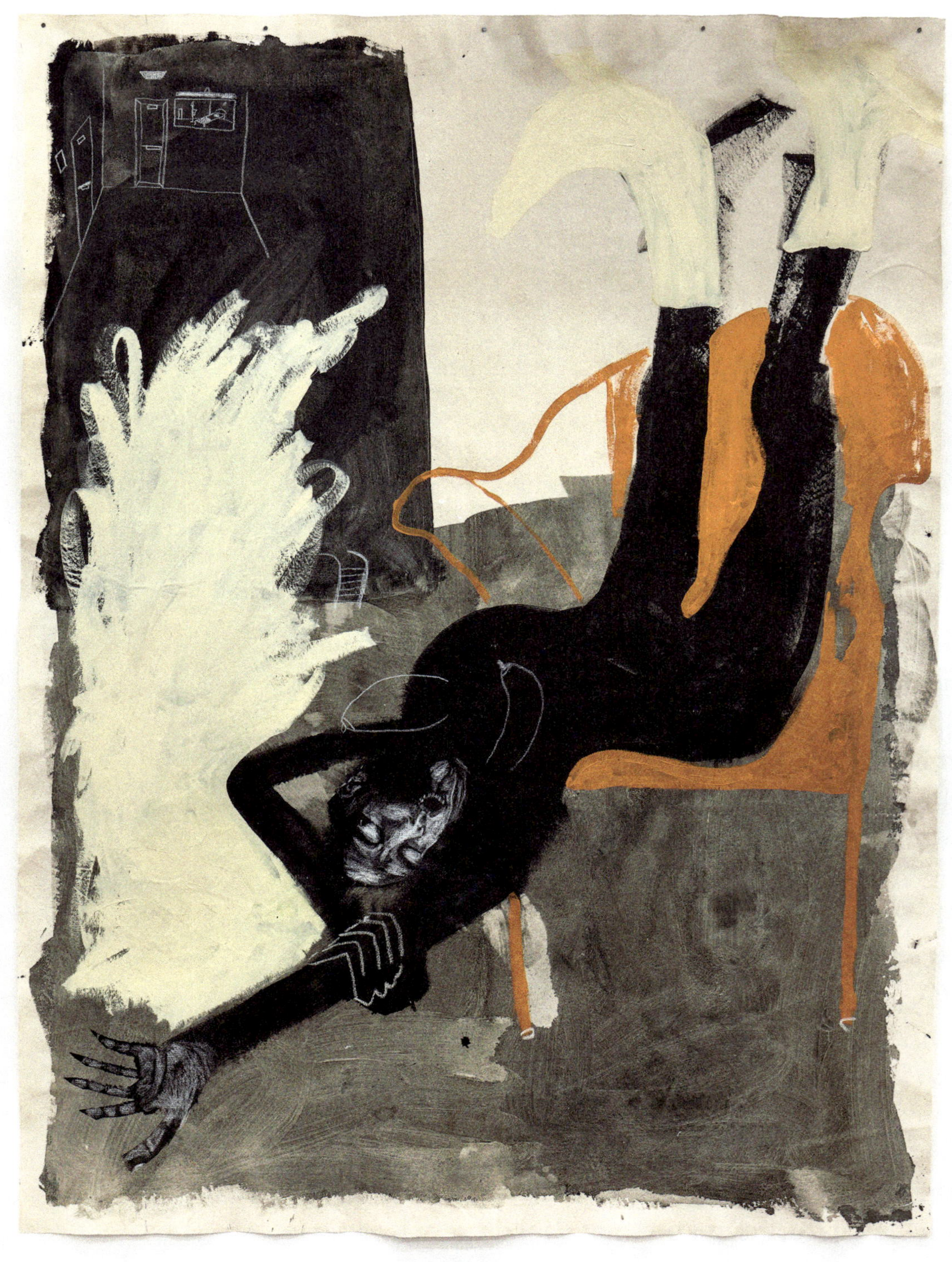

Abb. 4

Abb. 4
Shadi Al-Atallah
GROUP THERAPY AT 8 , 2021
Courtesy Shadi Al-Atallah und
Guts Gallery

Abb. 5
Shadi Al-Atallah
Kris croker stole my tears, 2018
Courtesy Shadi Al-Atallah und
Cob Gallery

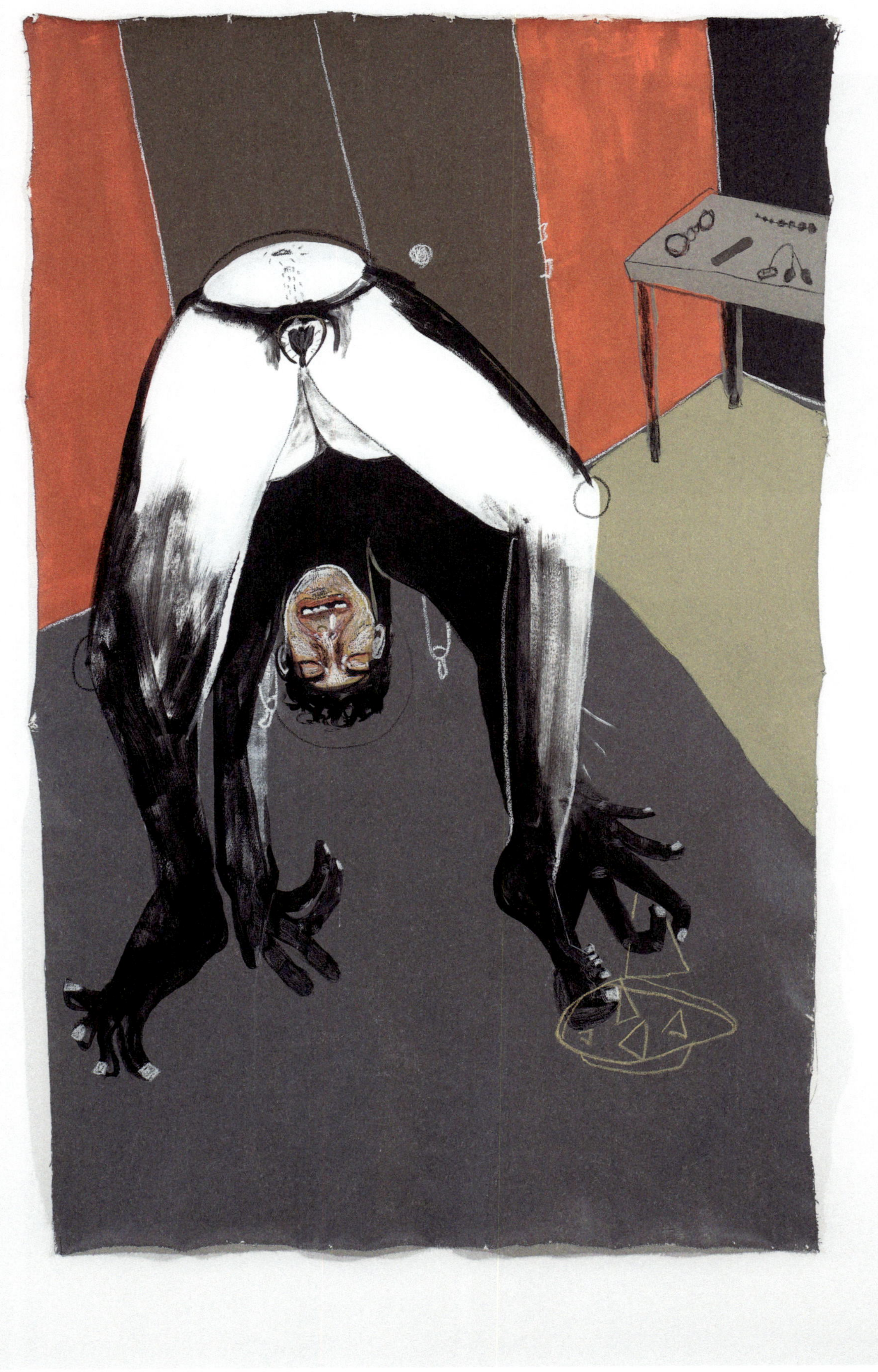

Abb. 5

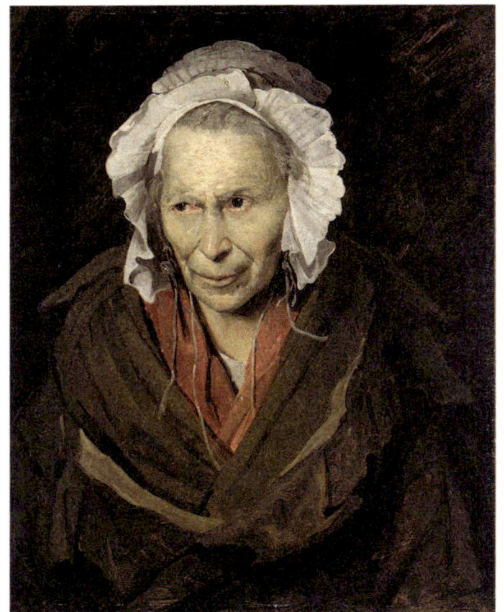

Abb. 6

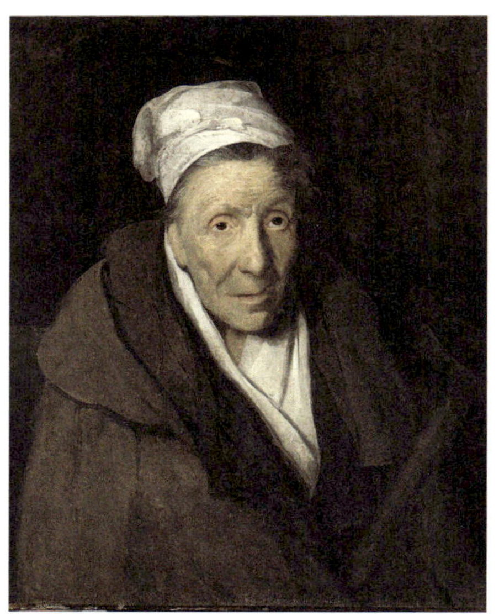

Abb. 7

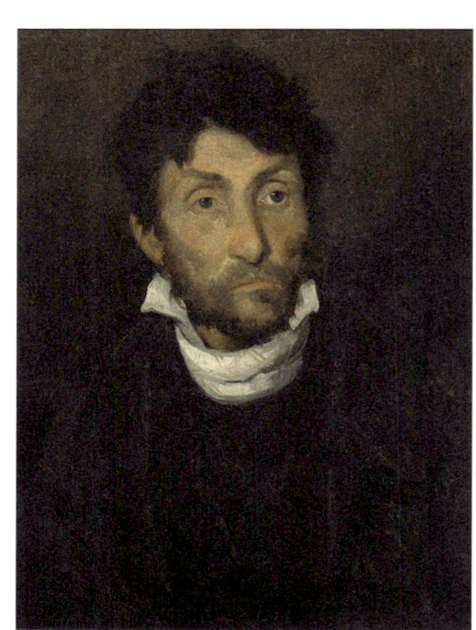

Abb. 8

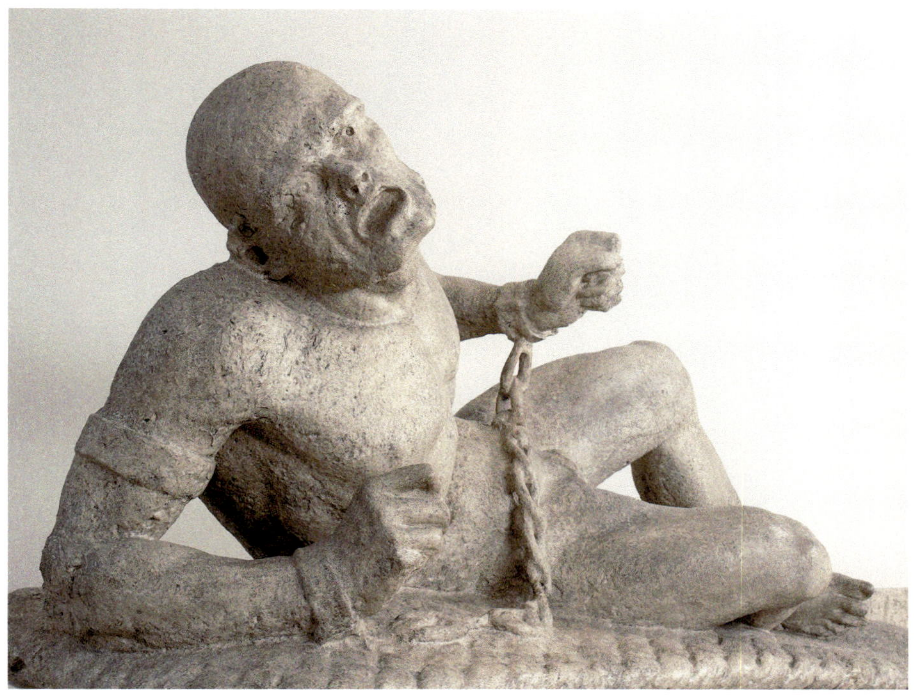

Abb. 9

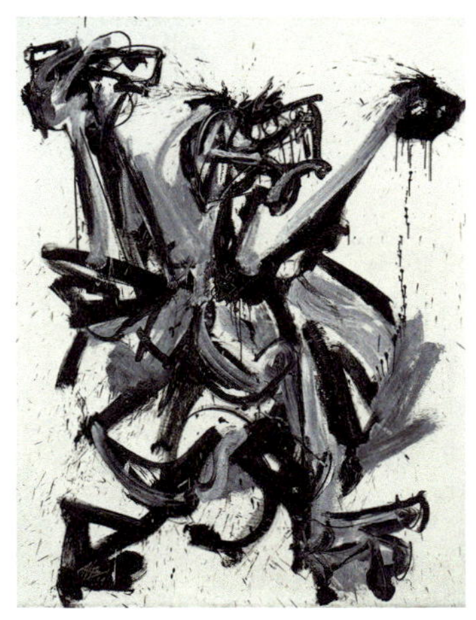

Abb. 10

Daher konzentrieren sich künstlerische Projekte über den Wahnsinn oft auf Gesicht und Mimik (*Der Schrei* von Edvard Munch, 1893, Abb. 1), auf den verzweifelt-traurigen Blick (*Melancholie I* von Albrecht Dürer, 1514, Abb. 2) oder auf Grimassen und barocke Gesten (*Der Werdegang eines Wüstlings* von William Hogarth, 1735, Abb. 3).

Desgleichen sind Synergien zwischen den Köpfen von Messerschmidt und Richard Avedons 1963 entstandenen Fotoporträts von Patient*innen des East Louisiana State Mental Hospital erkennbar – die Unterschiedlichkeit der Charaktere und Gesichter, die allesamt Spuren ihrer Traumata und Fantasien tragen, verschiedene Muskelgruppen, die sich je nach Situation, Erfahrung und Gesundheit auf tausenderlei Art spannen. Man sieht auch starke Ähnlichkeiten mit den lebhaften und doch introspektiven Arbeiten von Shadi Al-Atallah (Abb. 4, 5), eindrucksvollen Selbstporträts, in denen Themen wie geistige Gesundheit und Katharsis untersucht werden. Es sind Gesichter und Körper, die sich in Reaktion auf offenbar überwältigend schmerzliche Empfindungen winden, biegen und gestikulieren.

Von der Bildsprache her betrachtet könnte man Messerschmidts „Charakterköpfe" auch mit Théodore Géricaults Gemäldeserie *Porträts der Wahnsinnigen* (1819–24, Abb. 6–8) in Verbindung bringen oder sogar

Abb. 6
Théodore Géricault
Die Irre, 1819–22
Musee des Beaux-Arts de Lyon

Abb. 7
Théodore Géricault
Die Spielsüchtige, 1819–22
Musée du Louvre, Paris

Abb. 8
Théodore Géricault
Porträt eines Kleptomanen, um 1820
Museum of Fine Arts, Gent

Abb. 9
Caius Gabriel Cibber
Tobsucht, Portalfigur im Bethlem
Royal Hospital, London, 1676
Bethlem Museum of the Mind, London

Abb. 10
Antonio Saura
Grito n.º 7, 1959
Museo Reina Sofía, Madrid

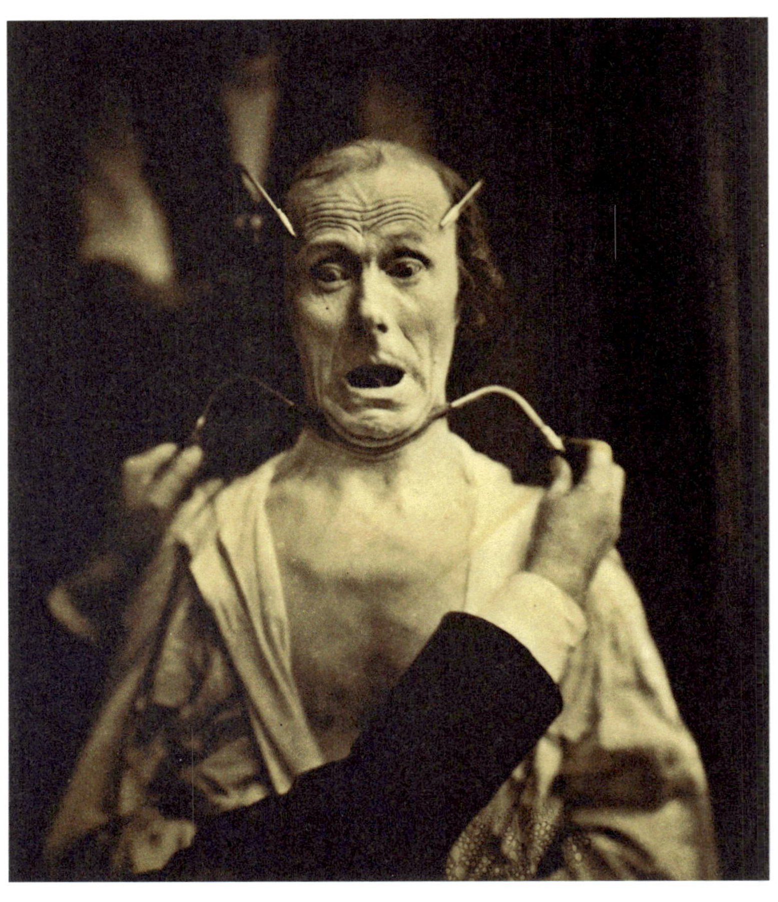

Abb. 11

mit Caius Gabriel Cibbers Skulpturen *Tobsucht* (Abb. 9) und *Melancholie* (beide 1676), die an den Toren des Bethlem Hospital in London aufgestellt sind und nicht nur die Ansicht, sondern auch Aussichten der dort Behandelten darstellen. Natürlich gibt es auch Ausnahmen in dieser Tradition – Werke, die gleichsam ein chemisches Ungleichgewicht oder starke Gefühle und Gefühlsausbrüche auf eine abstrakte Weise vermitteln. Antonio Saura *Grito n.º 7* (1959, Abb. 10) mit seinem gestischen Farbauftrag ist sicher eines der besten Beispiele hierfür. Sucht man nach Projekten zum Thema Wahnsinn, so findet man sonst in der Regel eine Fülle finsterer Gesichter, Schreie, Zähnefletschen und Grimassen. Sie können als Kommentare auf die Unfassbarkeit und auf das Geheimnis von Gehirn und Geist angesehen werden. Die Künstler*innen zeigen die Umstände – die körperlichen Anzeichen, die Symptome, die Nebenwirkungen psychischer Anspannung. Und sie zeigen, was sie sehen und verstehen können.

Messerschmidts „Charakterköpfe" sind mithin, wie viele der von ihnen angeregten späteren Kunstwerke auch, ein Ausdruck, dass Kunst und das Gesicht wie

Abb. 11
Duchenne de Boulogne *Terror*, 1854–56
Museum of Fine Arts, Houston, Texas

Abb. 12
Nach Franz Xaver Messerschmidt
Ein wollüstig abgehärmter Geck, vor 1923
Belvedere, Wien

Abb. 13
Nach Franz Xaver Messerschmidt
Ein schmerzhaft stark Verwundeter, vor 1923
Belvedere, Wien

Abb. 14
Nach Franz Xaver Messerschmidt
Der erboßte und rachgierige Zigeuner, vor 1923
Belvedere, Wien

kommunizierende Gefäße der Geheimnisse des menschlichen Bewusstseins sind. Sie sind Versuche zu sondieren, zu verstehen, sie suchen schmerzlich nach Antworten. Für Messerschmidt waren Gesichtsausdrücke offenbar eine universelle Sprache und eine Möglichkeit, das Unerklärliche zu erklären. So gesehen war er nicht nur künstlerisch, sondern auch wissenschaftlich ein Pionier.

So darf man nicht vergessen, dass er mit diesen Skulpturen etwa einhundert Jahre vor der Veröffentlichung von Charles Darwins *Der Ausdruck der Gemütsbewegungen bei dem Menschen und den Tieren* begann, das ursprünglich als Kapitel der *Abstammung des Menschen* gedacht war, dann aber monografisch erschien. Das Buch enthielt auch zahlreiche Zeichnungen und, was neu war, Fotografien von Duchenne de Boulogne (Abb. 11), die Experimente zu Gesichtsausdrücken und Gesichtsmuskeln dokumentieren, welche bereits mit elektrischen Sonden durchgeführt wurden und die wie Hommagen auf Messerschmidts „Charakterköpfe" aussehen. Darwin vertrat – wie wohl auch Messerschmidt mit seinen Köpfen – die Ansicht, dass die Mimik ein allgemein menschlicher Dialekt sei – gemeinsame Handlungen, die kultur- und sogar speziesübergreifend eine Verbindung zu unseren tierischen Vorfahren herstellen. Noch in den 1960er- und 1970er-Jahren formalisierte der bekannte US-Psychologe Paul Ekman diese Auffassung der Allgemeinheit des Gefühlsausdrucks durch den Nachweis, dass Menschen auf der ganzen Welt zuverlässig aus Gesichtsausdrücken auf emotionale Zustände zu schließen vermögen.

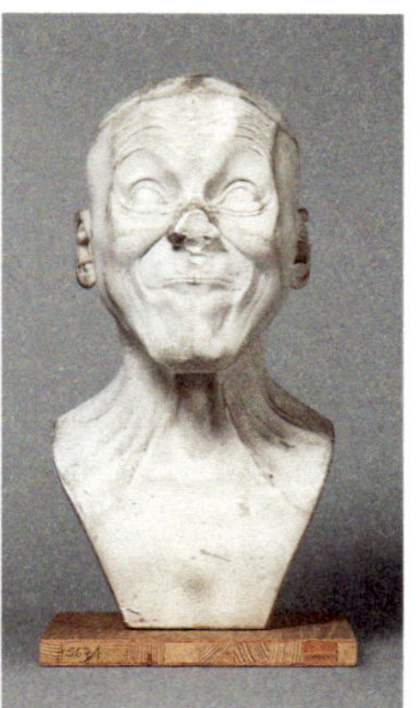

Abb. 12

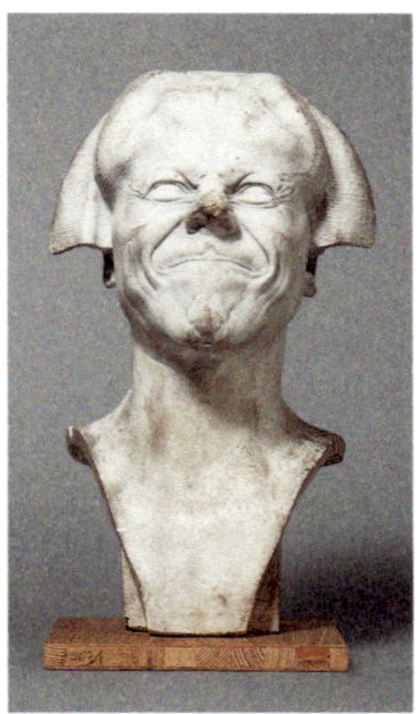

Abb. 13

Auch heute noch verstehen wir ein Lächeln oder ein Stirnrunzeln wie eine Lingua franca. Microsoft und Amazon verwenden Algorithmen, die Emotionen anhand des Gesichts erkennen können. Das nutzen die Unternehmen, die ihre Kund*innen in deren Bedürfnissen, Hoffnungen und Träumen besser verstehen wollen. Sie wollen dir in die Augen sehen, dir von den Lippen ablesen, wissen, was du fühlst, was dich bewegt, was dich

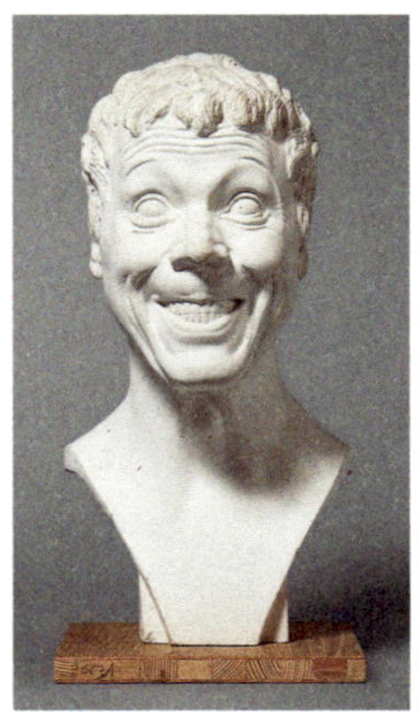

Abb. 14

3
Franz Strunz, *Merkwürdige Lebensgeschichte des Franz Xaver Messerschmidt, k. k. öffentlichen Lehrer der Bildhauerkunst*, Wien 1794, S. 3f., zit. nach Maria Pötzl-Malikova, *Franz Xaver Messerschmidt. 1736–1783* (Belvedere Werkverzeichnisse, Bd. 4), Weitra 2015, S. 118.

erschüttert, wer du bist. Ihre Ziele sind daher wohl nicht weit von jenen entfernt, die Messerschmidt laut einem viel besprochenen Essay von Franz Strunz anlässlich der Ausstellung der „Charakterköpfe" im Jahr 1793 zugeschrieben wurden. Er, Messerschmidt, könne wie manch anderer, so heißt es dort, „aus den Gesichtszügen der Menschen [...] gleichwohl den Karakter und die Leidenschaften derselben erforschen, beurtheilen und darstellen". [3]

Strunz war es auch, der die Köpfe nach Charakteren (*Der Erzbösewicht, Ein Heuchler und ein Verleumder*) oder Berufen (*Ein Gelehrter, Dichter*), nach geistigen oder körperlichen Zuständen (*Der Bekümmerte, Der Verdrüssliche*), andere wieder nach physiologischen Reaktionen betitelte (*Der Nieser, Ein aus dem Wasser Geretteter*). Strunz' Neigung zu klassifizieren und zu erklären ist wichtig im Hinblick auf die Tradition, die die „Charakterköpfe" Messerschmidts stifteten, aber auch auf die Reaktion der Kritik und auf ihn persönlich als Künstler. Der Hang zu diagnostizieren und zu kategorisieren setzt sich bis in die heutige Medizin und Kultur fort, wo er wie ehedem prägt, wie Künstler*innen psychisch Kranke und Andersartige behandeln und darstellen. (Es ist nicht unwichtig, dass Messerschmidt in einer Periode der europäischen Geschichte lebte und arbeitete, in der Geisteskranke zunehmend körperlich gezüchtigt, in geschlossene Institutionen gesperrt, ausgegrenzt und etikettiert wurden.)

Wie aber kann man mit Kunst Wahnsinn darstellen, ohne jemanden zum Objekt und zum anderen zu machen? Die Frage ist als solche schon problematisch, impliziert sie doch die Vorstellung, dass Geisteskranke überhaupt dargestellt werden *sollen* und nicht selbst schöpferisch sind. Das erinnert an die Tourist*innen, die am Eingang von Bethlem (oder „Bedlam", wie man sagt) ein paar Münzen berappten, um gaffen und bewerten zu dürfen.

Viel zu lange schon und auch heute noch mangelt es an echtem Interesse für die Kunst, die kranke Menschen, Menschen in Anstalten oder Menschen mit den entsprechenden Diagnosen schaffen. Als der französische Maler Jean Dubuffet 1945 Schweizer Asyle und Spitäler bereiste, um ihn mit ihrer Lebendigkeit und Authentizität des Ausdrucks verblüffende Werke von Anstaltspatient*innen zu sammeln und nach Paris zu bringen, stieß er nicht nur bei Galerien, sondern auch in Salons und bei Sammler*innen auf geringes Interesse und kaum Resonanz. Diese Werke und die Widersprüchlichkeit, mit denen sie aufgenommen wurden, brachten Dubuffet 1947 dazu, sein Manifest *Art Brut* zu schreiben. Darin legte er ihre Tiefe und Schönheit dar, die seiner Ansicht nach von der etablierten Kunstwelt glatt übersehen wurden. Doch wo gehört Messerschmidt hin? Zu Art Brut oder Kunstkunst?

Es gibt das Vorurteil, dass Kunst in den Wahnsinn führen, dass sie destabilisieren, entflammen und aus dem Gleichgewicht bringen kann. Und tatsächlich gilt es in den meisten Krankenhäusern als ausgemacht, dass abstrakte oder besonders gefühlsbetonte Kunst dort die Patient*innen irgendwie aufscheuchen und aufregen könnte und somit das Sanfte, das Naturthema sicherer sei. Die Kunst und die Künstler*innen, ob erst am Beginn stehend oder schon etabliert, sind immer gleichermaßen gefährlich wie auch in Gefahr.

Allgemein nimmt man tatsächlich an, dass Künstler*innen aufgrund ihrer Rolle, ihrer Einsamkeit, der introvertierten Suche und des inneren Drucks, etwas festzuhalten oder zu erklären, leicht in den Wahnsinn abrutschen können. Die Forschung steht zwar auf wackligen Beinen, doch noch 1993 hielt Kay Redfield Jamison, Professorin für Psychiatrie an der Johns Hopkins University School of Medicine in Baltimore, in einem Buch fest, dass bedeutende Künstler*innen zehn- bis dreißigmal häufiger an Depressionen erkranken als die Gesamtbevölkerung.[4]

„Ein so gesunder Mann, der beständig enthaltsam lebte, beständig seine Einbildungskraft anstrengte, beständig

4 Kay Redfield Jamison, *Touched with Fire: Manic-Depressive Illness and the Artistic Temperament*, New York 1993.

5
Nicolai 1785 (wie Anm. 1).

sitzend arbeitete, und fast beständig einsam war, mußte nothwendig Unordnungen im Körper, Folgen des stockenden Blutes, ängstliches Pochen des Herzens empfinden", so Nicolai über Messerschmidt, „und seine Einbildungskraft, vereint mit seinen Lieblingsvorurtheilen, bildete sich sehr bald allerley geistige Gestalten, welche vermeintlich diese Wirkungen, deren Ursachen doch in ihm selbst lagen, außer ihm hervorbringen sollten."[5] Für Nicolai kam Messerschmidts Kunst also von dessen Verrücktheit, verursachte diese aber auch.

Und doch ist der Zusammenhang zwischen künstlerischem Genie und Wahnsinn – Gefühlsausbrüche, Verantwortungslosigkeit für Tun und Lassen, Getriebenheit von der Kraft der eigenen Vision – beinah zum Klischee verkommen. Mit ihm sind wir gewohnt, das männliche Ego, Missbrauch und Fehlverhalten zu tolerieren und zu entschuldigen. Was hat das wiederum mit Messerschmidt zu tun?

Hin und wieder ist es am besten, die Dinge so zu nehmen, wie sie aussehen, nämlich für bare Münze. Man beachte: Die „Charakterköpfe" halten das Gleichgewicht zwischen Verfremdung und Vertrautheit. Wie die von ihnen dargestellten Gesichtsausdrücke und Bewusstseinszustände ermöglichen sie auch Empathie und Identifikation.

Daher werden sie auch weiterhin Kunstschaffende und Publikum inspirieren, und zwar gerade weil das, was sie zeigen, so gewöhnlich ist. Die in sie eingebetteten Folgen mimischer Widersprüche, Risse und Dehnungen leiten den Blick damals wie heute. Die Gesichtsausdrücke ergeben unser aller Biografie, ein Muskelnarrativ, das sich zu unterschiedlichen Zeiten bei jeder*jedem von uns auf die gleiche Weise zeigt, einen Gesellschaftstanz, der weltweit, ständig, allein, aber auch im Kreis getanzt wird.

Kurz, die „Charakterköpfe" erinnern uns, wie viele Leiden und Probleme wir gemeinsam haben. Manche konfrontieren uns mit einem ungewöhnlichen Abgrund, dem wir vielleicht wie auf einer schiefen Ebene entgegenschlittern. Aber die meisten fordern uns auf, einfach in den Spiegel zu schauen und eine Realität anzuerkennen, die bereits da ist und sich scheu und zögerlich auf uns selbst zurückwirft.

Franz Xaver Messerschmidt und seine Köpfe

Georg Lechner

Vermutlich im Jahr 1771 nahm Franz Xaver Messerschmidt die Arbeit an jenen Werken auf, die später als „Charakterköpfe“ (Abb. 1) bekannt wurden und große Popularität erlangten.[1] Zu dieser Zeit war der Mittdreißiger das, was man als einen gemachten Mann bezeichnet. Er hatte bedeutende Aufträge für die fürstliche Familie Liechtenstein und den kaiserlichen Hof ausgeführt, besaß ein Haus im heutigen dritten Wiener Gemeindebezirk und war als Nachfolger von Jakob Christoph Schletterer (1699–1774) als Professor für Bildhauerei an der Akademie in Wien vorgesehen. Doch als Schletterer 1774 starb, kam alles anders: Messerschmidt wurde bei der Wahl für diesen prestigeträchtigen Posten umgangen, wobei seine seelische Verfassung als Argument ausschlaggebend war.

Schwer gekränkt verließ Messerschmidt im Jahr 1775 Wien und ging erst nach München, dann an seinen Geburtsort Wiesensteig. Dort verbrachte er längere Zeit in Abgeschiedenheit und arbeitete an seinen Köpfen. Nach dieser Klausur entschied er sich, in die damals aufstrebende Stadt Pressburg (Bratislava) zu übersiedeln, wo er ab 1777 bei seinem Bruder Johann Adam (1738–94) in dessen großzügigem Domizil lebte und später ein eigenes Haus erwarb. Große Ansprüche scheint er nicht gehabt zu haben, und er bestritt seine Lebenskosten offensichtlich mit der Anfertigung kleiner Porträtmedaillons, vorzugsweise aus Alabaster, von denen heute einige in verschiedenen europäischen Museen verwahrt werden.[2]

Von seiner stetig wachsenden Köpfe-Kollektion wollte er sich jedoch nicht trennen, obwohl es Angebote dafür gab. Er fertigte sie aus Alabaster sowie aus Legierungen, die in unterschiedlichen Anteilen Blei und Zinn enthalten. Blei war im 18. Jahrhundert ein einigermaßen wertvolles Material, da es für verschiedene alltägliche Zwecke benötigt wurde. Doch auch die Bildhauerei hatte dieses Material für sich entdeckt, und gerade in Wien wurde dessen edle Dunkelheit sehr geschätzt. Zu den bekanntesten Beispielen zählt dahingehend der Providentiabrunnen

1
Die biografischen Angaben im vorliegenden Beitrag folgen der Monografie zu Franz Xaver Messerschmidt von Maria Pötzl-Malikova (Maria Pötzl-Malikova, *Franz Xaver Messerschmidt. 1736–1783* [Belvedere Werkverzeichnisse, Bd. 4], Wien 2015).

2
Siehe dazu Pötzl-Malikova 2015 (wie Anm. 1), S. 259–272, 276–278.

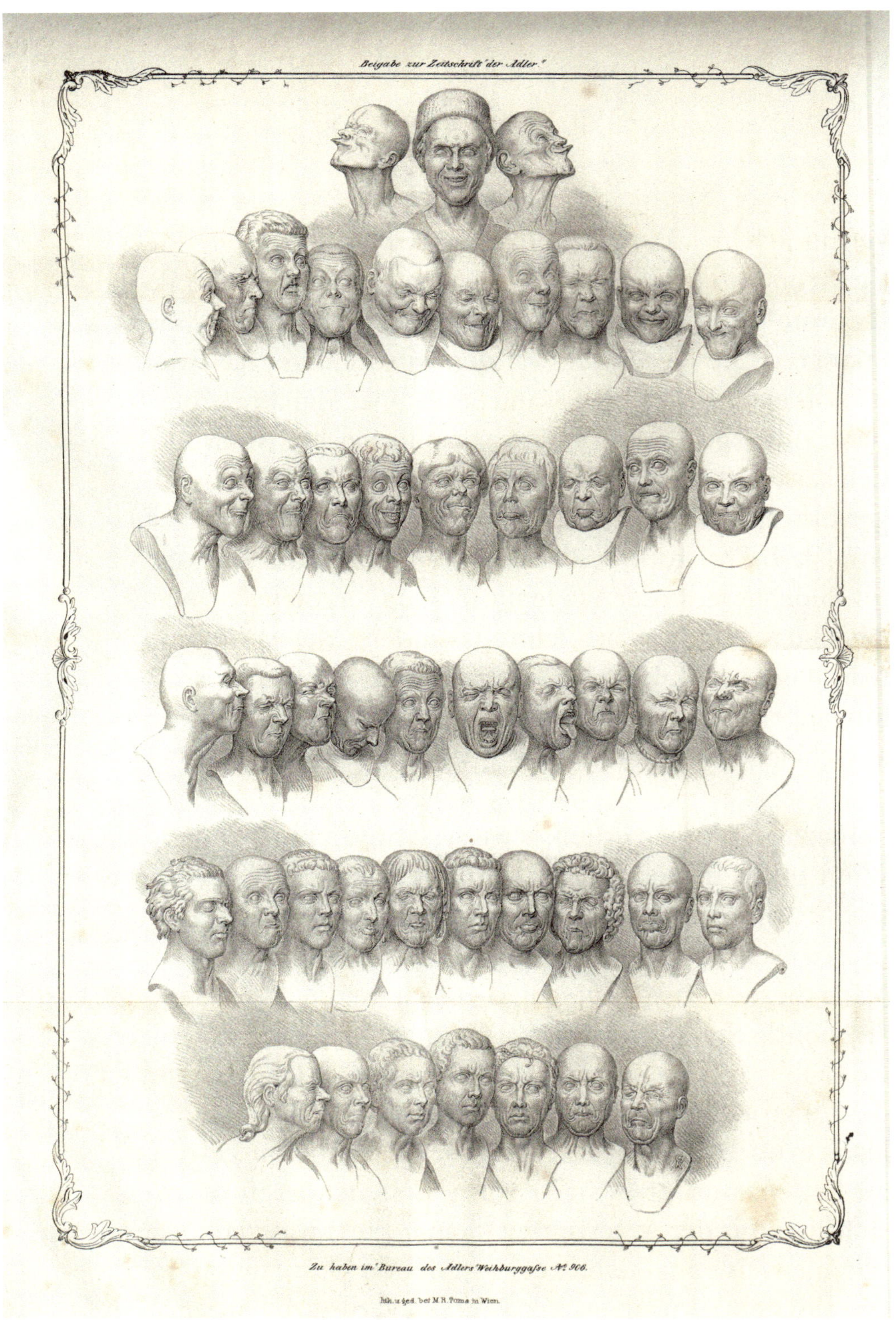

Abb. 1

von Georg Raphael Donner, der 1739 vollendet wurde. Dass Donner lediglich 47 Jahre alt wurde, mag auch auf das Arbeiten mit diesem giftigen Metall in Zusammenhang gestanden haben. Inwieweit auch Messerschmidt davon betroffen war, ist schwer zu beurteilen. Technische Kenntnisse hinsichtlich des Metallgusses besaß er wohl in ausreichendem Maße, da er seine Karriere als Stuckverschneider im kaiserlichen Zeughaus begann, wo er für die Bearbeitung und Dekoration von Kanonen sorgte.

Abb. 1
Matthias Rudolph Toma
Messerschmidts "Charakterköpfe", 1839
Österreichische Nationalbibliothek, Wien

Abb. 2
Franz Xaver Messerschmidt
Franz Anton Mesmer, 1770
Belvedere, Wien
(Dauerleihgabe aus Privatbesitz)

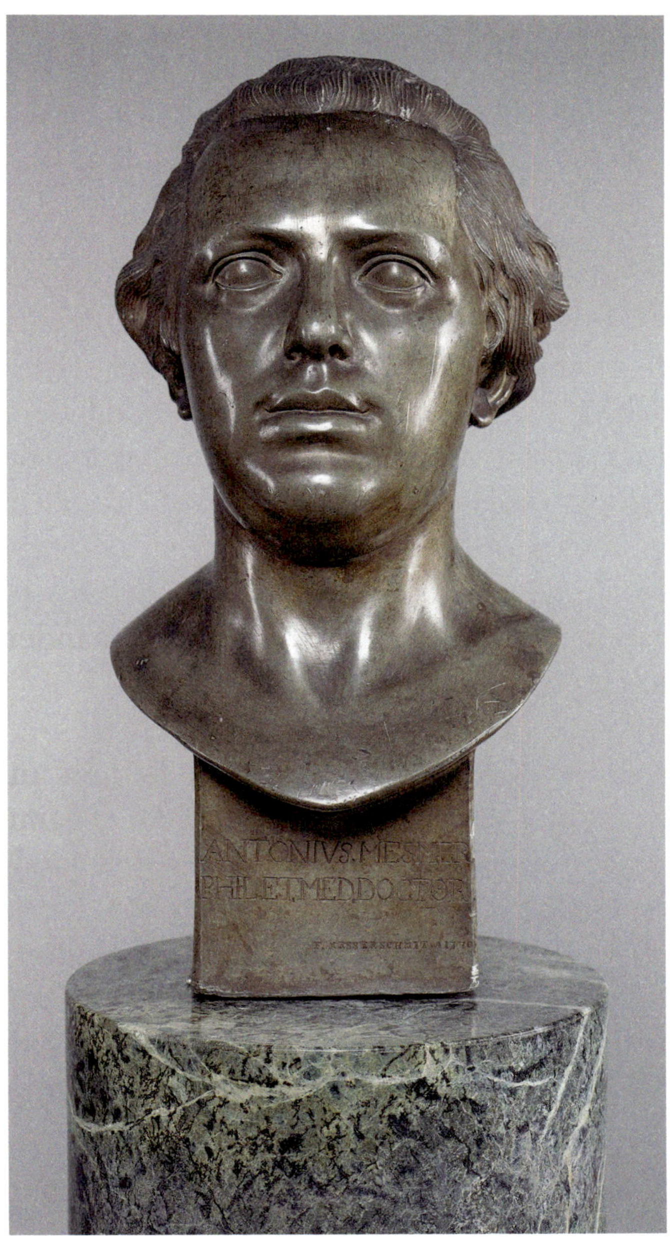

Abb. 2

Über lange Zeit wurde Messerschmidt in der Literatur meist als geisteskrank eingestuft, und die mitunter bizarren Köpfe wurden als logische Konsequenz dessen erachtet. Besonders brisant erscheint die 1932 publizierte Schrift des Kunsthistorikers Ernst Kris (1900–57), der sich zu diesem Zeitpunkt auch mit der gerade in Wien präsenten Psychoanalyse auseinandersetzte und dem Künstler Schizophrenie attestierte.[3] Derlei Urteile scheinen insofern problematisch, als die zeitgenössischen Quellen keineswegs ausufernd sind und Rückschlüsse nur schwer erlauben.

3
Ernst Kris, „Die Charakterköpfe des Franz Xaver Messerschmidt. Versuch einer historischen und psychologischen Deutung", in: *Jahrbuch der Kunsthistorischen Sammlungen in Wien*, N. F., Bd. 6, 1932, S. 169–228.

Eine ganz gute Vorstellung darüber, wie es um Messerschmidt tatsächlich stand, vermittelt uns der Bericht von Friedrich Nicolai (1733–1811), der den Künstler in Pressburg besucht hat. Einleitend fasst er Leben und

Schaffen treffend zusammen: „In seiner Kunst ein außerordentliches Genie; im gemeinen Leben ein wenig zur Sonderbarkeit geneigt, welches hauptsächlich aus seiner Liebe zur Unabhängigkeit entstand.“[4] Weiters schildert Nicolai, wie Messerschmidt sich kniff und Grimassen vor dem Spiegel schnitt, die Grundlage für seine Arbeit an den Köpfen waren.[5] Auch dass der Künstler von Geistern geplagt wurde, wird erwähnt. Insgesamt scheint es ein angenehmes wie aufschlussreiches Gespräch zwischen zwei ein[illegible] freundlich gesinnten Herren gewesen zu sein.

Wenn wir in Franz Xaver Messerschmidt keine[illegible] Schizophrenie Erkrankten sehen wollen, wie kam es [illegible] zu seiner doch außergewöhnlichen Serie der sogenannten „Charakterköpfe“? Bereits Albert Ilg (1847–96) hatte vorgeschlagen, das Wirken des Arztes und Magnetiseurs Franz Anton Mesmer (1734–1815) nicht außer Acht zu lassen.[6] Diese Idee verfolgte auch Michael Krapf und erachtete die Köpfe als Dokumentation der von Mesmer durchgeführten Therapien.[7] Damit publizierte er eine These, die nicht ohne Widerspruch blieb.[8] Inwieweit die Lehren Mesmers Einfluss auf den Künstler ausübten, ist schwer zu beurteilen. Bekannt waren die beiden Herren jedenfalls miteinander, denn Messerschmidt hatte für Mesmers Garten Brunnenfiguren geschaffen, die leider nicht erhalten sind, sowie eine Büste des Arztes angefertigt (Privatbesitz, als Dauerleihgabe im Belvedere, Abb. 2).[9]

In der jüngeren Vergangenheit widmete sich der tschechische Psychiater Michal Maršálek der Genese dieser bemerkenswerten Kunstwerke und führte ins Spiel, dass Messerschmidt an Dystonie gelitten haben dürfte. Zu diesem Schluss gelangte er aufgrund der von zeitgenössischen Quellen beschriebenen Verhaltensweisen des Künstlers sowie der merkwürdig verzerrten Gesichter, die sich mit Krämpfen, wie sie an Dystonie erkrankte Menschen durchleiden, in Verbindung bringen lassen.[10]

4
Friedrich Nicolai, *Beschreibung einer Reise durch Deutschland und die Schweiz im Jahre 1781*, Bd. 6, Berlin/Stettin 1785, S. 401.

5
Nicolai 1785 (wie Anm. 4), S. 413f.

6
Albert Ilg, *Franz Xaver Messerschmidts Leben und Werke. Mit urkundlichen Beiträgen von Johann Batka*, Wien/Leipzig 1885, S. 18–20.

7
Michael Krapf, „Die Auftraggeber und der Freundeskreis“, in: ders. (Hg.), *Franz Xaver Messerschmidt. 1736–1783* (Ausst.-Kat. Unteres Belvedere, Wien, 11. Oktober 2002 bis 9. Februar 2003), Ostfildern-Ruit 2002, S. 65–76, hier: 69–72.

8
Claudia Maué, „Franz Xaver Messerschmidt 1736–1783“, in: *Frühneuzeit-Info*, 13. Jg., Heft 1, 2003, S. 169–178, hier: 171–178. – Maria Pötzl-Malikova, „Zur aktuellen Situation in der Messerschmidt-Forschung. Anmerkungen zu einer Präsentation“, in: *Österreichische Zeitschrift für Kunst und Denkmalpflege*, 57. Jg., Heft 2, 2003, S. 253–264, hier: 263f.

9
Siehe dazu Pötzl-Malikova 2015 (wie Anm. 1), S. 233f., 247f.

10
Michal Maršálek, „Dystonia in Art: The Impact of Psychiatric and Neurological Disease on the Work of the Sculptor F. X. Messerschmidt“, in: Petr Kanovsky / Kallash P. Bhatia / Raymond Rosales (Hg.), *Dystonia and Dystonic Syndromes*, Wien 2015, S. 227–244.

Nachdem Franz Xaver Messerschmidt im August 1783 – mutmaßlich an einer Lungenentzündung – verstorben war, gelangten die Köpfe in das Eigentum seines Bruders. Es folgten mehrere Besitzerwechsel, deren Abwertung bis zur Praterattraktion und in weiterer Folge deren Zerstreuung. Schließlich wurde der Architekt Camillo Sitte (1843–1903) auf diese außergewöhnlichen Kunstwerke aufmerksam und veranlasste den Ankauf von zehn Köpfen für die Staatsgewerbeschule. Für einige Jahre gerieten sie in Vergessenheit, bis acht Stück davon im Jahr 1907 in der 22. Ausstellung des Hagenbunds neben Elaboraten damals lebender Kunstschaffender gezeigt wurden. Von dort aus traten sie den Weg in das Museum für angewandte Kunst in Wien und zu guter Letzt in das Belvedere an, wo sie sich beim Publikum zunehmender Beliebtheit erfreuten und heute als das gelten, was sie sind – unvergleichliche Werke eines genialen Künstlers.

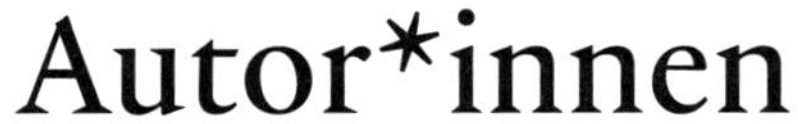

Autor*innen

Georg Lechner studierte Kunstgeschichte an der Universität Wien. Seit 2009 ist er im Belvedere in der Sammlung Barock tätig. Zu seinen Forschungs- und Publikationsschwerpunkten zählen neben der österreichischen Barockmalerei im Allgemeinen die Porträtkunst, die Wechselwirkungen von Malerei und Druckgrafik sowie die Geschichte des Belvedere und seiner Sammlungen. Georg Lechner kuratierte zuletzt im Belvedere folgende Ausstellungen: *Martin van Meytens d. J.* (2014/15), *Himmlisch! Der Barockbildhauer Johann Georg Pinsel* (2016/17, gemeinsam mit Maike Hohn), *Maria Theresia und die Kunst* (2017), *Der Kremser Schmidt. Zum 300. Geburtstag* (2018) und *Johann Jakob Hartmann* (2021).

Cat Marnell lebt als Autorin und Redakteurin in New York. Ihr Lebensbericht *How to Murder Your Life* wurde 2017 umgehend zu einem *New York Times*-Bestseller. Marnell war Beauty-Redakteurin bei Condé Nast und Mitgründerin von xoJane.com. Für *VICE* verfasste sie die Kolumne „Amphetamine Logic". Ihre neue Kolumne „Beautyshambles" erscheint exklusiv auf Patreon.

Stella Rollig ist seit Jänner 2017 Generaldirektorin und wissenschaftliche Geschäftsführerin des Belvedere. Sie studierte Germanistik und Kunstgeschichte an der Universität Wien und war als Kunstpublizistin tätig (unter anderem ORF, *Der Standard*). Von 1994 bis 1996 war Stella Rollig österreichische Bundeskuratorin für bildende Kunst, in dieser Zeit gründete sie auch *Depot. Kunst und Diskussion* im MuseumsQuartier Wien. Von 2004 bis 2016 leitete die Ausstellungsmacherin das Lentos Kunstmuseum Linz, ab 2011 zusätzlich das Nordico Stadtmuseum Linz. Neben ihrer kuratorischen Tätigkeit lehrte Stella Rollig an zahlreichen Instituten.

Lou Stoppard ist eine britische Autorin und Kuratorin, die bereits für *The Financial Times*, *Aperture*, *The New York Times* und *The New Yorker* schrieb. Als Kuratorin verantwortete sie zahlreiche Ausstellungen, darunter *North: Fashioning Identity* in der Open Eye Gallery in Liverpool und im Somerset House in London und *The Hoodie* am Het Nieuwe Instituut in Rotterdam. Zu ihren Publikationen zählen ein 2019 veröffentlichter Rückblick auf die Kunst der Straßenfotografin Shirley Baker, das 2017 erschienene Buch *Fashion Together* über Kollaborationen sowie *Pools* über das Motiv des Schwimmens in der Fotografie (2020).

Tim Smith-Laing lebt als Autor und Kritiker in London. Vormals Dozent für Literatur am Jesus College in Oxford, fungiert er nun regelmäßig als Gastredner an der Royal Academy of Arts in London und schreibt für Periodika wie *Apollo*, *Frieze* und *The Daily Telegraph* über Kunst und Literatur. Smith-Laing promovierte am Merton College in Oxford über die Literatur und Mythografie der frühen Neuzeit und veröffentlichte zu Themen, die von Hieronymus Bosch bis zu den Monkees reichen. Zu seinen laufenden Projekten zählt ein Roman, der auf dem Leben Franz Xaver Messerschmidts und seines Zeitgenossen Franz Anton Mesmer basiert.